Part I

The Masters Runner

Chapter 1

Masters Running:
The Never-Ending Pursuit

Sometimes life doesn't turn out as you expect. Sometimes it's worse. But sometimes it's better, "beyond belief" better. You experience the fun and achievement you hardly thought possible 30 years ago.

That's the case with many masters runners. Depending on the country, governing body, and event—road, cross country, track, mountain, trail, or ultradistance race—runners usually are considered masters when they reach the age of 35 or 40. In track and field events, some refer to those aged 30 to 34 as submasters.

Masters running has nothing to do with experience or performance. Masters runners include everyone from beginners to Olympians, people through age 100, and runners who are considered seniors and veterans (terms used for runners over 50 and 60, respectively). Masters running is both a category in itself, with events for masters only, and also one that is included as a division in races for all ages. Runners younger than masters age are considered open runners.

WHO ARE MASTERS RUNNERS?

Masters runners come from a wide range of athletic backgrounds. Some, including successful masters runners, were never involved in sports when young. One 2013 world masters age group champion, 54, started running at 43. "I never participated in sports when in high school or college. I was just 5 feet, 2 inches tall when I was 17 and too small for sports," he said. Some runners who have jogged for decades have decided to compete in their 50s and are now faster than they were in their 20s or 30s. Some, like former semiprofessional soccer player Amanda Loomis, 31, came to running from other sports. Some have returned to running after competing in high school and college. Some have competed since their youths or even, like Jeff Galloway, Colleen De Reuck, and Joan Benoit Samuelson, since they competed in the Olympics. In November of 2013 four-time Olympian De Reuck, 49, qualified for the 2016 U.S. Olympic Marathon Trials with a time of 2:39:22.

Masters runners train and race for different reasons. The sport offers many rewards, satisfying many motivations. It gives objective, undisputable results that quantify improved fitness and progress while aging. Want a masters ranking? Masters running can satisfy competitive drives. Races like national championships, the Boston Marathon, and many other events provide a sense of community, accomplishment, and prestige. Many masters combine running with altruistic drives, raising money for charities. The number of masters in charity events has increased dramatically. With hectic, pressured lives, many runners over 30 run not just because running offers the rewards just mentioned but also because it is efficient. If you have sneakers, you can run anywhere.

Finally, many masters run because the running community provides a sense of balance and stability. "In our lives we can think of ourselves as supported by a stable structure like a tripod," said Tom Derderian, president of USA Track & Field New England in a phone conversation in December of 2013. He has a broad perspective on the running community, gained by coaching and running competitively for more than 50 years, including participation in the 1972 and 1976 U.S. Olympic Marathon Trials. "Three supports can be family, work, and play. There are certain ways you have to act in your family and in your job. But when you are in your grown-up athletics you have a freedom with the people you train and compete that you don't have in the other parts of your life. That adds a stability to your life."

Susan Zwerling Cohen, 51, is an example of thousands who run for stress relief as well as stability. Shortly before her divorce, the mother of three ran her first race at 48. She ran a personal best half marathon at 50 in 2:12:33. "Running gives me time to reflect and is also a great anxiety reducer," she told me in December of 2013. "Reviewing my weekly mileage I feel a real sense of accomplishment and well-being overall. My kids think it's kind of cool too!"

GROWTH IN MASTERS RUNNING

To understand masters running today, it is helpful to understand the growth of running as a sport. The first running boom hit the United States in the early 1970s, inspired and promoted by a range of intense, elite runners and coaches—1972 Olympian Frank Shorter, marathoner Bill Rodgers, Dr. George Sheehan, Nike cofounder and University of Oregon coach Bill Bowerman, among them. Their followers were mainly highly competitive runners gifted with athletic talent and obsessed with race performance. Times, not fitness, were their focus. Logging 70 miles (112 km) and more a week was a norm for this running era.

From the mid-1980s to the present we've been in a second running boom, one in which masters have played an increasingly large role. This boom is different from the first one. This second boom is woven into mainstream culture; it is focused on running for everyone interested not just in achieving a personal best but also in fitness, overall health, life balance, community, and even fashion. Running today—even racing—is a way of life for many people. It has become a subculture.

"Running is not just for skinny ectomorphs," Ryan Lamppa, media director and researcher for Running USA, told me in 2012. Running USA is a nonprofit organization that promotes distance running and racing to benefit athletes, events, and running-related businesses. According to Running USA (2013), from 1990 to 2011 the number of road race finishers in this country grew by almost 300 percent (from 4,797,000 in 1990 to 13,974,000 in 2011). Within one year alone, from 2010 to 2011, U.S. road race finishers increased by 7.4 percent. The increase continues.

Masters running is one of the main reasons that this second boom is still growing. Oprah Winfrey, who ran her first marathon at 40, was one of the first "faces" of this boom. "More masters are doing road races than at any time in our country's history," Lamppa told me in a 2012 e-mail. He also said that in 1976, 28 percent of U.S. road race finishers were 40 or over. That jumped to 35 percent in 1990 and then again to 40 percent in 2011.

A growing percentage of these masters runners are women. In 1992, 7.7 percent, or 376,000, of U.S. road race finishers were women 40 and older. In 2011, approximately 19 percent, or 2.6 million, finishers were women 40 and older, according to Lamppa.

You'll likely see more and more older female runners in all races, including the Boston Marathon. According to the Boston Athletic Association, from 2001 to 2011 the number of female entrants age 40 to 49 more than doubled (1,490 to 3,868 entrants), the number of female entrants age 50 to 59 increased more than five times (280 to 1,416 entrants), and the number of female entrants age 60 to 69 increased almost six times (37 to 210 entrants).

The number of masters runners is increasing throughout the world as well. More masters are entering marathons than ever. At the 2011 New York City Marathon, 25,004 of the 47,133 finishers, 53 percent, were 40 and older. International championships for masters running that include competitions in track, road races, and cross country are attracting more masters than ever. The first such championships were held in August of 1975 in Toronto, Ontario, and included 1,427 men and women from 32 nations. The World Masters Athletics (WMA) championships are now held indoors and outdoors on alternating years. The most recent championships, the 2013 World Masters Athletics (WMA) outdoor championships in Porto Alegre, Brazil, hosted 4,158 competitors from 82 countries, said the event media representative, Lisiane Machado, in October 2013.

MEASURING PROGRESS

Whether or not you want to compete, you're a serious masters runner if you want to better your performance. Three ways to measure your progress are through your absolute times, your age-graded results, and how you place in your age group.

Your Absolute Times

Some runners who started running in their 40s have reached their best times in their 50s. No matter when you start, if you are starting, a personal best is waiting for you. Dr. Anders Ericsson, a psychologist who specializes in the study of expertise, states that it takes 10 years or 10,000 hours of focused practice in any field to achieve extraordinary performance (Ericsson et al. 1993). This research is supported by Bill Rodgers and Priscilla Welch, who write in their book, *Masters Running and Racing,* that masters runners achieve personal bests between 7 and 10 years of starting running, regardless of when they start. Welch started running at age 34 and ran a marathon in 3:26:12. At 42, 8 years later, she ran her fastest marathon, 2:26:51 (Rodgers and Welch 1991). My own research shows that masters who started running after age 30 improved their absolute times after 7.5 years of training no matter when they started running. Some of my athletes who ran casually in their 20s and 30s and who started focused training at 40 have achieved their personal best times in their mid-40s and even mid- to late-50s.

Your Age-Graded Results

Age grading, used since the mid-1970s, has grown in popularity. In masters championship races more prize money is often awarded to age-graded champions than to top finishers. Many other races post age-graded results as well.

What is age grading and how does it work? Age grading measures your running performance in a specific distance (e.g., 5K, 10K, half marathon) by taking into account your age and sex. It enables you to compare your performance against the performance of other runners in the same running distance, regardless of their age or sex or the time and location of the event.

The age-graded calculation takes world record performances for each age and distance, using data collated by the World Association of Veteran Athletics, to adjust your performance for age and sex. Your calculated age-graded score shows your performance as a percentage of the world record performance for your age and sex and the distance of your event. Say you are a 40-year-old man who has run 10 miles (16 km) in 58:30. The age-graded calculator would base your performance on the world record for a 40-year-old man running 10 miles, which is 46:31. Your age-graded performance would be 79.5 percent (46:31 divided by 58:30).

Using the score, you can compare yourself against runners of different ages from all over the world in the same event, even over a period of years. You can also track your performances over time, compare your results with men and women of all ages, identify your best events, and set goals for the future. (You can even, for better or worse, compete with your children!)

Calculation of the age-graded score is straightforward, although it is important to use the updated calculator, which you can find at www.usatf.org/statistics/calculators/ageGrading. The calculator requires you to insert your age and sex, the event distance, and your finish time. The calculator then produces an accurate age-graded evaluation of your performance. Standard track and field events as well as long-distance running events are included in age-graded tables.

The following relative standards apply:

100% = world record level

90% = world class

80% = national class

70% = regional class

60% = local class

How You Place in Your Age Group

If you're already competing in races, you may want to improve how you place relative to others your age. Most races list place finishers by age category, breaking masters into 5- or 10-year age divisions (e.g., 35 to 39 or 40 to 49, 50 to 59). Within each of these categories awards are generally given to first-, second-, and third-place finishers. Sometimes awards are given to the top five age group finishers.

If you now finish in the top half of your age division, you may aim to finish in the top third or quarter of your division or in the top five or better. Who doesn't want to win?

With new divisions—and therefore competitions—beginning with advancing ages every 5 or 10 years, masters runners often look forward to aging when it places them in a new age category. They are inspired anew by a chance to "recompete" and become the best as the youngest in a new division.

MASTERS EVENTS

First, you need to choose which events to enter. Know that while, as a masters runner, you can enter open races for all age groups, there are races for masters only. Information on masters events can be found at the international levels through World Masters Athletics (www.world-masters-athletics.org), and through national organizations such as USA Track & Field (USATF), United Kingdom Athletics, and Athletics Australia. Many of these, like USATF, have masters divisions themselves. Furthermore, within USATF are 57 associations covering their respective geographic regions. These associations, such as USATF New England, list regional and local masters events. All categories of races are offered regionally, nationally, and internationally. You can access a list of these associations at www.usatf.org/About/Associations.aspx. The remainder of this section lists events that you can enter.

Road Events

Road running is the sport of running on a measured course over an established road (as opposed to track, trail, or cross country course). Generally, a road race may be as short as a mile or as long as a marathon (26.2 miles [42 km]) or farther. Numerous kinds of championship events specifically for masters are available. These include 5K, 8K, 10K, 15K, half marathon, and marathon. Well-known races popular among masters in the United States include the New York City Marathon, Carlsbad 5000, Peachtree Road Race, Lilac Bloomsday Run, Boston Marathon, Crescent City Classic, and the Twin Cities Marathon. Thousands of road races take place all over the world.

Cross Country Events

Cross country races are run outdoors over natural terrain (as opposed to a track or the roads). The racing surface may include grass, dirt, mud, and sometimes gravel roads and may pass through woodlands and open country over hills and flat ground. Often occurring during the autumn and winter, cross country races are held in all kinds of temperatures and weather conditions, including snow, sleet, hail, and rain. Cross country events for masters generally include 5K, 6K, 8K, and 10K distances, although there can be other distances. Cross country is both an individual and a team sport. Individual results are based on times, and team scoring is based on runners' places. Cross country racing includes trail races; the major difference between the two is that trail running often covers longer distances (12K or more).

Mountain Events

Mountain races are run up and down mountains, some smaller, some larger. In New England, for example, you can try the 10K race up and down Wachusett Mountain. Well-known, longer mountain runs in New England are Mount Washington (7.6 miles [12.2 km]) in Gorham, New Hampshire, and Mount Cranmore (7.2 miles [11.6 km] for men and 4.8 miles [7.7 km] for women) in North Conway, New Hampshire. Both were recent sites for the U.S. Mountain Running Championships. Numerous challenging mountain races are run throughout the world. The 2012 World Masters Mountain Running Championships were held in Bühlertal, Germany, a 9.5-kilometer (6 miles) race that climbs 776 meters (2,546 feet).

Track Events

Track events take place on outdoor and indoor tracks over standard distances and can include obstacles such as hurdles and the water barrier in steeplechase. Track events range from sprints such as 55 meters indoors and 60 meters outdoors to distance events such as 3,000 meters indoors and 10,000 meters outdoors. Masters track relays include 4 × 100, 200, 400, 800, and 1,600 meters and 4 × mile (1.6 km). Track events also include the hurdles—60 meters indoors and 80, 100, 110, 200, 300, and 400 meters outdoors—and the steeplechase, an event that combines distance with hurdles and a water barrier. The steeplechase distance for women of all ages is 2,000 meters. The steeplechase distance for men 30 to 59 is 3,000 meters, and men 60 and older run 2,000 meters. The placement and height for hurdles and the steeple barriers vary depending on sex and age groups. Another event, the pentathlon, includes the 60-meter hurdles indoors and the 100-meter hurdles outdoors along with high jump, shot put, long jump, and the 800-meter run.

Ultradistance Events

Ultradistance running events include races longer than a marathon, or 26.2 miles (42 km). They may take place on paved roads, dirt roads, wooded trails, grass, or mountain paths and involve obstacles or rugged terrain.

Generally, there are two types of ultradistance events: those that cover a specific distance and those that take place during a specified time and the winner determined by who covers the most distance in that time. The most common distances are 50K (31 miles), 100K (62 miles), 50 miles (80 km) and 100 miles (161 km). Timed events may last for hours—6, 12, 24, 48—or even 6 or 10 days.

One of the most popular ultradistance events, covering 89 kilometers (55 miles), is the Comrades Marathon in South Africa, capped at 13,000 entrants. Others are the Marathon des Sables, a ten-day, 149-mile (240 km) ultramarathon across the Sahara Desert; the Spartathlon, the 246-kilometer (153 miles) ultramarathon held annually in Greece since 1983 between Athens and Sparta; and the Western States, the oldest and largest 100-mile (161 km) trail run in the United States.

Running and the Meaning of Life: Amby Burfoot

Cathy Utzschneider: You're a legend in the running world: runner, author, speaker, and *Runner's World* editor at large. Can you give a bird's-eye summary of your running and writing?

Amby Burfoot: I had the good fortune to begin running at age 16 at Fitch High in Groton, Connecticut, under the coaching of John J. Kelley, the 1957 Boston Marathon winner, and most influential individual in my life. I won the Boston Marathon in 1968, the first American winner since Kelley, and have finished the Manchester Thanksgiving Day Road Race 50 years in a row.

Victah Sailer/Victah@photorun.net

I began working at *Runner's World* in 1978 and have been there ever since, currently as editor at large. I have written four books, including a popular little manual called *The Runner's Guide to the Meaning of Life*. It's not heavy; it just talks about themes that run through every runner's life.

Cathy: You write in *The Runner's Guide* about meaning and connections. Can you elaborate a bit?

Amby: Running gives us time to think about life's important issues. I have always found that my miles lead me to connect with the physical environment around me—land, water, air, food—and the people I run with. I treasure both relationships and wouldn't exchange one for the other. Every run makes me richer, either through observation, internal conversations, or actual exchanges with my running partners.

Cathy: What are your thoughts on winning?

Amby: Winning is great. I'll take it every time. But it's not essential. No one wins every race, no one gets faster every year (certainly not after 20 or 30 years), and no one outruns Father Time. So it seems to me that the essential issue in running is how to enjoy and appreciate it without concern for performance, for winning. That's why I tell everyone they should focus on building their mental muscle even more than their cardiac and skeletal muscles. It's all about motivation.

(continued)

Amby Burfoot *(continued)*

Cathy: You talk also about running and losing. Can you share some thoughts here?

Amby: When I was young, I won more than my share of races. That was a glorious time, and I'll always treasure the memories. But the last 30 years, I've been losing way more than my share. And that's okay too. If you can't learn how to be a good loser, in every sense of the words, then you're not going to continue running for long. For me, longevity was always the goal. "Old John" A. Kelley, who finished Boston 58 times, was one of the first serious runners I ever met and a great role model.

Cathy: What do we learn about courage from running?

Amby: We learn that courage has many forms. It takes courage and toughness to win races, but it takes even more courage to keep running when you don't win. I have absolutely as much respect for people in the back of the pack—more or less where I am now—as I have for winners. They differ much more in talent than they do in courage. Talent makes you fast. Courage keeps you going.

Cathy: You write about materialism in a chapter called "What You Really Need, You Already Have" and include a chapter on simplicity. Can you comment on these?

Amby: I learned about the value of simplicity from both John J. Kelley and from Charlie "Doc" Robbins, who finished the Manchester Road Race 56 times. Kelley was a great follower of Henry David Thoreau. I'm not sure who inspired Robbins, a psychiatrist, or where he got his ideas from. I can't speak for anyone else when I talk about materialism. I can only talk about my own life. And I have always found that I am happiest when I focus on what I have, not what I don't have. I've been finding that tough of late. Everyone else seems to have lots of cool Apple products and to do amazing things with them. I think I might like to do similar creative things. But I remain happiest with my health, my family, my friends, my fitness, and a simple, mostly vegetarian diet.

Chapter 2

Understanding Running and Aging

Masters runners often ask how aging affects their running. They want context to understand and appreciate their performance. If you're over 30, and particularly if you're over 40 or 50, you're probably beginning to encounter the effects of senescence: normal physiological aging. While aging and the deterioration of the various systems ultimately affect performance, masters runners who understand it can learn to delay it to some degree.

AGING AND THE PHYSICAL DEMANDS OF RUNNING

Aging and running each places its own demands on our bodies. Understanding their interrelated effects will help you plan your training and set your goals. You'll be able to remain optimistic but also realistic. If you're just starting a training program, you should always check with your physician first.

INEVITABLE EFFECTS OF AGING

It's true that some masters runners we read about turn out unforgettable, inspirational performances that make us wonder, "Is that person immune to the aging process?" How can Ed Whitlock, for example, run a 3:15:54 marathon at age 80? But, we all know that no one—not you, me, or Ed—can escape the inevitable effects of aging. Aging may not look the same from individual to individual, but neither does growing. Given that the aging process follows general patterns—and that knowledge is power—you might as well know what to expect.

Effects on Vital Signs

Masters runners should understand the basics about vital signs—heart rate, respiration rate (the number of breaths you take in a minute), blood pressure, and body temperature. Running obviously increases your body's demand for energy, affecting some of these signs. Knowing what happens to them during running as you age can help you understand what is healthy and what isn't, what to look out for.

Resting Heart Rate

Resting heart rate (RHR), the number of heartbeats per minute at rest, stays fairly constant through adulthood, provided that fitness level stays fairly constant. (Resting heart rate generally reflects fitness level.) Sedentary adults have resting heart rates of 60 to 100 beats per minute compared to 40 to 60 beats per minute for very active adults. This is because the cardiovascular systems of active adults are more efficient than those of sedentary adults.

Clearly, however, running increases your need for oxygen. To get enough of it, your heart must pump blood more quickly. When you run fast or race, your heart rate approaches maximum levels. Unlike RHR, maximum heart rate (MHR)—the highest number of heartbeats per minute (BPM) experienced at the end of a race or in maximal exercise—decreases with age. Whether you are sedentary or active, MHR declines about one beat per minute each year, or about 40 beats per minute between the ages of 20 and 60. A simple method to calculate your MHR, accurate to within about 10 beats per minute, is the formula 220 minus your age. For example, if you are 34, your predicted MHR is 186 BPM, or 220 minus 34.

Frankly, few masters runners from Liberty Athletic Club, where I coach, base their efforts on heart rate, relying more on pace per mile or perceived exertion or both. That said, if you are pacing your runs according to percentage of maximum heart rate and incorporating intense sprints at an effort above 95 percent of your maximum heart rate, check with your doctor first if you have health issues. That intensity challenges the heart, joints, and muscles. I've also seen many masters runners who race distances from the 5K and up limit the intensity of their hard days to 90 percent of maximum heart rate, and they're posting excellent results.

For an accurate measure of your maximum heart rate, take a 10- to 20-minute stress test at a qualified facility, such as a hospital or fitness testing center. During the test you will exercise to your limit—often on a treadmill while someone periodically increases its speed or slope—while you're attached to a heart rate monitor or electrocardiogram (ECG). One or the other will show your maximum heart rate during the final moments of maximal exertion.

Respiration Rate

Like heart rate, respiration rate—the number of breaths taken per minute—increases with running. As you know, when you run you breathe faster and deeper to supply your heart, lungs, and muscles with oxygen. While respiration rate remains fairly constant with age, it's harder for older runners to extract as much oxygen with each breath than it is for younger runners.

Blood Pressure

And what about blood pressure? That's also affected by running. Blood pressure refers to the pressure of the circulating blood on blood vessel walls and is divided into systolic and diastolic pressure. Systolic pressure refers to the force in the arteries when the heart beats, pumping out blood. Diastolic pressure refers to the force in the arteries when the heart relaxes between beats. In healthy adults, blood pressure remains the same through the decades. Normal blood pressure is 120 over 80, and ideally less than 120 for systolic and less than 80 for diastolic pressure. You may, however, be among those 20 percent of adults or the almost half of adults over 65 who have slightly elevated blood pressure. In any case, running raises not your diastolic, but your systolic blood pressure. Like other kinds of exercise that involve intensity, running can cause normal blood pressure to increase to 200 over 80 and as high as 300 over 80. These readings are dangerously high, indicating too much pressure on the blood vessel walls. The bottom line is that your blood pressure should be checked before you start a training program, and clearance from your doctor is important.

If you're at risk for developing high blood pressure, you can take routine measures in your training to moderate it. A warm-up before and cool-down after running help your blood pressure adjust gradually to different levels of stress. Warm up by walking or jogging slowly for at least 10 minutes. Cool down by walking or jogging for at least 10 minutes. (Stopping too suddenly after your run can cause a sharp drop in blood pressure, resulting in lightheadedness and cramping.) Don't hold your breath while running because that can raise blood pressure. In terms of diet, limit your salt intake and avoid caffeine, which can raise blood pressure before and during a run.

Body Temperature

Body temperature stays constant throughout life, but a strenuous run can raise it. In addition, running in hot and humid conditions can raise core temperature in any runner, and masters are more affected by humid conditions than open runners. Middle-aged bodies are less efficient at sweating, a cooling mechanism for the body. Masters runners are also more sensitive to cold. Their skin is less likely to constrict (shiver) to preserve body heat, and their metabolism is generally slower.

Decreased Cardiopulmonary Function

You can appreciate performance as a master most if you know the effects of aging on your heart and lungs. You know the theme by now: heart and lung capacity declines with aging, too. Of all the physiological declines, those in the heart and lungs affect performance the most. One of the main reasons athletic performance decreases with age is that the heart and blood vessels become less efficient. As a review, the cardiopulmonary system includes the heart, both a reservoir for blood and a pump that circulates blood through the body, blood vessels, and the lungs, which deliver oxygen to and eliminate carbon dioxide from tissues.

What's useful to know about the heart, aging, and running? The heart weighs about .8 pound (363 g) in young, healthy adults. It grows as we age, and as it does, it decreases the size of the left ventricular chamber from which newly oxygenated blood is pumped through the body. During maximal exertion, stroke volume—the amount of blood pumped out with each heartbeat—also declines. Less blood means less oxygen for energy for running. Cardiac output, the amount of blood pumped out each minute, also diminishes with aging because our blood vessels (veins, arteries, capillaries) become less able to stretch and pump blood.

Regarding the lungs, ventilation—taking in oxygen and expelling carbon dioxide—decreases. The diaphragm, the muscle that helps the lungs expand and contract and therefore draw air into the lungs, becomes weaker and stiffer. Also the alveoli, tiny grapelike sacs where oxygen and carbon dioxide are exchanged, decrease in size and number. And the capillaries that carry blood to the alveoli decrease in number as well. The result is that by the time you're 80, your maximum breathing capacity will be about 40 percent of what it was at 30. That looks like more labored breathing, whether you're running or walking to the mailbox.

Decreased $\dot{V}O_2$max

$\dot{V}O_2$max, the single best measure of overall cardiovascular performance or fitness level, also declines. V represents volume, O_2 represents oxygen, and max is maximum. $\dot{V}O_2$max is usually expressed in relative terms, as milliliters of oxygen consumed per kilogram of body weight per minute (ml/kg/min). Essentially, $\dot{V}O_2$max is the greatest amount of oxygen that can be used at the cellular level by the entire body during physical activity. A high $\dot{V}O_2$max generally correlates with high endurance performance.

How much does $\dot{V}O_2$max decline with aging? In terms of percentages, it declines by an average of about 10 percent per decade in sedentary adults after ages 25 to 30. As an example, a 10 percent decline per decade translates to the equivalent of adding 30 seconds to a 10K personal best each year (or adding 5 minutes in 10 years). Despite the general decline in $\dot{V}O_2$max, though, continued vigorous training can slow the rate of decline per decade from 10 to 5 percent (Joyner 1993; Marti and Howald 1990). One 22-year longitudinal study found that while continued training can lower that decline to 5 to 7 percent, two exceptional elite male runners had declines of as little as 2 percent per decade between ages 22 and 46 (Trappe et al. 1996; Marti and Howald 1990).

Some studies of masters athletes have shown that this decline accelerates at certain times, from the mid-50s to mid-60s, and then again in the mid-70s. One study of 2,599 masters runners by Dr. Vonda Wright, orthopedic surgeon at the University of Pittsburgh, pointed to an unusually sharp decline at age 75 (Wright and Perricelli 2008).

Having watched women from their 20s to 70s run weekly quarter- and half-mile intervals over 20 years, I can see this decline clearly on the track. Here's just one example of two national-class middle-distance masters runners (with aliases) that shows how the decline can accelerate from the mid-50s to the mid-60s. At 52, Sarah typically ran 5 to 6 seconds behind 40-year-old Linda on half-mile (800 m) intervals. Both trained similarly and were equally talented. On those same intervals 12 years later, with similar continued training, Sarah, in her mid-60s, was 15 to 16 seconds behind Linda, then in her early 50s.

So what can you do to mitigate the decline in $\dot{V}O_2$max? Granted, some things are out of your control. You can't control genetics, which accounts for 25 to 50 percent of variance in $\dot{V}O_2$max. You can't always control disease, which lowers $\dot{V}O_2$max. And you obviously can't control aging. But you can gradually raise your level of activity—distance or speed—and you can control the quality of your diet. Excess fat lowers $\dot{V}O_2$max (So and Choi 2010). So take heart (and make the most of it)!

Bone and Muscle Loss

The theme continues. With aging, you lose bone as well. Men and women alike experience age-related bone loss sometime between ages 20 and 30, and that loss continues in later decades. You lose bone strength and flexibility. The rate of protein synthesis and the production of human growth hormone, both essential for the strength and flexibility of bone, decrease and your bones begin to lose minerals like calcium and phosphate. Your bones become more porous and more susceptible to fractures. Bone loss is accelerated by a sedentary lifestyle, hormone deficiencies, poor nutrition including calcium or vitamin D deficiency, excessive caffeine and alcohol intake, and smoking.

Some of the effects of bone loss are visible and some aren't. If you see someone whose spine is curved, you're seeing the effects of bone loss; vertebral discs become compressed and there's less joint space between them. Older people lose height. By age 80, you can expect to lose approximately two inches (5 cm) of height (about half an inch [1.3 cm] per decade after 40). What is harder to see is loss of bone density throughout the body, which is osteopenia or osteoporosis, discussed later in this chapter.

Skeletal muscle begins to decline after age 30, particularly if you are sedentary. The decline is more rapid after age 50, and still steeper after 60 (Williams et al. 2002; Booth et al. 1994; Grimby and Saltin 1983). Skeletal muscle fibers (muscle mass) atrophy—they weaken and die—as you age. We are born with all the muscle fibers we will have. A biceps muscle of a newborn contains about 500,000 individual fibers. An 80-year-old man has about 300,000 fibers. The term for the age-related decline in the number of muscle fibers and in the strength per unit of muscle is *sarcopenia*.

If you wonder why explosive running events seem more challenging as you age than endurance events do, know that it's related to what happens to the two basic kinds of muscle fibers in our bodies: Type I (slow-twitch) and Type II (fast-twitch) fibers. Type I fibers contract slowly and use oxygen efficiently and are used for endurance events like marathons. Type II fibers, of which there are two kinds—Type IIa and Type IIb—contract quickly and tire easily. These are used for strong, explosive events like sprints. As we age, Type II fibers decrease in size and number more than Type I fibers do.

As you lose muscle fibers and mass, you lose strength and power, particularly if you don't strength train. From 30 to 80, you lose about 40 percent of the muscle strength in the legs and back muscles and 30 percent in the arms (Grimby and Saltin 1983; Holloszy and Kohrt 1995). The good news is that you maintain considerable muscle mass in your legs just from running, and if you strength train a few times a week with a focus on your other muscles, you can minimize that muscle loss considerably. Chapter 9 discusses strength training.

Stress to Bones, Joints, Muscles, and Tendons

Yes, running is undeniably stressful on our skeletal muscles (all 640 of them), bones (206), joints (360), tendons (4,000 plus), and ligaments (900). It's said that we land with two to four times our body weight on every step and that the average runner takes approximately 1,500 steps per mile (1.6 km). That adds up. At 40 miles (64 km) a week, that's 60,000 steps a week and 3,120,000 steps per year. That stress on bones, joints, and muscles increases with age. I can see that at Tuesday-night track practice. The masters runners in their 70s often call it quits on intervals before the runners in their 30s, 40s, and 50s. They feel the impact of pounding earlier than younger runners. And they're smart to listen to their bodies, a skill to practice as a masters runner. As a result, they're successful runners. (One, Mary Harada, has won numerous national age group titles and set several world age group records. Another, Carrie Parsi, has won her age division in the Boston Marathon and set single age group records 14 times in the Mount Washington road race.)

How does running challenge your joints in particular? First, joints include bone, muscles, synovial fluid, cartilage, and ligaments. The repetitive motion of running can wear away the cartilage, the substance that lubricates joints, cushioning the ends of the bones. As cartilage erodes, bones rub together, causing a grating feeling, inflammation, and stiffness. Synovial fluid, a viscous fluid that reduces friction in joints, becomes thinner with aging. Despite these stressors, know that weight-bearing exercise like running, if not overdone, can keep your cartilage and ligaments healthy. It can promote absorption of nutrients into cartilage and increase its hydration. Exercise can increase production of synovial fluid. Balance and moderation are key.

As joints become stiffer, masters runners, as you probably well know, lose flexibility. If you could touch the floor with your palms at 20, chances are you can't at age 50. Most likely, you've lost range of motion. You're more limited in your ability to extend and flex your hips. Older runners have shorter strides than younger runners, as the results of one study showed, comparing strides in older and younger male marathoners (Conoboy and Dyson 2006). The strides of 40- to 49-year-old runners were 2.4 meters (7.8 feet). Those of the runners 60 and over were 2 meters (6.6 feet). Following a regular, focused stretching routine, especially after a run when your muscles are warm, can help you maintain flexibility. Chapter 6 discusses flexibility and stretching.

Masters runners are also more likely than open runners to feel soreness, strains, and tears in their muscles and tendons. As noted earlier, older muscles have lower percentages of Type II muscle fibers than younger ones and the mitochondria (the power centers in cells where nutrients are broken down to create energy) in older muscle fibers become increasingly dysfunctional. Hamstring and calf strains are among the most common muscle injuries that plague masters runners. In tendons, water content decreases with age, making them stiffer and less able to tolerate stress. Like many masters runners, I've had recurring Achilles tendinitis (inflammation of the Achilles) that sidelined me for four or five years in my late 40s. (I returned to periodic competition in my 50s.) A progression of Achilles tendinitis, tendinosis is a degeneration of the tendon that's common among masters runners. To alleviate soreness and help circulation, many masters swear by regular massages including a technique called active release therapy, physical therapy, yoga, chiropractic appointments, and acupuncture. If you follow a thoughtful training plan, listen to your body, and avail yourself of the wide variety of practitioners in sports medicine, you can meet most challenges you'll face.

Less Energy and Slower Metabolism

Decline also occurs in our metabolism and thus our levels of energy as we age. (That's hard to see in masters runners, though. Most masters runners are lean and energetic.) One of the main reasons basal metabolism slows is that the various enzymes crucial to metabolism decrease. After about age 25, metabolism begins to decline between 2 and 5 percent or more per decade. That feels like fatigue— you get more tired over the decades—and without exercise, that looks like fat. Between ages 25 and 75, sedentary adults can expect to see total body fat double as a proportion of the body's composition.

Like VO_2max and muscle loss, declining metabolism and energy involve factors you can control and some you can't. Age, size, and genetics determine 60 to 75 percent of your metabolism. You can, however, control what you eat and how much you exercise. Clearly, running burns calories, which is one of the main reasons many people start running in the first place. Of the 103 competitive masters female runners studied in my doctoral dissertation (Utzschneider 2002), all began running not for competition but for health and fitness. Furthermore, only 6 of the 103 runners, whose average age was 51, were unhappy with their weight. That's unusual for a population of middle-aged women. Formulae for calculating calories burned while running vary (and some are complicated) and depend on several factors, including speed, distance, body weight, genetics, and age. No one formula fits everyone. One easy formula I use is to multiply your body weight by .65 by the number of miles run. Say you weigh 120 pounds and run 5 miles. Multiplying 120 by .65 by 5 you can figure that you burn about 390 calories.

Prolonged Recovery

Recovery is one of the basic principles of training, particularly for masters runners. If you want to get more fit—to "up the ante" in your workouts—you have to learn how to recover. If you're increasing the intensity, duration, or frequency of your runs or races, you need more rest to let your muscles repair and grow stronger. The swimmer Dara Torres is a good example of someone who recognized the importance of prolonged recovery for a master. At 41 at the U.S. Olympic Trials for the 2008 Beijing Olympics, she qualified for the individual 100-meter and 50-meter freestyle, the 4 × 100-meter medley relay, and the 4 × 100-meter freestyle relay.

Running and the Brain: John Ratey, MD

Want to know about the effect of running on the brain? Dr. John Ratey, who is a guru on the topic, is the one to ask.

John Ratey

Psychiatrist and associate clinical professor of psychiatry at Harvard Medical School, Dr. Ratey has been researching, speaking, and writing about the effect of exercise on the brain for more than 30 years. He has published 60 peer-reviewed articles on issues in neuropsychiatry and written six books, including *A User's Guide to the Brain*, published in 2000, and *Spark: The Revolutionary New Science of Exercise and the Brain*, published in 2008.

Ratey's focus on exercise and the brain stems from a lifelong interest in athletics and exercise. Ratey was a competitive athlete, playing baseball, basketball, and tennis through high school, and a nationally ranked tennis player at age 16. Now he is a self-proclaimed gym rat. "I try to do something every day," he said. He lifts weights regularly, runs occasional 5Ks and sprints on the treadmill three times a week. "I usually do five to six 30- to 60-second sprints (with a walking break of two and a half minutes between efforts) at a setting of 8 and an incline of 8 depending on how I am feeling."

Ratey began focused research on exercise and the brain in the 1980s when several Harvard and MIT professors who happened to be marathoners, approached him, knowing he was a psychiatrist. "They were marathon runners who had to stop running because of injury. As a result they were depressed and couldn't focus and didn't know why. They were getting angry and they were procrastinating for the first time in their lives, all symptoms of ADD (attention deficit disorder)."

Cathy Utzschneider: What should masters runners (runners over 30) know about the effect of running on the brain?

Dr. Ratey: They should know that running is what our genes are coded for. Since the hunter–gatherer period, our brains have evolved to expect movement like running. We were expected to be movers, foragers, joggers, sprinters. When you're running, you're the head-of-the-tribe runner. What running and competition does is not just keep your weight down but also your brain up.

Cathy: How does it keep your brain up?

Dr. Ratey: Evolution's gift to us is that moving, more than any other activity, helps generate more brain cells. Moving increases the brain's concentration of a protein called BDNF, or brain-derived neurotrophic factor. I call it "Miracle-Gro for the brain" because it really is brain fertilizer. We have stem cells in our brain, and BDNF is one of those important proteins that helps the stem cells grow into new brain cells. BDNF also helps brain cells connect with each other.

Cathy: Isn't this discovery about being able to grow new nerve cells fairly recent?

Dr. Ratey: Yes, neurogenesis—the growth of brand-new nerve cells—in humans is something we didn't know about until 1999. Until then, it was thought that we were born with all the brain cells we were ever going to have.

Cathy: I read in *Spark* that exercise improves our ability to learn. You mentioned a 2007 study by German researchers whose subjects learned vocabulary words 20 percent faster after rather than before exercising. Is this true?

Dr. Ratey: Yes, more means you can improve both your ability to learn and your rate of learning. Learning means wiring cells together in cell assembly lines that are selectively connected. BDNF helps brain cells prepare to learn, learn new concepts, and develop new skills. Experiments with rats and mice have shown that exercise helps learners be more alert, motivated, and focused and less impulsive, more willing to overcome frustration.

Cathy: In *Spark*, you mention that regular exercise like running helps build up neurotransmitters and receptors of neurotransmitters, which deliver the equivalent effects of drinking coffee or taking Ritalin and Prozac.

Dr. Ratey: Yes, when you run, you release dopamine, norepinephrine, serotonin, and endorphins. Among other things, dopamine improves mood and motivation. Serotonin improves mood, lessens impulsivity, and moderates anger. Norepinephine improves attention and perception, and endorphins modulate pain, relieve anxiety, and calm the brain.

Cathy: You also mention that exercise helps us become more social. How is that?

Dr. Ratey: Exercise promotes our brains to be more receptive to others. It raises our neurotransmitters and makes us less socially anxious and more motivated. And it raises our oxytocin levels. Oxytocin is our love and bonding hormone. Exercise boosts our self-esteem, and exercise in a pair or group automatically increases our interaction with others. Many people who get involved in ongoing exercise with a trainer, a masters group, a running or walking partner, or a CrossFit-type of environment make new connections that often become an important part of their lives.

Cathy: I encourage runners to do drills requiring coordination before they start running. Do they deliver benefits that are different from those derived from endurance and interval running?

Dr. Ratey: Yes. Exercise that incorporates coordination challenges actually uses the most of your brain. Getting your heart rate up to a maximum of 90 percent for short periods is important, but so are periods of exercise involving coordination challenges.

Cathy: What's next for you?

Dr. Ratey: I'm working on three more books, one with a working title called *Human 1.0* about how we should be living according to our hunter–gatherer genes. It covers how we should eat, exercise, love, live, and play. Another is called *Spark in Action,* and includes stories of people who have triumphed over mental health problems (depression, anxiety, addictions, and stress).

But she withdrew from the 100-meter freestyle precisely because she knew that prolonged recovery from so many events would hurt her chances of succeeding in the 50 meters and the relays. The lesson: as a masters runner, be selective about what and how much you do.

What qualifies as recovery for masters runners? It may mean time off before or after a race, time easing off between seasons, cutback weeks when preparing for a major event, or rest after a track interval. It may be running easy instead of hard, cross-training (riding a bike, swimming, or water running, for example), weight lifting, or yoga, anything that gives your legs a break from intensive pounding so you avoid injury and illness.

What about examples of recovery? First, know that genetics, training history, and how you feel on a particular day all influence how much time you need for recovery. Sometimes recovery doesn't depend on age. I coach a world-class runner in her late-60s who's often ready for another interval sooner than some of the runners in their 20s. The following are my guidelines regarding recovery.

Age

The older you are, the more recovery you should take, no matter how fast you run. Train yourself to listen carefully to your body. Your own judgment trumps any rule. (If you're on the track with others, don't get distracted by their energy levels.)

Planning Your Race Year

Your year as a masters runner should include several periods of relaxed weeks to recharge your mind and body and help you stay free of injury. There is no hard-and-fast rule for what relaxed weeks should look like. That depends on you and your race experience. Too much time off from running can make reentry difficult. Some rest during the year is helpful. Too much is not. In relaxed weeks, my runners typically reduce their mileage by 30 to 40 percent, cut out intense workouts and races, cross-train, and focus on other life priorities.

John Barbour, 60, has perspective on that balance for masters, having run since he was a freshman in high school; coached middle school, high school, college, and club teams; and been named USATF runner of the year among men 45 to 49. His personal bests are 14:42 for the 5K, 29:33 for the 10K, 1:07:05 for the half marathon, and 2:19:25 for the marathon, he told me recently. Comparing his days of running as an open runner to today, he said that "those days when everything clicks and you feel smooth and easy are fewer and further between. I've learned that, while rest is valuable, too much rest (i.e., long breaks) makes one more prone to injury during the comeback, so maintain some level of running activity even on down periods, whenever possible."

Cutback Weeks

While you can generally increase mileage by 10 percent each week, also incorporate cutback weeks every fourth or at least every fifth week. These refresh your training and prevent overload, not only in training but also in fitting it into the rest of your life. In cutback weeks you might lower your training by 10 to 25 percent and then return the following week to the level before the cutback week. If you're feeling unusually tired or if you feel a nagging soreness in a particular spot, have the courage to lower your running by as much as 50 percent and either cross-train or rest instead.

Hard Workouts of the Week

Some competitive masters runners include two hard workouts a week. Runners in their 30s, 40s, and mid-50s should take at least two recovery days between intense workouts. A Tuesday track workout may be followed by a Friday track workout, for example. Many runners in their mid-50s and older are better off with at least three recovery days between intensive training.

Intervals (All Paces)

If you're unsure whether or not you're ready for another speed interval, check your heart rate. It should be at least 120 beats per minute. If it's over that, wait until it returns to 120.

Gender

If you're a woman and you need more recovery time than some of your male running friends, know that hormonal differences give them an advantage. Men have more testosterone, the hormone that helps not only protein synthesis but also muscle repair and growth, including recovery from tough workouts.

Declining Motivation

You think? Who wouldn't be surprised to hear that staying motivated can be a challenge for masters? Times slow, injuries threaten more often, and energy diminishes. Numbers of participants in older masters age groups—55 and particularly 60 and older—decline in all kinds of races. Running USA's 2011 road race age group distribution records of male and female finishers confirm this.

What helps masters runners stay motivated? First, don't take on too many responsibilities. Too many responsibilities, not injury, was the major obstacle faced by the masters runners in my doctoral study (Utzschneider 2002). Keep a journal and write down goals. Find a club. Train with a partner. Ask your family to help you stay motivated, schedule your runs, and eat healthily. I wrote my first book, *MOVE! How Women Can Achieve Athletic Goals,* precisely because motivation is such a major challenge for masters. It addresses the above issues.

WEATHER AND ENVIRONMENTAL CONDITIONS

Here's more not-so-good news about the effect of aging on our bodies. They're more susceptible to extreme heat and cold. Older bodies are less able to regulate core temperature. In hot and humid conditions, they're more susceptible to heatstroke. Older bodies sweat less readily so they're unable to cool down as efficiently. Beginning signs of heatstroke vary but may include an extremely high body temperature (above 103 degrees F or 39.4 degrees C); red, hot, and dry skin (with little or no sweating); rapid, strong pulse initially, followed by a weak and rapid pulse; throbbing headache; dizziness; nausea; shortness of breath; and confusion. To avoid heatstroke, stay out of the sun, drink plenty of water, slow down, and wear light-colored clothing made of fabrics like CoolMax or Dri-Fit that wick moisture away from your skin so cooling evaporation can occur.

Older athletes are also more sensitive to cold. They're less able to differentiate changes in temperature well and are more susceptible to hypothermia, which occurs when core body temperature is less than 95 degrees Fahrenheit (35 C). In older people, vasoconstriction, the narrowing of blood vessels to maintain body heat, and shivering, a muscular response to generate heat, function less efficiently (Collins et al. 1980; Young 1991; Young and Lee 1997). Beginning signs of hypothermia are shivering and increased breathing rate, heart rate, and blood pressure. Below a core body temperature of 95 degrees, symptoms worsen and include confusion, lack of concentration, and slurred speech. At the worst stages, the heart beats irregularly. Hypothermia can be fatal. Side effects include chilblains, superficial ulcers of the skin, and frostbite.

Wearing the right kind of clothing in wet, cold, and windy conditions can help you withstand the most adverse conditions. If you run in the rain or wind, you want clothing that is water resistant or waterproof, breathable, and wind resistant. In cold weather, you want thermal, breathable underwear (look for polypropylene fabric). Breathable gear for everything—neck warmers, hats, socks, gloves, even face masks—helps wick sweat away from your skin so it stays dry and you stay warm. One winter during a three-week double-digit subzero cold spell, two of my masters runners discarded their egos and donned face masks to train for the February Hyannis Half Marathon. "We were toasty after 15 minutes!" one of them said recently.

Dress for your run as if it's 10 degrees Fahrenheit warmer than the actual outside temperature. You'll be slightly chilled for the first 10 minutes or so, but then toasty warm for the duration. Among materials that many runners like are Gore-Tex, Activent, and Dryroad. Materials like these can keep you smiling on the coldest, wettest, or windiest days.

SPECIAL CHALLENGES FOR WOMEN

Masters female runners face unique issues for a range of reasons. Women's physiology, with monthly hormonal changes and menopause, presents its own issues, one being susceptibility to anemia from blood loss. Less obvious but also apparent are societal pressures for women of all ages to be thin. Some women masters runners do struggle to hold an "ideal" weight to race their best.

Female Athlete Triad

The female athlete triad—the three-part syndrome consisting of eating disorders, amenorrhea, and premature osteopenia (a mild form of osteoporosis)—is not just a young woman's condition today. More and more women in their 30s and 40s and even 50s are joining the ranks of young female runners, gymnasts, and skaters who suffer from at least a few aspects of the triad. While there's little research on the triad in masters female runners, there are aspects of it in some who are gaunt and apparently not fueling their bodies to the extent they should given their activity level. Signs of the female triad are bony hips and shoulders, brittle hair, and dry skin. Some women say that they appreciate the fact that light weight will help them run faster, and many of them have had children, so irregular menses is not a concern. These women generally take calcium, knowing that they don't eat enough calcium-rich foods, such as milk and cheese.

I've occasionally noticed what I'll call a lemming effect in groups of female runners, including masters: if a faster runner in a group starts losing weight, it's not discussed but others around her also start losing weight. A Division I college runner recently confirmed the lemming effect, saying that it works both ways with female athletes. Her college team was unusually free of eating disorders because its captain, one of the fastest runners, modeled and encouraged healthy eating habits.

Coaches shouldn't hesitate to tell women whom they suspect are underfueling themselves that eating enough and getting proper nutrition, including calcium and fat, can mitigate signs of the syndrome. If you eat more calcium, you'll be less susceptible to osteopenia. I've occasionally asked women who appear too thin—the main sign of the triad—to check their body mass index (BMI). BMI is a number calculated from your weight and height. According to the National Institutes of Health, if your BMI is less than 18.5, you fall in the malnourished category. (A BMI of 18.5 to 24.9 is in the normal and healthy weight range.) You can calculate your BMI by dividing your weight in pounds by your height in inches squared and multiplying that result by 703. Using a metric equation to calculate BMI, divide your weight in kilograms by the square of your height in meters. There are numerous web-based BMI calculators to help you calculate your BMI, if you don't want to do the math yourself. Of course skinny doesn't always mean healthy (something many women already know), and it doesn't always mean fast. Healthy nutrition and a body mass index in the healthy range are the goals. Sometimes heavier is even faster. I've seen quite a few masters runners post personal bests in races after gaining a few extra pounds. (I ran my personal best mile and 5K carrying a few extra pounds.)

Diet and Self-Image

Related to the female athlete triad, diet (to achieve low weight) and self-image are growing concerns for women in middle age. Driving the increase is a sometimes unrealistic societal expectation that women should be too thin in middle age: the skinny ectomorph is the ideal body image, our advertisements and movies suggest. At the same time, slowing metabolisms and menopause threaten waistlines with the midriff "spare tire." Some women do everything possible—including running, weight training, walking, and limiting caloric intake—to avoid it. Focus on diet and thinness also gives a sense of control at a time when mounting responsibilities, such as juggling the demands of a full-time job with the pressures of caring for children, grandchildren, and ill parents, leave women little time for themselves. Interestingly, more than a handful of elite masters female runners have said that the "spare tire" of five additional pounds (2.3 kg) that appeared during menopause miraculously disappeared 5 to 10 years later.

Increasingly, women of middle age are determining their self-worth by their weight and body image. According to a study of 1,849 women 50 and older published in the *International Journal of Eating Disorders* (Gagne et al. 2012), 62 percent said their weight or shape negatively affects their life, and 64 percent think about their weight at least once a day. They used several unhealthy methods to become thin, including diet pills (7.5%) and excessive exercise (7%). "Fifteen years ago, it was very rare to have a patient with an eating disorder at midlife," said Ann Kearney-Cooke, PhD, a Cincinnati psychologist who specializes in eating disorders. "Now, half my patients are women 35 to 70." (Moyer 2012, p. 1)

One of the worst eating and control disorders, anorexia, is increasingly common, unfortunately, among middle-aged women in many countries, including the United States, Britain, and Australia. According to Holly Grishkat, PhD, director of The Renfrew Center, an eating disorder treatment center, eating disorders among middle-aged women have increased by 42 percent from 2001 to 2010 (Sheridan 2012). An Australian study found that from 1995 to 2005 the rate of fasting and binge eating increased significantly among women age 55 to 64 (Hay et al. 2008).

Iron Issues

With all that women masters runners are juggling in their lives, it's not unusual for them to be tired. While fatigue may be caused by many things, including crazy schedules and insufficient sleep, you may find you're anemic, or low in iron. If you are, in addition to being generally exhausted, your running times are likely to rise (you'll get slower). Other symptoms of low iron levels are pale skin, headaches, being unable to recover from a poor night's sleep, and unexpected shortness of breath during exertion. Iron deficiencies are also difficult to detect because they develop gradually.

Masters female runners are more prone to anemia than many groups for several reasons. First, not many of them (as far as I can see) eat a lot of red meat, one of the best sources of iron. Second, foot strike during running destroys red blood cells, the cells that "grab" oxygen and distribute it throughout your body. Third, iron loss occurs not just through menses but also through sweating. Several runners I coach at the Liberty Athletic Club found they were anemic after they felt unusually tired and slow. All of a sudden their 5K running times increased. After learning from blood tests that they were anemic, they took iron supplements and were back to full energy levels and improved race times in three to six weeks.

To stave off anemia, be sure you're consuming enough iron-rich foods. In general, you should consume at least 15 milligrams of iron daily if you are a premenopausal woman and 10 milligrams if you are postmenopausal.

How can you prevent iron depletion?

- Eat foods like liver, lean meat, oysters, egg yolks, dark-green leafy vegetables, legumes, dried fruit, and whole-grain or enriched cereals and bread.
- Eat three to four ounces (85-113 g) of lean red meat or dark poultry a couple of times per week.
- Eat or drink foods rich in vitamin C with meals to increase iron absorption.
- Know that drinking coffee and tea with meals reduces iron absorption.
- Use cast-iron pans for cooking. They increase the iron content in your food.

Finally, if you have found that you are low in iron, retest your blood every three months. Three months gives you time to build up iron stores and evaluate progress.

Osteoporosis and Osteopenia

Masters female runners should be aware that they're not immune to osteoporosis and its milder precursor, osteopenia. These conditions result in low bone mass (density) and diminished strength. Osteopenia and osteoporosis are common among both men and women over 50, 55 percent of whom have one or the other (Pray and Pray 2004). If you are one of the many masters female runners who don't consume enough calcium, consider supplements. As always, consult your physician first.

The causes of osteopenia and osteoporosis, considered silent diseases because they have no obvious symptoms, are many and complex. They include genetics and a history of irregular menses, stress fractures, taking corticosteroids for one year or more, and smoking. Other causes include body weight less than 127 pounds (58 kg) for women and inadequate nutrition, including too much caffeine, which can strip calcium from bones, and getting too little protein, vitamins, and minerals such as calcium and vitamin D (which helps your body absorb calcium). Excessive exercise that leads to irregular or nonexistent periods and too little weight-bearing exercise are also causes. Menopause, which causes women to lose the estrogen that helps their bodies absorb calcium, is another cause.

The good news is that you can take action to ascertain your bone mass and to reverse the effects.

- Check with your doctor and ask for blood work to check your calcium and vitamin D levels and ask how much you should take given your medical history.
- Ask for a bone mineral density (BMD) test to learn the density of the hip bones and spine. If you haven't already, start a weight-lifting regimen at least twice a week, particularly for the back, abdomen, and upper body.
- Limit alcohol intake to no more than two drinks a day and limit your coffee or tea intake to three 8-ounce (237 ml) cups a day. (Limit those grandes!)
- Check your diet to be sure you're eating enough calories.
- Eat at least .8 grams of protein per 2.2 pounds (1 kg) of body weight daily.
- Maintain a healthy body weight at a body mass index of 18.5 to 24.9.
- If you smoke (I don't know a masters woman runner who does), give it up.

Menopause

Mention menopause and women roll their eyes. (How many 45- to 55-year-old women have nothing to say about menopause?) They visualize night—and day— sweats, moods fluctuating because of hormones, sleepless nights, weight gain, and bloating. Menopause is at the least a nuisance for most female masters runners. The new bloating around their waistlines is irritating. Despite training and eating well, they wonder where that tire came from. (Some say trying to maintain their premenopausal weight feels like they're fighting World War III). Even elite masters female runners may put on two to five pounds (1 to 2.3 kg) that often disappear by the late-50s.

The good news is that most masters female runners don't think menopause negatively affects their running times (which were slowing with age, anyway). In fact, the average age of the 103 female runners in my doctoral study was 52, and only 10 percent felt that menopause was an obstacle to competition (Utzschneider 2002). Most all masters runners feel that running helps alleviate the symptoms of menopause. It helps them control their weight and, even more important, it helps them sleep and regulate their moods.

Female Endurance Advantage

With the long-term physiological challenges women face—childbirth being the ultimate one—it's no wonder women are particularly strong in events requiring perseverance and patience. Given their smaller size relative to men, they're unusually strong in ultrarunning, distances longer than the marathon. Women are quickly becoming the fastest-growing segment of endurance athletes, and they do well against men in these races. Consider the 2010 Hardrock 100 Endurance Run in Silverton, Colorado, where 39-year-old Diana Finkel finished second overall in the 100-mile (160 km) race. Or the 2010 Vermont 100 Endurance Run where Kami Semick placed third overall, just 41 minutes behind the overall winner (whose winning time was 16:01:40). By contrast, how many marathons see women finish second or third overall?

The reasons that women have advantages when running ultradistances are not clearly understood. Perhaps one is that ultracourses often include considerable downhill sections, which are less demanding on smaller bodies than on larger bodies. Or perhaps women's greater fat stores give them a competitive edge. Increased body fat may be a fueling asset. We know that after about 18 miles (29 km) of running, the body begins to get low on glycogen and hits the wall, turning increasingly to other energy stores to continue. Could women be more efficient at using that body fat early in a race and saving the glycogen for the long haul? Whatever the advantage, consider it.

Chapter 3

Meeting the Challenge of Aging

Ask masters runners about the benefits of age and experience and the typical response is a smile, shake of the head, shoulder shrug, and then, "There aren't any!" Later, they're off for a run or they'll tell you enthusiastically about their next race. Masters runners are about as determined as any population, and most have (and need) more than a minor dose of humor. Mary Harada, a former world record holder for women 70 to 74 and 75 to 79 joked with me that she's going to run until she's chasing after her casket. Others say the same (that's one reason chapter 1 is called Masters Running: The Never-Ending Pursuit). Facetiousness aside, masters runners say there are advantages to years of experience.

BENEFITS OF AGE AND EXPERIENCE

Physiological declines aside, age has advantages. You know more now than you did decades ago: either about your body, your habits that affect training and performance, or what motivates you. Chances are that you are wiser and more patient than you once were. These qualities will help you and you should use them to your benefit. Occasionally, for example, masters runners have mentioned that young personal trainers have demanded too much from them in terms of weight training. If even an expert asks you to do something that you feel is too much for you,

Runner Profile: Pete Magill

Date of birth: June 19, 1961

Personal Information

- Senior writer and columnist for *Running Times* magazine
- Consultant for Seebach and Seebach legal firm
- Author of *Build Your Running Body* (The Experiment, scheduled publishing date of summer, 2014, with coauthors Tom Schwartz and Melissa Breyer)
- Started focused training at age 14 and training included intermittent serious stretches through age 29; started training for masters at age 39

Open Personal Bests

- 1,500 meters 3:48.03 (age 28)
- Mile 4:07.3 (29)
- 2K (road) 5:09 (29)
- 5K (road) 14:44 (34)
- 10K (road) 30:05 (29)

Personal Bests at 40 to 49

- 1,500 meters 3:56.42 (40)
- 3,000 meters 8:31.08 (40)
- 5,000 meters 14:34.27 (46)
- 10,000 meters 31:27 (45)
- 5K (road) 14:47 (42)
- 10K (road) 31:23 (42)

Courtesy of Dianna Hernandez

Personal Bests at 50 to 59

- 5,000 meters 15:06.82 (50)
- 5K (road) 15:02 (50)
- 10K (road) 31:11 (50)
- Half marathon 1:10:19 (51)

Age-Graded Personal Bests

- 5K (road) 98.10% (15:02 at age 50)
- 10K (road) 98.43% (31:11 at age 50)
- Half marathon 96.03% (1:10:19 at age 51)
- Numerous other marks 95-97%

Cathy Utzschneider: You clearly have a lot of talent. Are there other runners in your family?

Pete Magill: My son Sean ran high school track, winning his school's "Frosh-Soph" sprinter award when he was a sophomore. The next year, he trained with dad for eight weeks following football season, dropping from 195 pounds to 175 and recording a 4:34.9 in his first 1,600 ever. His high school coaches weren't supportive of his new training focus, so he returned to sprints for one season before dropping the sport to concentrate on football, which he continues to play in college.

Cathy: How often do you race?

Pete: I race far less than most of my masters peers. My focus is on big performances rather than frequent racing. If I race a dozen times in a year, that's a big year. Some years I only race five or six times. While it increases pressure to run well every time out, it also allows me to build better fitness between races and to recover more fully from previous efforts.

Cathy: What is your favorite distance?

Pete: My favorite distance isn't a distance at all. It's a type of race: cross country. I love cross country because it takes the time out of the race and turns it into a true competition, racer against racer. It also allows for the type of team experience that's only available in relays on the track and rarely exists on the roads. But if I have to pick an actual distance, it'd be the 5K. The 5K requires all elements of training:

endurance, strength, speed, and psychological control (pacing and effort), but the recovery is far less than for other races. We can put all our training to the test without having to pay with a prolonged recovery period postrace.

Cathy: What is your favorite race?

Pete: My favorite race is the USATF Club Cross Country Championships. Year after year, our men's masters race is the most highly attended of the day's races (including open and masters divisions), with 400 to 500 very serious distance runners spread across the start line. Top clubs from all over the country make the annual trek to compete, creating friendships and rivalries that span decades. Best of all, after competing head-to-head with our rivals, we can cool down on the course while watching the top young open runners in the country battle it out.

Cathy: Do you have a coach?

Pete: I've coached myself since my early 20s, and I continue to do so today. After less-than-satisfactory coaching experiences growing up, I decided to take the reins in my mid-20s. Starting up again at age 39, I expected to train and race for about two years, so it didn't seem important to find a coach. A few years later, I'd learned so much about masters training that I felt confident I could steer my own training as well or better than anyone else. It's worked well so far.

Cathy: Do you have a role model?

Pete: I don't have a role model, but that doesn't mean that there aren't people within the sport whom I admire and from whom I draw inspiration. The third race I ever ran as a master, at age 40, was an indoor mile. Finishing only a few seconds behind me in 4:25 was Nolan Shaheed, then 51 years old. I couldn't believe a 51-year-old could run that fast! It gave me hope that I might have a few years left in me. Now 51 myself, I hope some younger masters feel the same way when they race me.

Cathy: How has your training changed over the decades? Can you give an example of a typical training week for a 5K? Examples would be helpful.

Pete: When I was a youngster—teens and 20s—I trained like an idiot. If I ran 100 miles (162 km) per week, I ran 100 hard miles per week. Interval workouts were like miniraces. Easy distance referred to volume, not effort. Every day was a test. And every attempt to get race fit predictably resulted in burnout, injury, or illness.

As a new master, at age 40, I emphasized lower volume, higher quality, and greater recovery. My mileage varied from 35 to 70 miles (56-112 km) a week through my mid-40s, then began to climb as I simultaneously climbed toward my late-40s. Now in my 50s, I've maintained volume (I don't count miles, but probably log 85 to 95 miles [137-153 km] per week in nonrace weeks), but I've drastically eased up on easy days and lowered the intensity of quality days, favoring tempo intervals on the road over faster intervals on the track and using short and longer hill reps in place of speed work.

Sample 5K Training (Two Weeks)

- Sunday – long run (90-150 minutes)
- Monday – easy 90 minutes
- Tuesday – a.m. easy 50 minutes, p.m. 3 × 10-minute tempo intervals with 3-minute jog rest (70-80 total minutes)
- Wednesday – easy 90 minutes
- Thursday – a.m. easy 50 minutes, p.m. easy 90 minutes
- Friday – a.m. easy 50 minutes, p.m. short hill repeats: 8 × 8-10 seconds up steep hill at 95 percent effort with walk back to start plus 8 × 12-15 seconds down steep hill at 95 percent effort with walk back to start (includes 15-minute jog warm-up and 10-minute jog cool-down)
- Saturday – easy 80-90 minutes
- Sunday – long run (90-150 minutes)

(continued)

Pete Magill *(continued)*

- Monday — easy 90 minutes
- Tuesday — a.m. easy 50 minutes, p.m. 3 × (5-minute tempo interval, 1-minute jog recovery, 2 minutes at 5K effort), 3-minute jog recovery between sets (70-80 total minutes)
- Wednesday — easy 90 minutes
- Thursday — a.m. easy 50 minutes, p.m. easy 90 minutes
- Friday — a.m. easy 50 minutes; p.m. long hill repeats: 6 × 90-second repeats at 3K race effort with jog back downhill then walk for 4- to 5-minute total recovery (includes 20- to 25-minute jog warm-up and 10- to 15-minute jog cool-down)
- Saturday — easy 80-90 minutes

Cathy: What advice do you have for other masters?

Pete: Remember that the goal of training is to build better fitness, not to test the fitness we already possess. And repeat over and over: the best workout we can run today is one that allows us to run again tomorrow.

you're probably right. Trust your judgment. It will serve you well. (And, if you can, hire experts who have experience with masters athletes.)

Perspective and Wisdom

As a masters runner, you have both perspective and wisdom. You've seen more of life, and scanning the general population of others your age, you probably feel grateful that you're able to run at all. You also know that running is for a lifetime, and that at different stages in life—depending on what else is going on—running can fulfill different goals. There are times when you're fit and ready to race and others when a training run with friends is all you want. Personal bests, friendships, championship titles, vacations, and stress relief are all reasons to run.

You have more perspective regarding the challenges of running. Estimates of percentages of all runners injured each year vary considerably, depending on the study, usually ranging from about 40 to 70 percent of all runners (van Mechelen 1992; Jacobs and Berson 1986). As a masters runner, though, you have more perspective on setbacks and injuries. You can use your experience to your advantage. If you have a setback, you know it's not forever (whereas when you're younger, you think it's the end). You're more likely than open runners to back off when you feel a warning twinge, and you know running is for a lifetime so you'll be back.

Knowing Your Body

You know your body's idiosyncrasies, its strengths and weaknesses. Each person has his or her own vulnerabilities. Whether you have a muscle imbalance, a leg-length discrepancy, or tight hamstrings or Achilles tendons, you know your weaknesses and are better at knowing how to weave around them than you were when you were younger. You know whether you pronate or supinate, or you've found running shoes that fit your feet or orthotics that help. You know what workouts exacerbate a weakness or whether you're more vulnerable to tight turns on the indoor track, hill workouts, or long runs. You're more likely than younger runners to know whether or not a niggling spot in your foot or knee is a precursor to something more serious.

More Confidence and Trust in Your Own Judgment

As a masters runner, you probably have confidence in your own judgment. The views of others, including your coach, teammates, and friends, matter less than they used to. You do your own thing, in your own way. If you're on the track and feel you've had enough, you probably are confident in making that call regardless of what others are doing.

Masters runners are also more discerning about advice from health specialists and about whether a diagnosis feels right. If a specialist says something that doesn't feel right, masters are more likely to seek a second opinion. A second opinion has saved many masters, including me. A well-known orthopedic surgeon told me in my late 40s that I had arthritis and should only run two miles (3.2 km) a week henceforth. I sought a second opinion from another doctor who said my bones were those of a 30-year-old and I could continue to run 30 to 40 miles (48-64 km) a week. The second diagnosis felt right. That was about eight years ago and I've continued running since then. As a masters runner, have confidence in your judgment regardless of the expertise of specialists.

Tried-and-True Strategies

When you have a question about training or racing, you know what's worked in the past. You know everyone is different and one size doesn't fit all and that even though your training partner might run four or five days a week, your body feels best when you run six. You know what forms of cross-training work best, what you enjoy, and how much you can reasonably handle.

More experience means you know how you race best. If you're a middle-distance runner or a marathoner, for example, you know what it feels like to be at mile 4 (6.4 km) of a 10K or at mile 20 (32 km) of the marathon. You may know that for you, even splits work better than negative splits (where miles are run at increasingly faster paces) or vice-versa. You know which eating and hydrating routines work.

More Disposable Income

"Towanda!" Kathy Bates says in the 1991 movie *Fried Green Tomatoes*, exclaiming that she may not be in the prime of life but she's proud that she has more disposable income. Chances are you can spend more on running—clothing, GPS watches, running shoes, and races—than you did when you were in your 20s or 30s. You can occasionally pay for a trip to a race in a vacation destination or afford hotels and restaurants that might once have been out of the question.

Advantage of Patience

As a runner over 30, you have a longer-term perspective than someone who's younger. You know—not just from running, but from other areas of life—that achievement requires persistence and consistency through ups and downs. When I started masters running, the best advice from a veteran runner was to have patience.

Ten Years or 10,000 Hours to Excellence

The importance of focused practice over many years has been demonstrated again and again. Dr. K. Anders Ericsson, a professor at Florida State University and one of the world's leading theoretical and experimental researchers on expertise, has studied it in most fields, including mathematics, athletics, and music. He and his colleagues have found that 10 years or 10,000 hours of deliberate practice leads to excellence (Ericsson et al. 1993). Deliberate practice is practice aimed at reaching goals just beyond your present level of competence; it involves focusing on your weaknesses and specific needs, practicing your skills repeatedly, and continually adjusting them with feedback from a coach or teacher.

The limited research that exists on numbers of years to personal bests in masters running generally supports the rule of 10 years or 10,000 hours, showing that they are achieved within 7 to 10 years, regardless of when you start. Masters runner Priscilla Welch started running at age 34 and achieved her personal best in the marathon 8 years later, at age 42, running 2:26:51 (Rodgers and Welch 1991). Older legs can be fresher legs. It took the female masters runners in my doctoral dissertation an average of 7.5 years to reach their best times, whether they started running in their teens or after age 30 (Utzschneider 2002).

If you're a masters runner who is starting really late—not just after 30, but after 40 or 50 or even 60—and if you have genetic ability as well, you can catch up to others after 10 years of deliberate practice. As Rodgers and Welch wrote in *Masters Running and Racing*, "a 50-year-old novice racer is promised the same span of progress as a 15-year-old," (1991, p. 4). Figure 3.1 from my research found that after 10 years, masters runners who started after 30 or even after 50 could be just as fast as those who started when young.

One reason it takes more than a few years to achieve one's best result is simple: it takes that long to figure out the mix of physical and mental training habits, including strength training, patience, and race strategy that work best for you, and that mix changes over time. Joe Navas, 43, started running at age 30. "It took me the better part of eight years to even begin to wrap my head around the idea of patience in all aspects of running," he told me in December of 2013. When he first started running, "training meant running faster every time out. How could one expect to get faster without running faster? I had no concept of time or pace, beyond what I was beginning to learn about how to not just plain blow up in a race, which still took a long time to wrap my head around. I was the guy in the Cape Cod Athletic Club who could be counted on to lead for the first mile and fade. Every time."

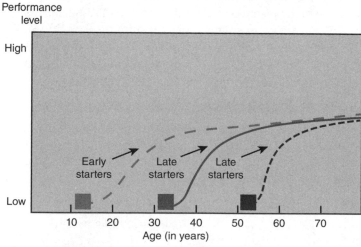

Figure 3.1 Late starting masters female runners can catch up to women who start running in their earlier years.

Personal bests for Joe came 8 to 10 years later. "I began to think that training more and racing less could have benefits. I approached every race with an idea about pace," he said. At 38, he ran 1:10:26 at the New Bedford Half Marathon. That year he also ran personal bests in the Lone Gull 10K (32:18) and in the Falmouth Road Race (36:63). In his ninth year of running, he ran a personal best marathon at the Boston Marathon (2:33:18) and in Fairhaven Father's Day 5K (15:29). Now, at 43, his perspective on running and racing is focused beyond time. Personal bests don't come forever. "Hubris is, essentially, the enemy," he said. "I run to reason, to examine, to enjoy what I am, not what I should, could, or would be."

PRACTICING HEALTHY LIVING HABITS

Just as 10 years or 10,000 hours of deliberate practice leads to excellence, so can consistent, healthy living habits keep you at your best at any age. A good first step to review your habits is to write down a schedule of your week to see how you are spending your time. Are you trying to do too much? Do you have enough downtime? When do you eat, sleep, work, and run? One habit affects another.

Better habits can be learned and less-healthy ones can be unlearned. Charles Duhigg, author of *The Power of Habit* (2012), explains habits in terms of loops—cues, routines, and rewards—and maintains that if you identify the cues and rewards, you can change the routine, the behavior, or habit itself. In my own practice I've seen people who once indulged regularly in ice cream substitute it for light ice cream, which they then replaced with yogurt. (One person even replaced yogurt with 1 percent milk with honey.) Some runners who once refused even to step on what they called the "dreadmill" now look forward to running fast intervals on it. Habits can be changed.

You're more likely to succeed if you choose an obvious cue and a clear reward. If you want to get in the habit of running right after you get up in the morning, put your running shoes and running clothes right by your bed (the cue). Reward yourself consistently, whether a reward means a cafe latte afterward or a feeling of accomplishment when noting miles in a training journal.

Sleep

Keeping your sleep consistent—whether that's 6 or 10 hours a night—will help you run your best. Of course, avoid extreme sleep deprivation of less than 4.5 hours. That affects moods and lowers production of hormones important for performance, such as human growth hormone essential for repairing sore muscles and other soft tissue. A few nights of little sleep can interfere with glucose metabolism and raise levels of the stress hormone, cortisol.

To help you sleep, avoid caffeine (coffee, tea, chocolate, soft drinks), a stimulant, at least six hours before bed. If you drink alcohol, drink it four hours before you want to sleep. Being a depressant, alcohol may initially put you into a deep sleep. As your body absorbs the alcohol, however, you may experience mild withdrawal symptoms. You may wake up before you ordinarily would. Because alcohol is dehydrating, you may wake up at night, thirsty.

If you have problems falling asleep, try a simple muscle-relaxation exercise using mainly your arms and hands. As you are lying down, create tension by pressing your fingers into the palms of your hands and making fists. Focus on and feel the tension. Then relax your hands and arms, allowing them to be heavy. Breathing slowly and deeply, think about the word *relax* each time you breathe out. You'll find that that your hands and arms relax more and more. Repeating this exercise has helped many runners fall asleep.

Recovery

As a masters runner, you'll do best if you understand both how important recovery is and what it actually means. You need more recovery than younger runners just to ward off injury. The recovery phase of training, including rest and easy days, is when you become more fit, when you adapt after the stimulus of hard workouts. Regeneration occurs in this recovery phase. Depending on how intensely and how much you run, muscle fibers and connective tissue that have been worked hard need at least 48 hours to repair and rebuild. Fluids, enzymes that help muscles contract and relax, and muscle glycogen need to be replaced. The older you are, the more time you need. Working muscles again too soon leads to tissue breakdown and injury instead of buildup. Without recovery, adaptation may occur in the short term, but ultimately it will fail. And because most injuries come from overuse, a day of yoga, rest, massage, or easy miles can prevent three- or four-week forced breaks.

Chapter 2 mentions recovery as it applies to hard and easy running, and chapter 5 discusses recovery in depth as it applies to staving off injury. What about recovery days after a race? Here are general guidelines based on age and race distances. I don't recommend recovery days by age groups because readiness for the next workout depends more on fitness, although, generally speaking, the older you are, the more days you should take. Knowing your own body is key.

Race Distance	Recovery Days Between Race and Next Workout
1 mile	3-4
5K	5-6
5 miles to 10K	6-8
15K to half marathon	10-14
Marathon	35 or more

The point here is that knowing the many forms of recovery and building in time for it will keep you healthy. Recovery includes cooling down, stretching, soft-tissue work, cross-training, napping, body work, steams, and saunas. As a rule of thumb, masters runners should take 15 to 30 minutes of recovery for every hour of training. Many masters runners see some kind of body worker, whether that's a massage therapist, chiropractor, or acupuncturist, at least once every two to four weeks.

You need recovery not just after running but in life in general after stressful periods at work or at home. While positive stress (eustress) can benefit the body, too little recovery can turn training into negative stress (distress). Don't overschedule yourself. If you have more than three major obligations in your life in addition to a serious running goal, you have too much on your plate. Cut out something.

Hydration

You need to drink enough fluids, particularly water, to run your best at any age. Not drinking enough can lead not just to dehydration but to slower running as well. A 2 percent drop in body weight during a run often correlates with a 10 percent decline in performance.

General hydration guidelines for daily living follow:

- Thirst is sometimes, but not always, a good indicator that you need to drink. If you're thirsty, you may well already be dehydrated.
- According to the Institute of Medicine of the National Academies (2004), of people who are adequately hydrated, women consume an average of 2.7 liters (92 oz, about 11.5 cups) and men consume an average of 3.7 liters (125 oz, about 15.5 cups) of water from all beverages, including caffeinated beverages *and* foods daily. Given that about 20 percent of those amounts come from food, the average adequately hydrated woman drinks about 74 ounces or 9 cups of water daily and the average adequately hydrated man drinks about 100 ounces or 12.5 cups of water daily.

How much should you hydrate while running? That depends on the following:

- How much you run. The more miles, the more fluid you should drink.
- The weather. Drink more when it's hot and humid.
- Altitude. The higher the altitude, the more you should drink.
- Your weight. The more you weigh, the more you should drink. Because men generally weigh more than women, they should drink more, and, of course, pregnant women should also drink more.
- Your sweat rate, the amount of fluid you lose through sweat in an hour of running. The more you sweat, the more you should drink.

While hydrating is important for all distance races, the marathon is where it's most important to follow a hydrating pattern, as opposed to drinking when you feel thirsty. A recent study (Dion et al. 2013) on hydrating and performance during a half marathon found that performance was just as strong in those who drank according to thirst as in those who drank according to a set plan. The runners who drank according to thirst did, however, experience more physiological stress than those who drank regularly; they lost 3 percent of their body weight and experienced higher heart rates and body temperatures than those who followed a set plan.

If you're looking for a set hydrating plan and don't know your sweat rate, drink four to eight ounces (118-237 ml) of fluid every 15 to 20 minutes of running. As a general rule, faster or heavier runners competing in warmer climates should drink more than slower or lighter runners competing in cooler climates (American College of Sports Medicine 2007). Know also that cool water is absorbed faster than warm water, so drinking plain cool water for runs of one hour or less is the best option. Sport drinks help you maintain energy on runs of more than one hour. While many sport drinks are 6 to 8 percent carbohydrate, many runners dilute these with water, using 50 percent sport drink and 50 percent water, for easier digestion. Avoid carbonated beverages, sugary drinks, and highly concentrated fruit juice; they may cause stomach cramps, nausea, and diarrhea. The issue of hyponatremia, the result of drinking too much fluid, is also discussed in chapter 13.

One way to assess whether you're drinking enough is to check your urine. Although bladder size is a consideration, you should urinate five to eight times a day, and the color should be light straw yellow. If it's bright yellow, that's the first stage of dehydration and it's time to drink a glass of water.

Nutrition and Weight Control

Eating a balanced diet and maintaining a healthy weight are essential not just for good health but for peak performance as well. Almost every issue of *Runner's World* has a cover feature related to nutrition: healthy seasonal meals, nutrition tips, strategies for losing five pounds. To see results, your diet doesn't have to be perfect. Use the 80/20 rule by eating well 80 percent of the time. Numbers of calories you consume will vary depending on several factors, including your weight and activity level.

How many calories should you consume to maintain weight and fuel workouts? The most efficient, accurate way to answer that question is to use an online calculator that asks you to input not simply your sex, age, weight and height in either U.S. or metric units and your level of daily activity (sedentary, somewhat active, active, or very active), but also your calories burned from additional exercise and from training for different sports. A calculator that can tell you how many calories you burn not just from running but more specifically from running 6 miles in 12-minute miles (5 miles per hour) versus 5.5-minute miles (10.9 miles per hour), as well as how many calories you burn in over 100 activities including walking, swimming, biking, weight lifting, hatha yoga, jumping rope, and even basketball at different levels of intensity will give you the closest answer to the question. The calculator at www.nutritiondata.self.com/tools/calories-burned incorporates all these variables. If you play golf, you can even calculate how many calories you burn using a power cart versus how many you burn walking and carrying your clubs.

If you want to lose weight, an average of one to two pounds (.4 to .9 kg) a week is a reasonable goal. To average one pound lost per week, you need to create a daily 500-calorie deficiency, either through exercise or calorie cutting or a combination of both. In the previous example, if the runner continues with running four miles (6.4 km) a day and limits her caloric intake to 2,150 calories, she'll lose about a pound (.4 kg) a week.

Major Nutrients

If you regularly follow a few dietary guidelines, you'll increase your chances of staying healthy and running optimally. A balance of the three major nutrients—carbohydrate, protein, and fat—will minimize the need for supplements.

About 55 to 60 percent of your daily calories should come from carbohydrate. It provides energy for exercising muscles, regulates the metabolism of fat and protein, and digests easily. Carbohydrates are essential because all food—whether steak, broccoli, or chocolate—is broken down into glucose, which is used for immediate energy or stored as glycogen in the muscles and liver.

There are two kinds of carbohydrate, and your body needs both. Simple carbohydrates are absorbed quickly into your bloodstream, and can give you fast fuel. Simple carbohydrates can also cause dramatic swings in blood sugar levels if taken in large amounts quickly. Examples of simple carbohydrates are fruit, fruit juice, jams and jellies, milk, table sugar, honey, molasses, and candy. Complex carbohydrates have more nutritional value than simple carbohydrates; many contain iron, antioxidants, B vitamins, and fiber. Complex carbohydrates also take longer to be broken down into glucose, so their effect on blood sugar levels is much less dramatic and variable. Sources of complex carbohydrates are bread; pasta; legumes like beans, peas, and lentils; cereals; and grains such as corn, rice, and oats. About 45 percent of your daily calories should come from complex carbohydrates and 10 to 15 percent from simple carbohydrates.

While recommendations for daily protein intake call for 10 to 15 percent every day, protein needs should be based on your body weight, not your caloric intake. (If your caloric intake is unusually high, 10 to 15 percent of that equals too much protein.) While the recommended protein intake for the average American is .4 gram of protein per pound body weight (.8 g/kg), runners need to replenish the amino acids oxidized during exercise and to replace exercise-induced muscle damage by consuming .5 to .8 grams of protein per pound (1.2 to 1.7 g/kg).

In addition to helping to build and repair body tissues, including muscles, protein also replaces red blood cells, facilitates hormone production, helps with muscle contractions, forms antibodies for disease protection, and regulates water balance. Because many masters runners are vegetarians, it's helpful to remember that protein is made up of building blocks called amino acids. Twenty amino acids join to make all kinds of protein. While the body can make most of these, there are several it cannot. These are the essential amino acids (EAA), which you must include in your daily diet.

If you eat meat, getting enough protein is not complicated. Protein from animals—meat, poultry, fish, milk, eggs, and cheese—is considered complete because it provides all the essential amino acids. If you are a vegetarian, you get much of your protein from incomplete protein sources, such as legumes, grains, nuts, and seeds. These are low in one or more of the essential amino acids and should therefore be eaten with other complementary proteins. As an example, rice and dry beans are complementary proteins. Eaten together, they provide adequate amounts of all the essential amino acids the body needs. Other complementary proteins are peanut butter and whole-wheat bread and bean soup and bread.

About 20 to 30 percent of your daily calories should come from fat, found in meat, cheese, eggs, nuts, seeds, oils, butter, margarine, desserts, and snacks. Fat is critical for everyone and especially athletes because it provides a concentrated source of energy, helping to delay fatigue. Fat also helps satisfy hunger; absorbs fat-soluble vitamins A, D, E, and K; supports vital organs; and helps maintain body heat. While fat is necessary, focus on consuming more unsaturated, or healthy, fat: sources that come mainly from vegetables and are usually liquid at room temperature. Limit saturated fats, those that are usually solid at room temperature because a high intake can lead to high cholesterol, some cancers, and heart disease. Also limit trans fats, those created when liquid fat is processed into semisolid fat and used to increase the flavor and shelf life of foods. Like saturated fat, trans fat raises LDL, or bad, cholesterol and increases the risk of heart disease. But unlike saturated fat, trans fat lowers HDL, or good, cholesterol and may do even more damage. To see percentages of monounsaturated, polyunsaturated, saturated, and trans fats in various oils and spreads, see figure 3.2.

Few masters runners have difficulty maintaining a healthy weight, although the challenge to be at your leanest to run your fastest is greater as metabolism slows with the decades. No more all-you-can-eat nachos. If you're in your 40s, 50s, or 60s, you may not be able to eat as much as you could decades earlier without gaining weight. As mentioned in chapter 2, you can use body mass index, a calculation that

Types of fat in various oils, spreads

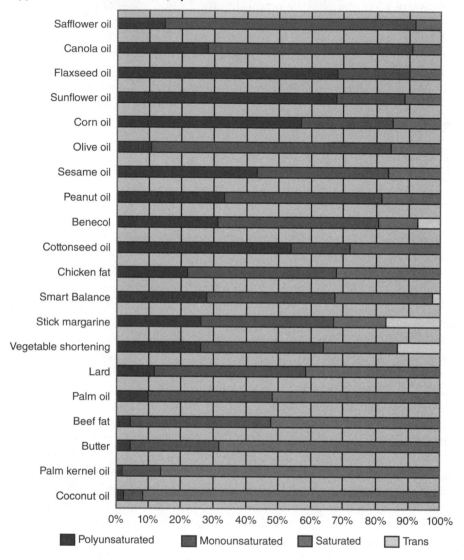

Figure 3.2 Percentages of monounsaturated, polyunsaturated, saturated, and trans fats in various oils and spreads.

Adapted with permission from the *Harvard Heart Letter* and © Harvard University. For more information visit: **www.health.harvard.edu.**

uses your height and weight to estimate your body fat, to determine whether you're at a healthy weight. If your BMI is 18.5 to 24.9, you're in the normal and healthy weight range. If you're over that and are carrying a few extra pounds, losing a few could help your running times. The following guidelines from an article in *Runner's World* may help you (Burfoot 2007).

How Does Losing Weight Affect Your Running Times?

If you want to lose weight, seek the advice of a professional (sport nutritionist, your doctor) and lose weight gradually.

- Losing 2 pounds (.9 kg) can take off 12.4 seconds in a 5K, 25 seconds in a 10K, 52 seconds in a half marathon, and 1:45 minutes in a marathon.
- Losing 5 pounds (2.3 kg) can take off 31 seconds in a 5K, 1:02 minutes in a 10K, 2:11 minutes in a half marathon, and 4:22 minutes in a marathon.
- Losing 10 pounds (4.6 kg) can take off 1:02 minutes in a 5K, 2:04 minutes in a 10K, 4:22 minutes in a half marathon, and 8:44 minutes in a marathon.
- Losing 20 pounds (9 kg) can take off 2:04 minutes in a 5K, 4:08 minutes in a 10K, 8:44 minutes in a half marathon, and 17:28 in a marathon.

Vitamins and Minerals

Knowing why vitamins and minerals are important can help you be sure you're eating a healthy diet. Table 3.1 shows the roles and sources of vitamins and minerals essential for runners. Obtaining vitamins and minerals from whole foods is preferable to supplementation; there's no strong evidence that taking supplements improves either health or athletic performance. If you're concerned that you're not getting enough of a vitamin or mineral, check first with your doctor and ask about the amount that's best for you. Even with minerals like calcium and iron, I've learned that the right amounts vary from person to person.

Reframing

Reframing is one of my favorite words, and one that masters runners seem to like. It's a concept that helps them meet the challenges of aging and the demands of life while they continue to run. Reframing means looking at running goals with a new set of eyes, considering new circumstances and interests. Say you have a family reunion and others in your family like to run. Reframing might mean setting a goal not of running a personal best but of corralling family members to run. You're reframing also if you've been a road runner and you want to try cross country or you have a friend who's been ill and you want to run for a cause. Regardless of the situation, reframing is a skill that you can use to your advantage in infinite ways, given your experience, perspective, and wisdom.

Table 3.1 Vitamins and Mineral Chart

VITAMINS		
Vitamin	**Role**	**Best sources**
Vitamin A	It helps develop bones and prevent stress fractures. It also helps maintain eyesight by providing nutrients to the retina and it contributes to the function of the immune system.	Dark-green leafy vegetables; yellow-orange vegetables and fruits such as carrots, sweet potatoes, cantaloupe, and peaches; liver; milk; butter
Vitamin B-complex	Broken into eight types of vitamins (e.g., B_1 B_6, B_{12}), vitamin B-complex helps convert carbohydrate into glucose; promotes the growth of red blood cells, which prevents anemia; helps metabolize fat and protein; and assists in growth.	Whole-grain cereals, green vegetables, poultry, fish
Vitamin C	Boosts the immune system. It helps prevent the common cold, and, as an antioxidant, it assists in cancer prevention and warding off heart disease. Vitamin C also helps the body form scar tissue.	Oranges, tomatoes, broccoli, grapefruit, cantaloupe
Vitamin D	Develops bone and bone strength, helps maintain a normal and strong heartbeat, strengthens the immune system, and assists in blood clotting.	Sunshine, fortified milk, egg yolks, tuna
Vitamin E	Lessens damage to the muscle tissues in the body after hard training. It also helps the immune system and prevents lung damage from many kinds of pollutants.	Vegetable oils, rice, leafy vegetables
Vitamin K	Helps bone metabolism and prevents blood clotting.	Green leafy vegetables, vegetable oils, fish
MINERALS		
Mineral	**Role**	**Best source**
Calcium	Builds and maintains bone strength, helps regulate heart function, and prevents muscle cramps.	Milk and fortified juices, beans, oranges, broccoli
Chloride	Maintains the body's nerve impulses that control muscles. As an electrolyte, it plays a key role in maintaining water balance in the body. (One of the ingredients of sport drinks is chloride, which is easily lost through sweat.) Chloride also is needed for the production of stomach acid.	Table salt (sodium chloride)
Iron	Helps form hemoglobin, essential for carrying oxygen from the lungs to the muscles. Low iron levels lead to anemia, characterized by lack of energy and general lethargy.	Beef, lamb, pork, leafy green vegetables, nuts, shrimp, scallops
Magnesium	Plays a key role in generating energy, helping bone growth, and regulating body temperature. Magnesium works as a counter to calcium's role of facilitating muscle contraction by assisting in muscle relaxation. Cramped muscles are sometimes caused by magnesium deficiency. Magnesium's role in muscle relaxation also helps in relieving overall stress in the body.	Bananas, green vegetables, corn, apples, whole-wheat bread
Phosphorous	Assists in almost every chemical reaction in the body and assists in using carbohydrate, fat, and protein for energy. Phosphorus also stimulates heart and muscle contractors and prevents tooth decay.	Meat, fish, chicken, eggs, whole grains, chocolate
Potassium	Helps to convert glucose to glycogen, the main energy source for muscles. Also stimulates the kidneys to get rid of body wastes.	Bananas, green leafy vegetables, oranges, potatoes, raisins
Sodium	Helps the body retain fluids to prevent dehydration and helps cause the thirst sensation, alerting us to drink fluids.	Table salt (sodium chloride), seafood, poultry, carrots, beets
Zinc	Helps remove carbon dioxide from exercising muscles, boosts the immune system, and protects the body from pollution.	Beef, lamb, chicken, sunflower seeds

Chapter 4

Biomechanics of Good Form

Let's face it. Just the word biomechanics might make you want to skip this chapter. Why care about good running form? You're fast enough. Who cares about dorsi-flexing? Truth is, knowing about and practicing good form will help you when you need it most: at the three-quarter section of a race, the slowest section of any race, quarter mile to marathon. Knowing correct biomechanics will help them become more of a habit, and a habit of correct biomechanics will make you faster.

Running brings out the uniqueness in all of us, including our unique form. From a distance, you can pick out your friends running even if you can't see their faces. Our form, or gait, is hard wired into us, dictated by nature, not something we're taught. It depends on many variables, not the least of which are the curve of the spine, musculature, height, leg length, foot structure (Are you flat footed? Do you have a high arch?), and flexibility. And not one of those alone predicts good form. Some long-legged runners have short strides, for example.

Talk about biomechanics and you enter controversial territory. Coaches and other experts debate about what correct form is, including ideal foot strike. Some say runners should be taught to run correctly. Others say let nature take care of itself: run the way it feels best, they say.

My view is that tweaking your form can be helpful, although I don't advise changing it radically unless you are injured frequently or are uncomfortable. Over the years, I've helped runners who wanted to change an aspect of their form: everything from foot strike to breathing patterns. Sometimes runners naturally change their foot strike from a heel- to a mid-foot strike as they develop greater muscle, tendon, and ligament strength. One asthmatic runner insisted on breathing only through her nose. She ran slower and continued to breathe through her nose. If you want to change your form, learn what you're doing first. Look at your image in the next store window you run by. Better yet, ask a friend to video you from different angles (phones work well for this). Still better, ask an exercise physiologist to analyze your gait.

Reminding yourself of the principles of optimal running biomechanics can help you adjust your running form, optimize your performance, and lower your risk of running injuries. In general, I tell runners of events from the mile up to focus on running

- tall,
- relaxed,
- with economy of motion, and
- quietly.

Or I suggest they remember the acronym TREQ: tall, relaxed, economy, quietly. Running tall means running with an erect posture so your head and upper body are aligned properly. If your weight is balanced so that your head is over your shoulders, hips, and legs, your lower body and stride are more likely to be correct. Your diaphragm will also be open so breathing is easier. You'll be less likely to jut out your head, slouch your shoulders, or stick out your rear end. Periodically shaking tension out of your arms and hands can help you relax, preventing your face, shoulders, and neck from tensing and consuming energy. Running with economy of motion helps you minimize movements that don't propel you forward. Avoid bouncing, for example, because too much up-and-down movement wastes energy and can be hard on your feet and legs. Think of running with a beanbag on your head. Exaggerated pumping of arms (except on hills) also wastes energy. If you imagine running on eggshells (and trying not to break them) your feet are likely to hit the ground quietly and lightly. If you hear thumping, you're probably putting undue stress on joints, tendons, bones, and muscles. Running should be quiet, soft, and springy.

ENHANCE YOUR UNIQUE FORM

In addition to knowing the principles of optimal running biomechanics, it is helpful to know correct posture. This includes the position of the head, shoulders, and hips. Knowing how to drive the arms, including hand position, and to stride forward, including ankle position, and knowing the possible foot strikes (there are several) also contribute to correct posture.

Posture

Hold your head high and your back straight, imagining a string attached to the top of your head. If you look ahead about 10 to 20 feet (3-6 m) you'll straighten your neck and back. Looking down can lead to fatigue and tightness in your neck. Keep your head as steady as possible without bobbing or rotating side to side. Relax your jaw and neck. Too much tension there can create tension throughout your body. An exaggerated yawn can help relax your jaw and face. Practice smiling as you run; this helps relieve overall tension. Keep your shoulders low and loose rather than high and tight. Carrying your shoulders too high can lead to fatigue, a shorter stride length, and increased shoulder tension; carrying them too low can lead to bouncing and a forward lean. If your shoulders feel tight, shake them out to release tension. Shoulders should remain level and not dip from side to side with each stride.

Your entire body should have a slight forward lean (but do not bend at the waist). Keep your head in line with your shoulders. If you think about running tall, you will stretch yourself to your fullest height with your back straight. If you begin to slouch, take a deep breath and feel yourself naturally straighten. Leaning your head too far forward leads to fatigue and tightness in the neck, shoulders, back, and even hamstrings. A slight forward lean means that your head is balanced over your shoulders, which are balanced over your hips, which are balanced over your legs (see figure 4.1). Your hips are the center of gravity.

Figure 4.1 Proper running form includes proper positioning of the head, shoulders, and hips.

Arm Drive

Arms should swing mostly forward and back, not across the midline of your body, between waist and lower-chest level (see figure 4.2a). Tuck elbows in, and bend them at about a 90-degree angle. On the back swing, your wrists should be next to the side of your pelvis, grazing your hips as if you are reaching for your wallet. Let your arms fall naturally back to the forward position. If you feel your forearms tensing, drop your arms to your sides and shake them out to release tension.

Keep your wrists loose, and lightly cup your hand as through you're holding an egg or a potato chip that you don't want to crush. Don't make a tight fist or keep your hands so loose that they become floppy (see figure 4.2b).

Forward Stride

Unlike sprinters who need to lift their knees high to achieve maximum leg power, efficient distance runners don't need an exaggerated knee lift. It requires too much energy over a long period. Efficient endurance running requires a slight knee lift, quick leg turnover, and a shorter stride than that of a sprinter (see figure 4.3). Your feet should land directly under your hips, not too far ahead of them. The knee of the leg striking the ground should be slightly flexed. Allowing your lower leg to extend in front of your body means your stride is too long. When your foot hits the ground, your ankle should be flexed to allow your foot to roll forward to create more force for push-off. You should feel your calf muscles powering your forward steps.

Figure 4.2 *(a)* Arms should swing straight back and forward; *(b)* lightly cup your hand as if holding an egg you don't want to break.

Figure 4.3 A distance runner's forward stride requires slight knee lift, quick leg turnover, and a shorter stride than a sprinter's.

Foot Strike

As mentioned earlier, foot strike—how, where, and when the foot hits the ground— is somewhat controversial. There's some disagreement about what is best, and unless a runner is frequently injured or clearly lands with a heel strike in front of his or her body (which is often the case), I don't generally suggest trying a new foot strike. The three types of foot strike are heel, midfoot, and forefoot. Most distance runners are heel or midfoot strikers.

- **Heel strikers** land lightly first on the heel of the foot, usually the outside of the heel, with the ankle dorsiflexed (toes pointed up) and then roll forward to push off with the toes. Avoid jamming your heel into the ground. This can result in overstriding and landing in front of the body and center of gravity, which creates a braking effect and slows you. Overstriding stresses your body and increases the risk of injury (Daoud et al. 2012).

- A **midfoot striker** lands on the heel and ball of the foot simultaneously, although the ball of the foot handles most of the impact. The heel touches the ground just slightly, and the runner lands with a bent leg, which offers greater shock absorption and more momentum for push-off than the heel strike does.

- A **forefoot striker**, more common among sprinters than distance runners, lands lightly on the outside ball of the foot with the ankle plantarflexed (toes point downward) and the foot slightly inverted (sole angled inward) to maintain balance. The ankle then begins to dorsiflex and the heel lands, controlled by the Achilles tendon and calf muscles. The runner then pushes off with the big toe. Strong and flexible Achilles tendons and calves are essential for a healthy forefoot strike.

Because running form often breaks down with fatigue, it's helpful to visualize it or remind yourself of the acronym, TREQ, periodically on long runs. For example, visualizing correct form once every mile can remind you to run tall and keep your arms from swinging across the midline of your body.

BREATHING

Steady, relaxed breathing is essential for running rhythm. If you find yourself breathing too quickly or hyperventilating or if you can hear your breath, you are probably running too fast or feeling out of control and you should slow until your breath is quiet.

Some runners find it helpful to breathe in time to their foot strike, while others find it annoying. If you want to try to establish a cadence, count footsteps in time with your breathing. I recommend trying a 2-2 breathing pattern. Force your breath out and then slowly breathe in. Breathe in while stepping right foot, left foot, and then breathe out while stepping right foot, left foot. Continue the pattern. If you feel out of control, either because of your breathing or your pace, try different breathing patterns. Practice patterns such as 3-2, 3-3, 2-3, or 3-4 to see what works best.

Breathe in and out of your mouth from your diaphragm or belly. Your abdomen should expand as you breathe in and flatten as you breathe out. You can get more air in and out of your mouth than your nose. As your abdomen expands, your diaphragm is fully lowered and your lungs are inflated to the maximum, allowing more oxygen intake. Getting enough oxygen also helps ward off side stitches that result when the diaphragm does not get enough oxygen.

STRIDE LENGTH VERSUS STRIDE RATE

Knowing about stride length and stride rate will help you as a masters runner. You can run faster by increasing one or both, because both determine speed. They depend on numerous variables including flexibility, height, weight, hip mobility, and biomechanics and cannot be attributed to one factor alone. Some shorter runners, for example, have longer strides than taller runners do. As a general rule, the more fit you become, the more your stride length and rate are likely to increase.

Stride rate (cadence or frequency) is the number of times your feet hit the ground and it is usually measured in right or left foot strikes per minute. As a general rule, cadences of 80 to 85 foot strikes per minute are common in recovery and easy-pace runs, cadences of 90 foot strikes per minute are more common in moderate running paces and races of 5K or longer, and cadences of 95 or more foot strikes per minute are seen during speed work on the track and in races under 5K. Many elite runners, including masters, have a stride rate of 90 to 95 foot strikes per minute. A higher stride rate, or turnover, is ideal because it pushes you forward quickly and strongly.

Stride length measures the distance from where the right heel (or left) hits the ground to where the same heel hits the ground again. Stride length depends on running technique, including foot strike, and leg length. It also depends on strength: how much force you can produce in the push-off and knee drive. Stride length is generally longest during 100-meter sprints and shorter in distance events. Studies of elite marathon runners show that they have run the second half of their marathons faster by shortening their stride length and increasing their stride rates (Conoboy and Dyson, 2006).

One of the main reasons masters runners become slower is that generally declining muscle mass and flexibility and slower reflexes contribute to shorter strides and slower stride rates. Stride length in masters runners decreases because rear-leg propulsion is weaker. The masters runner's return phase of the free leg as it leaves the ground and travels to a forward position for the next foot strike is less dynamic and responsive than it is in younger runners. The free leg needs to fold up toward the rear end and pull quickly and powerfully forward, relying on hip, gluteus, and hamstring strength. One study in the *British Journal of Sports Medicine* (Conoboy and Dyson 2006), for example, found that average stride length in male marathoners was 2 meters (6.6 feet) at age 60 and older compared to 2.4 meters (7.9 feet) for men 40 to 49.

Masters runners should focus more on increasing stride rate than stride length, which can lead to overstriding. Forcing a long stride length usually does not improve running speed or efficiency. The opposite happens. Instead of landing directly under your body with every step, when you overstride you reach out in front of your body with your foot and land heavily on your heel, causing a braking action. This will excessively stress your knees, hips, and back, in addition to slowing you down.

Know that you can work on increasing both stride rate and length with hill sprints, speed work, and weight training. Training with weights set at about 75 percent of one repetition maximum—the maximum amount of weight you can lift one time

Shoes? No Shoes? Minimalist Shoes?:
Scott Douglas

You can't talk about biomechanics without thinking about feet and what we put on them when we run. Nothing? Barefoot shoes? Flats? The big bulky variety? Scott Douglas is an expert on running, editor, journalist, author, and accomplished runner. He is editor of *Runner's World Newswire* and a former editor of *Running Times* and has been covering running professionally since the early 1990s. He has written or cowritten six books, including two editions of *Advanced Marathoning* (2008) and the *Runner's World Complete Guide to Minimalism and Barefoot Running* (March 2013). A runner himself (of course), he has run more than 100,000 miles (160,934 km) and competed in distances from 800 meters to the marathon.

Courtesy of Stacey Cramp

Above and beyond those credentials, Scott knows footwear and his feet. "I've tried everything from running barefoot to the FiveFingers to more substantive minimalist shoes," he said. "I've 'wear tested' at least 400 pairs of shoes in the past couple of decades."

Cathy Utzschneider: What sparked your interest in shoes?

Scott Douglas: It stems from my own running. I've always instinctively gravitated to running in light, low shoes. Especially in the late 1990s and early 2000s, shoes were getting bigger and bigger, both in terms of how high they were off the ground and in how much higher the heel was than the forefoot. I found it harder to find normal running shoes that didn't feel as if I was suspended off the ground and tilted forward. When *Born to Run* became a bestseller in 2009, suddenly everyone became aware of a topic that a lot of longtime runners had been grappling with for years.

[In *Born To Run*, author Christopher McDougall—motivated in part by injuries he incurred while running—explores the history and benefits of and joy derived from barefoot running. He travels to Mexico to find the Tarahumara, a tribe known for running long distance barefoot. He visits science labs at Harvard University to understand the biomechanics of running. McDougall himself trains for a 50-mile race with the Tarahumara. The book is a journey and celebration of barefoot running which inspires readers to consider the possibility that they were born with all the foot gear needed for running.]

Cathy: What's a way we can begin thinking about what kind of shoe to wear—if at all?

Scott: First, think about functionality. My interest is in people being healthy and happy runners. Shoes are a tool to help you achieve that goal, whether that's a minimalist shoe or barefoot. Other things help too, such as having a body with the right strength and flexibility for running, dedication, a healthful diet, and not being 50 pounds overweight.

Cathy: What do you think about barefoot running?

Scott: It's a great tool for learning good running form and strengthening the ankles and feet. But on a daily, real-world basis, it's not the most practical thing for most people. Who wants

(continued)

to spend entire runs worrying about every rock or piece of glass in the road? And it's hard to run barefoot when it's cold or snowy outside, obviously. In the real-world sense, minimalist shoes are a more worthy topic of discussion.

Cathy: What does minimalist running mean, really?

Scott: Very broadly, it means making a conscious decision to try to be able to run comfortably and injury free in shoes that are lower to the ground and are more level than many conventional running shoes. Many today have a lot of stack height—they're high off the ground—and have a high heel-to-toe drop, meaning there's a large difference in the height of the heel compared to the height of the forefoot. Both of those features of conventional running shoes can alter your running form in negative ways. Minimalists argue that a shoe that's close to the ground makes for more, not less, stability because your feet are closer to the ground and are better able to function naturally. After all, do people feel unstable when they walk around the house in socks? The same sort of thinking applies to stability in running shoes.

Cathy: How do you choose a minimalist shoe?

Scott: Think about the shoes you've felt best and most enjoyed running in. Think about their characteristics. Rather than looking for a particular shoe or category of shoe, it's better to look at the characteristics you're looking for since the categories of shoes are bleeding into one another. For example, you also could consider racing shoes, including a road racing flat, which is lower to the ground, a minimalist shoe. It's worth looking into everything that a shoe company might offer.

Cathy: What kinds of shoes might those include?

Scott: Vibram FiveFingers are the poster child for barely there shoes, but for most people, those are pretty extreme in terms of a transition from normal running shoes. All the running shoe companies have something would-be minimalists could consider; I include racing flats in that broad sweep.

Cathy: What points or questions should masters raise regarding what shoes to wear, or not?

Scott:

1. Why should you care about this topic? It's possible that learning to run well in lighter, lower shoes could lead to improved running form, which could lead to better performance and feeling better running. For me, at 48, feeling good on my daily run is more important than 20 years ago when I was trying to set PRs. It's possible that minimalist shoes could give you that feeling.

2. For how long have you run in conventional running shoes? The more years in those, the more cautious you should be in experimenting with minimalist shoes because your body has adapted to that kind of running shoe. Your calves and Achilles tendons have become tighter and shorter. Suddenly switching to a lower, flatter shoe would put strain on your muscles and tendons that they're not used to.

3. For a masters runner, are you at a good running weight? Lots of people could be at a better running weight. While they're using minimalist shoes they might also experiment with getting leaner if, like many masters runners, they've seen their weight creep up over the years.

4. If you're thinking about trying a minimalist shoe, think about what aspects of a shoe you like, and transfer that to what you like in minimalist models. Do you like a shoe

that's firm or one that has some softness in the middle of the shoe? Do you like a wide forefoot or a snugger fit? Find a minimalist shoe that you feel comfortable wearing.

Cathy: Can runners who wear orthotics because they overpronate or supinate wear minimalist shoes?

Scott: There's not enough hard data that this one thing—how much you do or don't pronate—should be the determining factor in how you should buy shoes. And even if pronation were the key to picking the right running shoe, a lot of people don't accurately describe how their foot lands when they run. People who have orthotics should consider whether they still have the original problem they got orthotics to address. If not, most sport podiatrists would say it's probably worth trying to wean yourself off them.

Cathy: What does your book add to the discussion about running?

Scott: I talked about the pendulum swing and how after the publication of *Born to Run,* people flocked too quickly from big, bulky shoes to barefoot running. Drawing on the knowledge of longtime running experts, I explain why minimalism is worth looking into while at the same time keeping it in perspective in terms of the overall performance of running. Some people spend more time debating minimalist shoes than they do running! Being in the right shoe is important, and many people can benefit from learning to run well in less shoe, but it's also important to pay attention to the many other factors that contribute to good running.

---

performing a specific exercise—helps offset the shrinkage of fast-twitch muscle fiber. You can also increase your stride rate through plyometric exercises, such as bounding and skips to build strength, activate reflexes, and stimulate fast-twitch muscle fibers.

FORM DRILLS TO ACTIVATE YOUR MUSCLES

With all the miles you run, spending 10 minutes a few times a week to practice drills will ultimately help not just your form but your speed as well. Drills imitate specific aspects of sound running form, including upright posture, arm drive, knee drive, leg action, the coordinated dynamic balance involved in the forward stride, and shifting weight from one leg to the other.

Drills also help strengthen the specific muscle groups essential for running. The ankle, knee, and hip joints undergo considerable flexion and extension during the running stride, and each of these joints is exercised through a similar, or greater, range of motion during the various drills. My runners perform the following drills after their warm-ups and before speed workouts on the track.

HEEL WALK

1 × 10 meters: Walk on your heels, dorsiflexing your toes (raising them toward your shins). As you look straight ahead, point your toes forward, and hold your arms at your sides, walk tall as if a string is holding your head to the ceiling. Variations of this drill include walking with your toes turned in and then with your toes turned out. This drill strengthens your feet, ankles, calves, and particularly the tibialis anterior, the muscles on the front of your lower legs. This drill helps prevent shin splints.

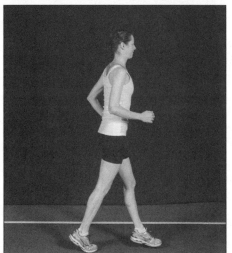

TOE WALK

1 × 10 meters; Rise onto your toes and walk with the toes pointed forward. Look straight ahead and again, walk tall, with your arms at your sides. Variations of this drill include walking with your toes turned in and then your toes turned out. Toe walking strengthens your feet, ankles, calves, tibialis anterior, and posterior muscles.

HIGH SKIP WITH ARM CIRCLES

1 × 20 meters; Skip while moving your arms first in forward circles and then in backward circles, taking the shoulders through a full range of motion.

SIDE SLIDE WITH ARM SWINGS

1 × 20 meters; Focused on lateral movement, this drill activates the iliotibial band and vastus lateralis on the outside of the legs. Begin by stepping to the right with your right leg and bring your left leg to its side. At the same time, swing the arms up and out to the side until they reach shoulder height. Then swing them across your body as if you are hugging yourself and repeat. Next move in the reverse direction, first stepping to the left and then bringing your right leg to its side.

A MARCH

1 × 20 meters; The marching high-knee drill emphasizes correct running mechanics: a driving knee lift, upright posture, and a coordinated arm swing. This drill should be performed deliberately and slowly. Stand tall, holding your chin and chest up and feet shoulder-width apart. Hold your hands at your sides. Simultaneously lift your right knee, keeping your lower leg under the knee, and lift your left hand to the level of your mouth. As you step with your right leg your right hand and arm will swing back, grazing your hip, as if you are throwing down a rock. Be sure that your arms don't cross the midline of your body.

A SKIP

2 × 20 meters; The A skip follows the same form as the A march, except that you skip on the balls of your feet rather than walking. This makes it more challenging. The drill improves coordination, balance, and strength in your feet, core, and legs. Be patient with yourself as you gain coordination, and then focus on balance as you build momentum. Stand tall, holding your chin and chest up and your feet shoulder-width apart. Lift your right knee, and then extend your lower leg as far and high as possible while keeping your core straight.

While you raise your left knee, raise your right hand to the level of your mouth and then swing it back, passing your hip. Then make the same motion with your right leg and left arm. Be sure that your arms don't cross the midline of your body.

B MARCH

1 × 20 meters; An extension of the A march, the B march stresses hamstring flexibility as well as knee lift and general running mechanics. Stand tall, holding your chin and chest up and feet shoulder-width apart. Do not bend at the waist. Raise your right knee to hip level and then extend your lower leg and foot to almost full extension so they are nearly parallel to the ground. Swing your leg back and down below your center of gravity, scuffing the floor as if you're scraping a wad of gum off the bottom of your shoe. You'll hear a pawing sound as your foot brushes the floor. While you raise and extend your right leg, raise your left hand to the level of your mouth. When you right leg swings back down, swing your left arm down and back, passing your hip. Keep your elbows close to your body. Then perform the same movement with your left leg and right arm.

B SKIP

1 × 20 meters; This B skip drill stresses an active foot strike to improve stride length. The drill also strengthens the hamstrings and gluteal muscles, improving coordination, balance, and upright running posture. This drill involves the same motion and coordination as the B march except that you are on your toes and it is faster. It is challenging to maintain a balanced, upright position while you master the coordination. Be patient while you practice this drill. Trying to do it slowly is a good way to begin. As with the B march, raise your right knee to hip level and then extend your lower right leg and foot to almost full extension so they are almost parallel to the ground. Swing your leg forcefully down past your center of gravity, scuffing the floor as if you're scraping a wad of gum off the bottom of your shoe. You'll hear a pawing sound as your foot brushes the floor. While you raise and extend your right leg, raise your left hand to the level of your mouth. When your right leg swings back down, swing your left arm down and back, passing your hip. Keep your elbows close to your body. Then perform the same movement with your left leg and right arm.

CARIOCA

1 × 20 meters in each direction; This drill focuses on lateral movement to loosen your hip flexors and increase their flexibility, which can improve stride length. You can practice this drill first by walking through it before you turn it into a skip. Hold your arms out to your sides and walk sideways, placing the right foot over the left. After the right foot goes over the left, the left foot steps in the direction you're moving. Your arms and upper body should rotate from your hips in the direction opposite your moving leg. Gradually turn this walk into a skip by speeding up and landing on the balls of your feet. After 20 meters, change direction and lead with the left foot.

HIGH KNEE

1 × 20 meters; This drill improves knee lift and leg turnover. Start by jogging slowly, and then with your feet dorsiflexed, try to raise first your right and then left knee to 90 degrees or as high as possible. Focus on landing on your midfoot or forefoot, and try to increase the cadence while maintaining an upright stance. As with the A and B drills, your left arm should swing down as your right leg comes down. Maintain an upright posture, aiming to maximize the number of steps.

BUTT KICK

1 × 20 meters; Butt kicks strengthen the hamstrings and focus on the recovery stage of your stride, helping increase leg turnover. Start by jogging slowly and then begin to kick your butt with your feet while holding an upright stance and landing on the balls of your feet. Don't worry if your feet do not hit your butt. Try to increase your stride rate, landing on the balls of your feet. Do not bend forward. Be careful with butt kicks if you have knee problems.

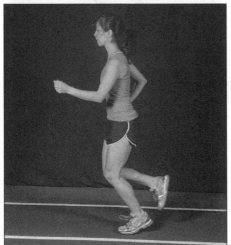

RUNNING BACKWARD

1 × 20 meters; Running backward helps restore balance to your body by using a counter (backward) movement. Standing in an upright posture and looking straight ahead, begin running in place. Slowly begin running backward, landing on the balls of your feet and swinging your arms as you would while running forward. Do this drill on a flat surface that's free of obstacles.

BOUNDING

10 steps per leg; Bounding develops balance, power, and strength, all of which improve stride length. After jogging a few yards to gain momentum, forcefully push your foot off the ground, bringing that foot forward and upward with a high knee lift while reaching forward with the opposite arm. Continue by alternating your push-off foot and arm, increasing your stride length and the time that you are airborne. Concentrate on keeping your head up and driving with your arms.

SHIN GRAB

1 × 20 meters; This drill stretches the gluteus and hamstring muscles and also focuses on balance. Stand tall and still, and look straight ahead. With your weight on your left leg, use your hands to pull your right knee to your chest. Lower the right leg and repeat with the left leg. Don't worry if you lose your balance at first. This drill takes practice.

FAST FEET

1 × 10 to 20 seconds; This drill activates muscles to prepare them for quick turnover. Taking as many steps as possible, move your feet up and down quickly and lightly, keeping them low to the ground and leaning slightly forward. Move your arms in time with your feet. It can help to say to yourself, "Quick, quick, quick."

"Hmmmm," you may think if you don't do drills now, "What else will motivate me to do drills?" Do them with a friend or a group. Do them after a warm-up and before a speed workout if it's a day for intensity. Running is one sport that is almost too simple to practice. Because many of us spend so many minutes running, it's easy to lose sight of our form. Our arms may cross the midline of our body. As we get tired, our shoulders start to slump. Focusing on drills at least once a week reminds us that running well and fast requires good form. Drills are the answer to that.

Chapter 5

Warding Off Injuries

Injuries are the bane of runners, their unwanted companions. Both younger and older runners get injured. If you have friends who are runners, chances are you know someone who is injured. One metanalysis that presented findings from many studies on the incidence of injury among runners reported that between 37 and 56 percent of all runners are injured every year (van Mechelen 1992). Masters runners are more susceptible to injuries than open runners (McKean et al. 2006). Wanting to seize the moment before the aging process interferes more with their performance, masters may forget sometimes that their flexibility and shock-absorbing capacity are not what they used to be.

As common as injuries are, they are challenging. First, runners are so afraid of injuries that they'll often deny them until the pain becomes so uncomfortable that they can't run. Often runners will wait to tell me for the first time about a discomfort they've been feeling for weeks. Determining their cause and diagnosing them are often more questions of art than science. Injuries often arrive suddenly from a unique combination of factors. It's a challenge to figure out what caused them and why they occurred at that time. Solving an injury mystery involves time, sometimes several opinions from different specialists, often tests (MRIs, X-rays, and so on), and trust in your own judgment. Different kinds of specialists often have different opinions on what the injury is and why it happened.

LISTENING TO YOUR BODY

Although it's obvious that you should listen to your body, sometimes it's not easy. It's difficult to maintain perspective on yourself, and listening to your body requires just that. There's no one else to confirm how you feel. Feel a discomfort, and you wonder whether you're imagining something. You focus intently on listening, but you may not want to hear. Hearing can lead to bad news: Yes, there is something wrong!

If you think you feel pain, track it immediately in a daily logbook on a scale of 1 to 5, with 1 being awareness and 5 being too painful to run and time to see the doctor. You'll know whether the pain is lessening or increasing. As soon as you feel even an awareness (a 1) in the same place for three days in a row, take off the next two days and cross-train. You'll stay in great shape, and save yourself a lot of time and needless pain in the future. The sooner you have the discipline to stop running—and it takes more discipline to stop than to continue—the less likely you are to aggravate the injury and the sooner you'll be back to running.

Cross-Training: Part of the Plan

Cross-training for running—participating in alternative forms of exercise such as biking, aquarunning, swimming, cross-country skiing, rowing—should be part of your plan whether or not you're injured. If you think from the beginning of your training that cross-training will be part of your success, and that it should be part of your plan to incorporate variety and build balance into your training, you'll be able to turn easily and confidently to cross-training when you're injured.

If you have to stop running, choose the cross-training activity that is most available, most similar to the specific movement of running, and the most "friendly" given your injury. Have plantar fasciitis? Try pool running. Pulled your hamstring? Try swimming or biking. Try various kinds of exercise until you find one you like. Many runners I coach have found great success with deep-water pool running. One year I trained three U.S. Olympic Trials marathon qualifiers with aquarunning for three months until the last month before the marathon, when they were able to begin running again. In the Trials, they performed as well as their counterparts who had not been injured. In terms of how long each cross-training workout should last, I generally recommend that you spend as much time cross-training as you would running.

Yoga

Yoga can help prevent injuries because it complements running and masters running in particular. Whereas running works in one direction with high impact, yoga works muscles in all directions without stress. While running strengthens muscles in the lower body, yoga builds overall body strength. Flexibility is not something running builds, but something yoga does. Many masters runners who practice yoga find their stride lengthens. Whereas racing can be intense, yoga encourages focus and relaxing under pressure.

The challenge for many masters is determining which kind of yoga you should practice and how you can fit it into your schedule. Do you take a class or practice it at home? If you can't find a class, I recommend a 10- to 15-minute practice at home two or three times a week. My favorite yoga routine involves a relaxation and then an abridged version of a sun salutation with eight poses that stretch, strengthen, and relax all muscles, including your back, quadriceps, hamstrings, and upper body. You can find this routine in chapter 6.

Low-Impact Machines

Low-impact machines like a cross-country ski machine, Arc Trainer, rowing machine, bicycle, and elliptical trainer are among cross-training equipment that help prevent injury and are therefore wise options to incorporate into your routine training. Some high-end physical therapy facilities also offer use of an excellent but expensive machine, the Alter-G antigravity treadmill, which allows you to run at 20 to 100 percent of your actual body weight. Low-impact equipment allows you to put minimal strain on your bones and joints, while still providing an effective cardiovascular workout.

Varying Your Training Distance

Varying your distances offers both physical and psychological benefits. Interspersing longer runs with shorter runs builds in variety to prevent monotony and boredom. Short runs give your body a chance to recover while long runs burn more calories and build a sense of accomplishment as well as endurance.

Varying Your Running Terrain

Your body is an all-terrain vehicle. Ideal training includes running on varied surfaces. Too much unevenness, though, carries risks such as a turned ankle. Vary your training to include roads, grass, dirt, and gravel trails. Your feet, shins, knees, and hips will thank you. While no studies have found a clear association between running surface and injury rate (particularly between running on concrete and injury), running on concrete is more jarring than running on asphalt, grass, or dirt. Pounding on a hard surface can lead to repetitive strain injuries such as stress fractures of the tibia, iliotibial band syndrome, medial tibial stress syndrome, and compartment syndrome. Even worse than pounding, the continuity of the surface may be just as bad or worse. A hard, flat surface exaggerates the stress of impact because the mechanics of every stride are exactly the same, stressing your muscles and joints in exactly the same way.

If possible, find a softer surface to run on at least once a week, be it a trail in the woods, grass field at your local high school, or path through the park. The advantage of irregular surfaces such as grass, trails, and even gravel is that no two steps are the same, which provides slight variations in the impacts on your body, reducing the chance of an overuse injury. Irregular surfaces engage more muscles, including lateral stabilizers like the gluteus maximus and minimus, which control side-to-side movement of the hips, and tiny muscles like the peroneus brevis and the flexor hallucis brevis. The peroneus brevis muscle wraps around the fibula and around the lateral and under side of the foot, helping to control lateral movement of the foot, and the flexor hallucis brevis, a small muscle on the sole of the foot, helps move the big toe and arch the foot. These muscles aren't needed much on a flat surface. The softer surface of trails and gravel roads not only keep the stresses of impact down but also allow faster recovery.

Training on a Treadmill

When it's snowy or icy outside, running on a treadmill can be a great alternative, and it's useful for logging miles, speed work, or tempo runs in a controlled setting. You may well find your pace on the treadmill faster than your pace outdoors. In addition to the absence of wind resistance, the treadmill belt assists leg turnover, making it easier to run faster. The treadmill provides a controlled, exact setting to run intervals interspersed with recovery jogs or walks.

Certain rules of form on the treadmill will help you avoid injury.

- Warm up by walking and then jogging for at least 10 minutes. Cooling down with a slow jog for at least 10 minutes will help prevent dizziness when you're finished.

- Avoid leaning forward at the waist and holding onto to the handrail or console.

- If you're a beginner on the treadmill, begin with no incline before you start running at 1 percent. Because there's no wind resistance indoors, a treadmill setting of 1 percent best reflects the energy cost of outdoor running. Don't set the incline too steep. And don't run at an incline of more than 2 percent for your entire run; this may lead to Achilles tendon or calf injuries.

Training on a Track

Tracks have helped many masters achieve their best times. Know, though, that some tracks have kinder, softer surfaces than others. Indoor tracks, just 200 meters in circumference as opposed to outdoor tracks that are 400 meters, can present particular challenges because their curves are tighter than the curves on outdoor tracks. When running intervals or in competition, athletes run counterclockwise. Running in the opposite direction during warm-ups and cool-downs balances your muscles and minimizes your risk for repetitive stress injuries. Look for softer surfaces. Most rubberized all-weather tracks provide enough cushion, although many masters distance runners find Mondo surfaces to be too hard. Dirt tracks lead to slipping and poor footing, which in turn can lead to injury.

WARMING UP AND COOLING DOWN

Masters runners require a longer warm-up than younger runners. Warm-ups should include 15 to 20 minutes of easy jogging, dynamic stretching, and four to six strides (runs at 70 to 80 percent of maximum effort over 50 to 80 meters). Dynamic stretching can include jumping jacks (shown to cut Achilles injuries up to 50 percent), skipping, marching with high knees, and butt kicks. Cooling down by jogging for 10 to 15 minutes and then stretching helps prevent injury and enhances future workouts, allowing your body to return to a resting state slowly.

Incorporating myofascial release (MFR) into cool-downs by rolling muscles, ligaments, and tendons with a foam roller, stick, or body-rolling ball can help break up tight areas of your body, decreasing muscle soreness and preventing injury.

Static and dynamic stretching, stretching while moving, particularly after a run, helps prevent injury and decrease muscle soreness. While a total-body stretching program is ideal, targeting the hips, hamstrings, quadriceps, hip flexors, and calves is crucial after each workout.

SYMPTOMS OF OVERTRAINING

While inadequate warming up or cooling down can lead to injury, so can overtraining. Overtraining is running so many miles and including so many hard miles that not only do you fail to progress, you regress. You may find it harder to maintain the pace you were used to running. Know the signs of overtraining:

- Headaches
- Fatigue
- Reduced concentration
- Apathy
- Insomnia or troubled sleep
- Irritability
- Depression
- Decreased performance
- Delayed recovery from training
- Decreased libido
- Digestive issues such as constipation
- Elevated morning rested pulse
- Increase in injuries
- Chronic muscle soreness
- Weight loss
- Frequent or never-ending minor infections or colds
- Appetite loss
- Decreased enthusiasm for training

DEALING WITH INJURIES

Once injured, be your own best advocate in seeking professional advice. Inform yourself about your injury by reading and speaking with others. (The website www.runninginjuryoracle.com is an interactive tool and one of many resources that can help you identify your injury). If you're not satisfied with advice from one professional, get a second or third opinion.

If, for example, you're not happy with the advice from an orthopedist, consult a chiropractor, physical therapist, or acupuncturist or get a second opinion from another orthopedist. As an example, four years ago one of my runners who was getting frequent shin splints was told at 41 by an orthopedist that she should stop running her usual 35 miles a week. She had rather flat feet which led to recurring shin splints. Rather than stop running, she sought out a second opinion from a physical therapist, who encouraged her to spend four weeks strengthening her feet with exercises (which included walking in sand) and then gradually build up her mileage. She has been running 40 miles a week since—without shin splints.

An injured runner has many treatment options. The following are approaches to healing injuries.

RICHE

RICHE—rest, ice, compression, heat, and elevation—should be started as soon as possible after an injury.

- **Rest** recharges you and allows your injury to heal. The amount of rest needed depends on your injury and its severity.
- **Ice,** when applied to the injured area, reduces inflammation. Generally, cold should be applied as soon as possible after an injury. Cold compresses reduce bleeding within the tissues and stop the swelling, whether they're due to acute injuries or overuse syndromes.
- **Compression**, or applying slight pressure or a pressure bandage to the injured area, limits bleeding into the tissues and swelling. Wrap the injured area with an elastic bandage, but not tight enough to cut off the blood. Take off the bandage every four hours and reapply it.
- **Heat** widens the blood vessels (causes a vasodilation) after the initial inflammation has subsided with rest and ice. Vasodilation delivers more blood to the area to remove injured tissue and helps repair the damage. Moist heat increases the effect of heat.
- **Elevation** also reduces inflammation and swelling. The injured extremity should be propped so it is above 12 inches (30 cm) above your heart.

Contrast Baths

Contrast baths, or alternating heat and cold (hihi: heat-ice-heat-ice), is an effective method of relieving inflammation. You can submerge the injured area in hot water for one to two minutes and then in cold water for one to two minutes, repeating that a few times. Hot water should be 95 to 100 degrees Fahrenheit (35-38 degrees C), cold water 55 to 65 degrees Fahrenheit (13-18 degrees C). End by putting the injured area in cold water for four to five minutes. Do this daily for 20 minutes.

Ice Baths

Particularly after long events like the marathon, ice baths help reduce swelling and inflammation by constricting the blood vessels and decreasing metabolic activity, flushing harmful metabolic debris out of the muscles. Cold-water immersion generally produces a greater and longer-lasting change in deep tissues than individual ice packs and is more efficient for cooling large groups of muscles simultaneously. Though many wince at the idea of sitting in a bathtub of 52 to 60 degrees Fahrenheit (11-16 C) water for 10 minutes, strategies like filling the tub waist deep and then putting on a down vest or fleece and a hat make you feel warm at least in your upper body. And you can sip a cup of hot tea at the same time. After you're out, your tissues warm up, causing a return of faster blood flow that helps repair damaged tissue more quickly.

Whirlpool

Using a whirlpool with water at of 98 to 105 degrees Fahrenheit (37-41 C) helps reduce inflammation because of the heat and the massaging of the water coming from the jets, which increase circulation in the injured area. Use the whirlpool daily for 20 minutes.

Massage

Massage reduces adhesions between muscle fibers and helps remove accumulations of fluid. You can administer massage yourself with your hands, a tennis ball, a foam roller, a stick roller, and so on. Or a licensed massage therapist can provide the massage. Many athletes with specific areas of tightness or pain feel that active release technique (ART) and trigger-point therapy are the most effective at releasing

---

Checklist for Possible Causes of Injury

Injuries are a challenge to figure out. What you might think at first is one injury may turn out to be another. Think you have strained your hamstring? Later you may learn you have a strained piriformis or iliotibial band. One of my runners thought she pulled her quadriceps. Later she learned she had a stress fracture in her femur. To diagnose your injury, you usually need the expertise of a professional for confirmation, and it helps you and your physician if you can figure out what might have caused the injury. Following is a list of questions to ask so you can learn what might have contributed to it. If you answer *yes* to any of these questions, consult your primary care physician, physiatrist, or physical therapist. The latter, for example, will suggest exercises to improve a structural weakness or an imbalance.

Your Biomechanics

- Is there a structural weakness in your feet and legs? Do you have a leg-length discrepancy?
- Do you have structural abnormalities? Structural conditions like lumbar lordosis, a forward curve in the lower spine, or patella alta, a kneecap that's higher than usual, are examples of abnormalities that can lead to running injuries.
- Are your opposing muscle groups (hamstrings and quadriceps) equally strong and flexible?
- Is your running form correct, and is your foot strike appropriate for your body weight?
- Have you changed your running gait when running in snow?

Your Training

- Do you warm up and cool down enough?
- Are you stretching enough and not too much?
- Have you made sudden changes in the quantity or quality of mileage or speed or changed the amount of training on hills or other surfaces? Are you running too much on concrete or are your ankles not strong enough to run on grass?
- Do you take enough time to rest and recover after long runs, workouts, and races? Are you racing too much?
- Have you increased your mileage by more than 10 percent a week?
- Do you hydrate enough and is your diet adequate for your training level?
- Are your running shoes giving you enough support?
- Has your weight changed significantly?

Other

- Are you under additional stress?
- Have you been involved in other physical activities that might affect your running?
- Have you been getting enough sleep?

Minimizing Injuries and Maximizing Biomechanics: Chiropractor Mika Tapanainen, DC

Cathy Utzschneider: You were a runner before you became a chiropractor. Can you talk about that?

Dr. Tapanainen: My love for running and running-related injuries goes far beyond my two decades of sports chiropractic. I grew up playing all the sports but at an early age realized my talents as a sprinter. I trained with Esbo-IF Track Club (actually at the time it was a subsidiary of Mazda Track Club) and ended up running as part of the Finnish Junior National Team and youth Olympic Program. My injuries stacked up and throughout my own experiences with the chiropractor, physical therapist, and rehabilitation professional, I found my passion and everlasting interest in solving running injuries.

Courtesy of Chris Morin

Cathy: As a chiropractor, how do you help runners most?

Dr. Tapanainen: As a chiropractor I've had the fortune to travel and work with the Finnish Olympic athletes and the Finnish National Ballet for almost a decade and of late, the Boston Ballet, for another decade. In Boston, I discovered a wonderful, active running community that has proven to supply plentiful injuries relating to running. In my experience, most running injuries are related to form, alignment, and overuse; therefore, during my sessions we try to understand the essence and root of the injury. Why is there an injury to begin with? It's often a simple truth with a complicated history. Clinical examination begins with an anatomical overview: a gait evaluation, which gives the clinician a basic understanding of your body mechanics during movement. Frequently there is a need for more precise evaluation of an athlete's running, which can be done on a treadmill and preferably videotaped for further analysis. The anatomical overview evaluates active and passive joint ranges of motion and muscle strength, balance, and flexibility and includes a palpatory examination to determine joint and the muscular static and dynamic relationship. During my two decades of working with athletes who present with various neuromusculoskeletal injuries, one thing rises above all during the initial evaluation: realization. Learning about your own biomechanics empowers you to improve as a runner by minimizing the faults and maximizing your potential.

Cathy: Working with runners on form and alignment, what are the common difficulties you observe?

Dr. Tapanainen: The biggest challenges lie in changing form or improving alignment. Alignment is driven by anatomical structure determined by genetics and later by learned movement patterns and muscular imbalances. Therefore, to change alignment, we are faced with a multitude of factors that are against the change. The earlier these are detected and dealt with, the better the outcome, in general. Alignment work is time consuming and frustrating at first, but the long-term prospect of fewer injuries and improved performance persists. Form is all about efficiency. Efficiency equals energy storage. I like going back to basics with drills known as running ABC's developed by coach Gerard Mach in the 1950s. Of late, the big question has involved minimalist running, which I find useful both for form as well as alignment. Forcing a midfoot contact associated with a shorter stride results in lesser loads to proximal joints and structures. My recommendation is time. Slowly build up with speed drills and striders as well as using minimalist shoes during the day. Get your body used to a minimalist shoe. Achilles tendon and plantar fascia pad injuries are commonly seen in my office as a result of a too aggressive changing to minimalist shoes.

Cathy: Several studies have found that stride length decreases over the decades more than stride frequency. Do you have suggestions for preserving stride length?

Dr. Tapanainen: Several studies suggest that aging results in reduction in stride length and increase in contact time. To battle the effects of time, we'll have to look at an umbrella approach: efficiency during running gait minimizes energy expenditure. Mix it up: intervals, fartleks, and striders to "get you off your heel;" yoga, Pilates, or Gyrotonics to improve dynamic flexibility; and cross-training to minimize overuse and maximize overall strength. Plan your runs: include a warm-up and dynamic stretching with a foam roller before the run and static stretching after the run. Include strength training and plyometrics as well as agility work to your weekly training regimen.

Cathy: If you had words of advice for masters runners, what would they be?

Dr. Tapanainen: The current research supports the notion that running prolongs overall health and slows the decline in physiological function. In my practice I've seen patients from age 4 to 96, and in my opinion if there is one truth that I've found it is as follows: keep moving!

tension to decrease pain and increase range of motion. The active release technique focuses on healing scarred muscles, tendons, ligaments, fascia, and nerves by applying deep pressure to the affected area, evaluating tissue texture, tightness, movement, and function and by trying to remove or break up the fibrous adhesions through stretching motions. Trigger-point therapy is similar to ART in that it targets injuries. Trigger points are essentially muscle knots to which therapists apply deep pressure to break them up and bring blood flow and oxygen to the injured area. Once a trigger point has been smoothed out, a nearby joint will likely have a greater range of motion.

CAUSES AND TREATMENT OF COMMON INJURIES

RICHE is helpful for all injuries listed in this section and, depending on the severity of the injury, physical therapy, massage, acupuncture, chiropractic, and other treatments may well be necessary.

Achilles Tendinitis

Achilles tendinitis is the inflammation or irritation of the Achilles tendon, a cord that connects your heel to your calf muscle. It is one of the most common injuries in runners, and particularly masters runners. If you've been running and racing since your youth, by the time you are 35 you may well be familiar with Achilles tendinitis. Many masters who were once sprinters or track racers switch to middle- or long-distance running precisely to avoid reigniting Achilles tendinitis, which may be aggravated by sprints, by the sudden movements common in tennis or soccer, or by shoes with little heel support. Achilles tendinitis may result from running- and nonrunning-related activities. A sudden increase in mileage and too much hill running are two main causes of Achilles tendinitis. In addition, if the muscles and tendons of your legs and feet are tight, or if you have flat feet that can cause excessive stretching in your muscles and tendons, you may be prone to Achilles tendinitis. Finally, high heels aggravate Achilles tendinitis. I've coached many runners who were sidelined for weeks or months with inflamed Achilles, the result of hours on the dance floor in high heels.

Achilles tendinitis presents as pain, swelling, and stiffness in the Achilles and sometimes in the calf as well. As someone susceptible to Achilles tendinitis from years of tennis and squash, I can say that it may feel so tender that a simple touch can startle you with a twinge. In general, pain from Achilles tendinitis diminishes as you warm up. Sometimes it completely disappears later in the run. Be careful, however. The pain may return afterward and feel even worse. You may aggravate it with running.

Although rest is critical, prolonged inactivity may cause stiffness. Move the injured ankle through its full range of motion and perform gentle calf and ankle stretches to maintain flexibility. If self-care doesn't work, seek treatment because if the tendon continues to sustain small tears through movement, it can rupture under excessive stress. A temporary shoe insert that elevates your heel may relieve strain on the tendon. Strengthen your calf muscles with exercises such as toe raises. Avoid hill running.

Ankle Sprains

Ankle sprains, or stretching or tearing of ligaments around the ankle, often occur when the foot twists or rolls inward. They may result after running on soft or uneven surfaces. If you twist your ankle, stop running. It's safe to resume running if the pain disappears completely after walking for a few minutes. In addition to applying the RICHE principle, wrap your ankle with an elastic bandage or even a boot for support. If swelling lasts for more than three days, get an X-ray to rule out the possibility of a fracture.

Black Toenails

Black toenails are caused by your toes rubbing against the front of your shoe. A blood blister forms under the toenail and the nail eventually falls off. High mileage and a lot of downhill running may cause black toenails, as may running in warmer weather when feet swell more. It helps to trim your toenails regularly and to wear wicking socks to keep your feet dry.

Once you have a black toenail, leave it alone. The pain is usually the worst on the first day and then lessens after that. The damaged part of the nail is gradually pushed off, and a new nail will replace it. Don't force the old nail off; it will fall off on its own. If you notice redness and infection, see a doctor.

Blisters

Small bubbles of skin caused by friction between skin and sock can form anywhere on the foot and fill with clear fluid. Some are painless, while others can cause enough pain to force you to stop running. Excessive moisture caused by sweat or wet conditions and wearing running shoes that are too tight can lead to blisters. Some runners wear a double layer of socks to deter blisters. The friction occurs between the two sock layers instead of your skin and the sock.

If you already have a blister and it's not painful, just leave it alone since the skin protects it. It will eventually break and the fluid will drain. If the blister is painful, you can boil a needle for 5 to 10 minutes in water and once cool, carefully pierce the blister. Press the fluid out and use an antiseptic cream on it. Cover the area with a blister blocking product or moleskin to protect against infection and provide cushioning. You can also spread antichafing balm or petroleum jelly on affected areas. As a preventive measure, some runners also put moleskin or athletic tape over hot spots on their feet that are prone to blisters. Make sure the moleskin or tape is applied smoothly with no wrinkles and is not too tight.

Chafing

Chafing caused by skin rubbing repetitively against loose fabric results in a painful stinging or burning sensation and usually a red and raw area. Chafing most often occurs at the inner thighs and under the arms and around the bra line for women and nipples for men. Moisture, either from sweat or rain, can worsen chafing.

Apply diaper rash ointment, antichafing balm such as BodyGlide, or petroleum jelly to the chafed areas before your run. Because chafing can be caused by loose clothing and clothes made of cotton, which stays wet once wet, wear running clothes that are snug and made of synthetic materials that wick away moisture. Some runners wear spandex bike shorts to prevent chafing between their legs.

Iliotibial Band Syndrome

Iliotibial band syndrome (ITBS) is a common running injury that may result from overtraining, running on a banked surface, inadequate warm-up or cool-down, and certain physical abnormalities. The iliotibial band is a fascia, a thick membrane, that runs along the outside of the thigh from the top of the hip to the outside of the knee. It stabilizes the knee and hip during running. When the band becomes tight, it rubs on the bone. ITBS is marked by sharp, burning knee or hip pain. Most people feel the pain on the outside of the knee as the iliotibial band becomes inflamed or the band itself may become irritated.

In addition to following the RICHE principles, taking anti-inflammatory drugs such as ibuprofen can reduce the swelling. Cut back on hill work, and make sure you run on even surfaces. Perform leg-raise exercises to strengthen your hips, and be conscientious about stretching your IT band.

Muscle Pulls or Strains

A muscle pull causes a sudden, searing pain and tightness in the muscle. You may not be able to bear full weight on the affected limb or bring it through the normal range of motion. Unlike a sprain, which affects ligaments, a strain is an injury to a muscle or tendon. Whether in the hamstring, quadriceps, or other muscle, strains or pulls may be caused by inflexibility, overexerting specific muscles, insufficient warm-up, too much hill work, or suddenly increasing your mileage.

RICHE is the best treatment for mild to moderate strains. If you don't see improvement within two weeks, you could have a muscle pull, in which case you should see your doctor.

Runner's Knee

Runner's knee, a common complaint among long-distance runners and also aggravated by climbing stairs, results in soreness around and sometimes behind the kneecap. Your knee may feel stiff and sore after sitting for long periods, and you may hear a clicking sound when you bend or extend your knee. Runner's knee is usually caused by weakness in the middle quadriceps muscles and tight hamstrings or IT band and sometimes overpronation (your feet roll inward when you run).

Treatment should include strengthening your quadriceps muscles with exercises such as forward lunges and straight-leg raises to help support and stabilize your kneecap. Stretching your hamstrings and IT bands also helps. In addition, make sure you have the right kind of running shoes for your foot type and that your shoes are not worn out. Replace your shoes every 300 to 400 miles (483-644 km). You may also want to buy over-the-counter arch supports. If you're still experiencing pain, see a doctor about getting custom-fitted orthotics.

Plantar Fasciitis

Do you feel severe pain in your heel, especially when you first step out of bed in the morning? Most commonly, heel pain is caused by inflammation of the plantar fascia, the tough band of tissue that supports the bottom of your foot and runs from the heel bone to the toes. Plantar fasciitis may be caused by wearing worn-out running shoes or ones that lack arch support, overpronation (when your feet roll inward too much), or tight calf muscles. Having flat feet or high arches may also add stress. High-heeled shoes may also lead to plantar fasciitis because they make your Achilles tendon contract and shorten, straining the tissue around your heel.

The stabbing or burning pain of plantar fasciitis is usually worse in the morning because the fascia tightens overnight. As you warm up during your run, the pain normally decreases and is more tolerable, but it may return after an hour or so of running.

Decrease your mileage until the pain subsides, cross-training until the pain gradually improves or disappears. In addition to RICHE, stretching your plantar fascia, Achilles tendons, and calf muscles may also provide relief. An anti-inflammatory such as ibuprofen may ease pain and inflammation, although it won't treat the underlying problem. You can also apply pressure to your heel by rolling a golf ball or tennis ball with the arch of your foot while you are standing and stabilized. This can help reduce pain and increase blood flow.

If self-treatment doesn't work, see a doctor for orthotics or night splints. A physical therapist can help you stretch your plantar fascia and strengthen lower-leg muscles, which stabilize your ankle and heel, and show you how to apply athletic tape to support the bottom of your foot.

Shin Splints

A pain in the front or inside of the lower leg along the shin bone (tibia), shin splints are common among beginning runners who increase their mileage too quickly. Shin splints may be caused by weak anterior tibialis muscles on the front of your lower leg, which are responsible for flexing the foot upward and are often underdeveloped in nonrunners. Running on hard surfaces and wearing shoes with poor support may put added strain on the muscles on the front of your leg. People with flat feet are also more likely to develop shin splints.

In addition to applying the RICHE principles, stretch your calf and shin muscles with toe and heel raises several times a day. Also, try inserting over-the-counter heel lifts so that your calves don't have to stretch as far, and make sure you use good running form. If you lean forward too much when you run, you may be pulling too hard on your calf muscles. If the pain does not go away after a few weeks of rest, check with an orthopedist to rule out a stress fracture. Otherwise, you can return to running after several weeks of healing.

Side Stitch

A side stitch is a sharp, intense pain under the lower edge of the ribcage, more often on the left side. It's more common in novice runners who take quick, shallow breaths. The cause of side stitches is not known, although some runners notice they get them when they eat just before their run. Running in extremely cold temperatures may induce side stitches because it's less comfortable to take in deep breaths with lungs full of frigid air until you're thoroughly warmed up.

Avoid eating within one hour of running. Drink plain water rather than sugary, carbonated drinks. Always warm up before your runs and when running, breathe deeply from your belly, not from your chest. Deep belly breathing allows you to take in more air.

If you're running in cold weather, try breathing through a scarf or neck warmer. Finally, practice good running form, maintaining good posture so you're not hunched over. If you do feel a stitch, gently pushing your fingers into the affected area and altering your breathing pattern may relieve some pain. Take a deep breath in as quickly as you can, to force the diaphragm down. Hold your breath for a couple of seconds and then forcibly exhale through pursed lips. If you get a cramp in the middle of a run, try changing your breathing pattern. If you always exhale when your right foot strikes the ground, try exhaling on the left foot strike. If all else fails, you may have to stop and walk briskly for a few seconds while concentrating on deep breathing. Continue running after the stitch goes away.

Stress Fractures

Stress fractures are tiny cracks in the surface of a bone and most often occur in the lower leg or the foot. They occur most frequently when runners increase the intensity and volume of their training over several weeks to a few months. A shortage of calcium or a biomechanical flaw in running style or body structure may contribute to the injury. Stress fractures commonly appear in the tibia (the inner and larger bone below the knee), the femur (thigh bone), the sacrum (triangular bone at the base of the spine), and in the metatarsal (toe) bones. You'll notice gradual muscle soreness, stiffness, and a pinpoint pain on the affected bone. Early diagnosis can prevent the injury from spreading and becoming a complete fracture. Pain gets worse with running, but you can maintain fitness by cross-training.

If you have symptoms of a stress fracture, stop running immediately. Ask a doctor for an X-ray or bone scan. A bone scan is more precise than X-rays for diagnosing stress fractures. You may also want to test bone mineral density to see whether it is low. Your doctor may recommend supplements to improve it, such as calcium and vitamin D, which is necessary for calcium absorption. Your injury will keep you off the roads for 6 to 10 weeks depending on the severity of the stress fracture, and you may need a cast. Cross-training will keep you in great shape, particularly if you incorporate workouts equivalent in time and intensity to what your running efforts would have been. Return to running gradually and when you do, don't increase your weekly mileage by more than 10 percent each week. You may want to have your gait analyzed at a running shop to ensure that you're wearing the right shoes for your foot and running style. As previously mentioned, replace your shoes every 300 to 400 miles (483-644 km). Finally, strengthening the muscles around your bones can keep them strong enough to prevent stress fractures. If, for example, you have a tibial stress fracture, strengthening your shin muscles and calves with toe and heel raises helps.

As much as you try to avoid injury and practice safe running, you may become injured at some point. My best advice is to "listen" carefully for pains that reoccur three days in a row. Runners don't like to acknowledge pain and many continue to run, refusing to accept the inevitable. The result is significant, sidelining injuries. If a pain is significant and persists in the same spot, back off from running immediately even if it's for a day or so. Cross-train or rest instead. And while you are cross-training, remember that you are still training. If the pain persists, see your primary care doctor or a sports medicine expert such as a chiropractor or physical therapist. The sooner you back off, the sooner you'll be running again.

Injuries do go away. Liberty Athletic Club runner Jan Holmquist, 70, has been plagued with Achilles tendinitis and sidelined several times over the last 10 years and was unable to run from two weeks to two months with her first flare-up. And that's not all. "Over the years, I have been sidelined with a broken neck, broken wrist (once the left and once the right), shin splints, stress fracture, sprained and fractured ankle (three times)," she said. "Never give up" is her motto. Why would she? She's running better than ever today, having been the top age-graded performer (over 100%) in several national masters road championships and the one mile outdoors. Her outstanding achievements are many. Jan, at the age of 69 in 2013, was named USATF masters athlete of the year for women 65 to 69. She's also been named number one runner in her age group in *Running Times* and by USATF at 60, 62, and 68.

Chapter 6

Flexibility and Stretching

"Stretching is my lifeline. I think that's probably the main reason I've kept a long stride and rarely get injured."

"Me? Stretch? I haven't stretched since the 1970s. And I just won my age group in a 10K recently."

Stretching evokes all kinds of reactions from masters runners, and it's a topic that's been debated for decades among all runners, all athletes, and physical fitness professionals. What kind of stretching should you do and when? How much does stretching really help your running? How can it help the range of motion possible in a joint? These questions and others may contribute to the fact that many runners, including masters, take little time to stretch. "I have so little time! Stretching is the first thing to go," I've often heard.

For masters runners in particular, though, and as the earlier chapter on physiology and aging notes, flexibility rather than tightness helps performance. Remember that with aging you lose elasticity in the soft tissues—an older muscle is inherently stiffer than a younger one—and limited range of motion limits stride. Between the ages of 30 and 80, you lose 20 to 30 percent of range of motion. And range of motion, along with leg turnover, is a central component of speed.

Many of you masters runners, particularly if you've run or been involved with other sports for decades, may be more confused than open runners about stretching. You have seen the change in opinions about what type of stretching is right to do when. You remember 20, 30, and 40 years ago when all kinds of athletic practices began with static stretches. Remember the years of reaching toward your toes or leaning against a wall to lengthen your hamstrings and calves, of holding those poses without moving for 30 seconds to a minute or more before a workout? The belief was that static stretching, muscles remaining stationary in the stretched position, as opposed to dynamic stretching, stretching while moving, was the best preparation for lengthening muscles, increasing flexibility, and enhancing performance.

But that belief is no longer held so strongly in the performance and physical fitness world. Beginning more than a decade ago, considerable research has found that static stretches—particularly those held for a minute or more—before intensive running or other demanding workouts actually make performances worse (Kay and Blazevich 2012). Studies found that subjects who performed static stretches before intense exercise, could not jump as high, sprint as fast, or swing a tennis racket as powerfully as they had before. Static stretches appeared to cause the nervous system to react and tighten, not loosen, the stretched muscle, the research showed (Young and Behm 2003; Wilson et al. 2010; Kay and Blazevich 2012). Static stretching before a workout can overextend those muscles and actually rob them of the power and strength necessary for the actual workout. In 2010 the American College of Sports Medicine warned against static stretching before workouts and competitions. The best time for static stretching is after a workout. Before a workout, practice dynamic, or active, stretching.

The benefits of stretching and of consistent stretching for masters runners are significant and several. Many runners, including masters, who often train on their own and are pressed for time, don't take the extra 10 or 15 minutes to stretch. If you remind yourself of the following benefits of stretching for masters runners, as for all runners, you will be more inclined to reserve time for it.

Stretching provides the following benefits:

- Increases range of motion and stride length. Those are essential for masters runners. Watch other masters run. Their strides are most likely shorter than those of younger runners. Stretching to help develop a longer stride ultimately can help speed and results.

- Improves your running form and posture while running, standing, and sitting. Stretching your back, shoulders, and neck relaxes those muscles so you can hold an upright, relaxed stance when running. Ever see runners holding their shoulders too high? That consumes energy and can be the result of tight shoulder, back, and neck muscles. Dynamic stretching can help you loosen those muscles.

- Helps you become aware of muscle tension you hadn't realized you had. How many times do you come to a workout after a day of being sedentary? By targeting all parts of your body, dynamic stretching helps you identify an area that is particularly tight and that may be susceptible to a pull in an intense workout.

PRERUN DYNAMIC STRETCHING

The best warm-up routine begins with 10 to 15 minutes of easy jogging followed by dynamic stretching. Dynamic stretches move your muscles through full, exaggerated motions, many of which mimic running. These stretches increase blood flow to your muscles, activate your central nervous system, decrease muscle tightness, and increase your heart rate.

You can dynamically stretch your muscles three ways in a warm-up: drills, sun salute poses from yoga, and leg swings. Many of the drills are plyometrics: exercises involving jumping or skipping. They increase the power in your muscles by rapidly lengthening and then shortening them. Drills and leg swings are part of every warm-up for runners in the club I coach, the Liberty Athletic Club. Sometimes we also incorporate some of the sun salute poses, like the downward dog.

1. *Running drills,* such as high knees and butt kicks, coordinate muscles, ligaments, and joints, challenging your flexibility, mobility, strength, and stability. (See chapter 4 for a full description of these running drills.) Allow 5 to 10 minutes for these.

2. *Sun salutes*, the yoga sequence that combines yoga poses, loosens your muscles, balancing all muscle groups in a relaxed effort. Relax into the stretch rather than making it an effort and never stretch it farther than the muscle wants to go. (See the Sun Salutes sidebar for photos of each pose in a sun salute yoga sequence.)

3. *Leg swings* loosen the hip flexors, hip extensors, hip adductors, and hip abductors, increasing stride length and frequency. Perform forward straight-leg swings, forward bent-leg swings, and side-to-side swings, doing 5 to 10 on each leg. Simple directions follow.

   - For forward straight-leg swings, brace your body against a wall or other support by holding one arm out to the side at shoulder height. Start with both feet directly under the hips and swing the outside leg forward and backward (figure 6.1*a*).

   - For forward bent-leg swings, perform the same motion as a straight-leg swing except allow your knee to bend (figure 6.1*b*).

   - For side leg swings, face a wall or other support, bracing your body with both arms outstretched and shoulder high. Swing one leg to the side of your body, extending to a comfortable height. Swing the leg back, crossing in front of the body (figure 6.1*c*).

   During all leg swings, both legs should be fairly straight but your knees shouldn't be locked. Swing your legs fluidly without bouncy or jerky actions. Gradually increase the range of motion until your leg swings as high as it will comfortably go.

Figure 6.1 *(a)* forward straight-leg swing, *(b)* forward bent-leg swing, *(c)* side leg swing.

POSTRUN STATIC STRETCHES

After a run, static stretches held for 10 to 30 seconds at most help maintain flexibility and relax tight muscles. Studies have shown that there's no need to hold a stretch for longer than 30 seconds and that stretches held for more than one minute result in lower performance afterward (Kay and Blazevich 2012; Bandy et al. 1997). Likewise, you achieve benefits in the first stretch, and after four stretches, the muscle's length changes little. There's no extra benefit from stretching a muscle 10 times in one session. One reason to do static stretching after a workout is that your muscles are warm. Stretching cold, tight muscles or improper stretching can lead to muscle strains, tears, and other injuries. Be careful not to overstretch. Breathe easily, and don't hold your breath.

Everyone has different needs, so you may want to focus on the stretch that targets your tightest, weakest areas. Of the following 13 stretches, the first 10 are the most critical.

STANDING CALF STRETCH

Tight calf muscles, consisting of the gastrocnemius and soleus muscles, lead to common injuries in all runners. Strained calves are painful and result in shortened strides.

Stand about an arm's length from a wall. Stand facing a wall with the forearms against it and your head resting on your hands. Bend one leg and place your foot on the ground in front of you, leaving the other leg straight, behind you. Slowly move your hips forward until you feel a stretch in the calf of your straight leg. Keep the heel of the foot on the straight leg on the ground and *your toes pointed straight ahead*. For a deeper stretch, move your foot farther back.

Sun Salutes Yoga Sequence

Doing even one sun salute before a workout is enough. "Sun salutes are my 'secret weapon,' if I have one," said Sue Gustafson, age group winner among women 50 to 59 in the 1997 Boston Marathon. "I do a dozen of these every morning before running or getting on with the day. Sun salutes harmonize and warm the body in a gentle, powerful way." Following are the yoga poses included in a sun salute yoga sequence.

Raised arms position.

Hand to foot position.

Equestrian position
(lunge with right foot forward).

Mountain pose.

Cobra position.

Return to equestrian position.

Return to hand to foot position.

Return to raised arms position.

HEEL DIP

Heel dips target the calf muscles (soleus and gastrocnemius) as well as the Achilles tendons, a prime area of vulnerability for masters runners. Tight calves and Achilles tendons also contribute to plantar fasciitis.

Balance on your toes on a platform or step. Your heels extend over the edge. You may need to hold onto something to keep your balance. Put all your weight on one foot, then slowly lower the heel of that foot, lengthening the calf. Rise back to your starting position. Start with 3 to 5 repetitions, and gradually build to 20 to 30. Repeat with the other foot.

ILIOTIBIAL BAND STRETCH

One of the most common running injuries is iliotibial band syndrome. The IT band, a layer of connective tissue on the outside of the thigh, becomes irritated from rubbing over the bump of the thigh bone near the knee. A tight IT band, along with tight muscles in your hip, pelvis, or leg and uneven leg length are among the causes of IT band syndrome.

Stand with your left leg crossed in front of your right leg. With your right arm extending overhead, reach to the left. Put your left hand on your hip. Push slightly on your left hip until you feel a slight stretch

along the right side of your torso, hip, upper thigh, and knee. For a deeper stretch, keep your feet farther apart, bend the knee of your forward leg, and keep the back knee straight.

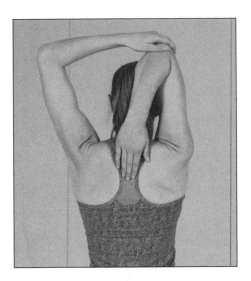

SHOULDER STRETCH

Tight shoulders lead to slouching, fatigue, and limited range of motion.

Stand up straight with shoulders relaxed and back. Reach your right arm over your head, bend your elbow and reach your hand behind your neck. With your elbow pointing toward the sky, slide your right palm down to your back. With your left hand, grip your right elbow and gently pull it toward your ear. Continue sliding your right palm down your back without straining. Keep your head up and resist the urge to bend your neck forward. Repeat with the opposite arm.

PLANTAR FASCIA STRETCH

Inflammation of the plantar fascia—the connective tissue that runs from your heel to the base of your toes—is a common running injury. Stretching the fascia and massaging and icing it help stave off plantar fasciitis.

Sit barefoot. Use an elastic band to pull the ball of the foot and toes back toward you. You will feel a stretch on the underside of the foot. Hold for a count of 10. Release. Repeat 4 times.

UPPER-BACK STRETCH

Stretched back muscles contribute to upright running posture.

Grab your elbow with the opposite hand and gently push the elbow up and across your body until your hand reaches down to "scratch" your back. Gently push on your elbow to guide your hand down your back as far as it will comfortably go, stretching your triceps and shoulders. Stretch both arms.

HAMSTRING STRETCH

Runners are notorious for tight hamstrings that can cause low-back problems and lead to pulled muscles. Tight hamstrings also limit your range of motion, which can affect running stride, form, and speed.

Lie with one leg straight up in the air, the other bent with the foot flat on the ground. Loop a rope or towel over the arch of the lifted foot, and gently pull on the towel as you push against it with your foot. Push only to the point where your muscles contract. Repeat with the opposite leg.

QUADRICEPS STRETCH

For powerful running, the quadriceps muscles (the vastus lateralis, vastus medialis, vastus intermedius, and rectus femoris) should not be tight. They are critical for stride length and responsible for extending the knees and flexing the hips.

Kneel on your knees (without resting back on your heels). Lean back with your body erect and your arms hanging down to the side. Hold the position for 15 seconds. Do this stretch 2 or 3 times.

HIP AND BACK STRETCH

Relaxed hip and back muscles help you maintain balance and keep you from slouching when you run. Upright posture with a slight forward lean contributes to good running form.

Sit with your right leg straight. Bend your left leg, and cross your left foot over and rest it outside your right knee. Bend your right elbow and rest it on the outside of your left thigh, just above the knee. During the stretch use the elbow to keep this leg stationary with controlled pressure to the inside. With your left hand resting behind you, slowly turn your head to look over your left shoulder and at the same time rotate your upper body toward your left hand and arm. As you turn your upper body, think of turning your hips in the same direction (although your hips won't move because your right elbow is keeping the left leg stationary). Stretch both sides.

GROIN STRETCH

Tight groin muscles, also known as the adductors, may limit your ability to move your hip joints in all directions, including hip flexion and extension, hip adduction (toward the body), and abduction (away from the body), and hip rotation. Some masters runners are sidelined for months from running because of tight groin muscles.

Seated, put the soles of your feet together. With your elbows on the inside of your knees, gradually lean forward and gently press your knees toward the ground.

PIRIFORMIS STRETCH

Your piriformis muscle is responsible for rotating your hip. If the piriformis becomes too tight or has spasms, it can irritate the sciatic nerve, causing pain in your gluteal muscles, low back, and thighs.

Lie on the ground with the left leg bent at the hip and knee and right ankle crossed at the knee in a number 4. Slowly bring your left knee (and, along with it, your right ankle) toward your chest. If and when your left knee gets close enough to your chest, clasp your hands around your left hamstring, just below your left knee, and slowly bring your left knee (and, along with it, your right ankle) toward your chest. Use your hands and your left hip flexors to pull your left knee and right ankle toward your chest even more until you feel a firm stretch in your left buttock. Just do one stretch per side per day. Repeat on the other side.

HIP FLEXOR STRETCH

The hip flexors bring the legs up toward the trunk; their strength is essential for best sprint performances and for running uphill. These muscles also become tight when you sit a lot at your desk or when driving. Tight hip flexors often lead to low-back and hip pain.

Begin in a forward lunge position and drop your back knee to the floor. Place your hands on your hips and look up. Press your hips forward and down toward the floor and feel a stretch through your torso, hip, groin, and thigh. Release and repeat on the other leg.

HAMSTRING AND BACK STRETCH

This is the final stretch to ensure upright posture and optimal stride length.

Lie on your back with your knees bent. Hug your knees to your chest to stretch your hamstrings and low back.

Runner Profile: William Riley

Date of birth: May 29, 1936

Personal Information

- Insurance and banking. Most recently, senior underwriter at Commercial Union Assurance Co. in Boston, Massachusetts.
- Loan officer at two banks on Cape Cod.
- Married to Deborah, two adult children from a previous marriage.
- Starting focused training at 40. Was a swimmer briefly at Brown University.

Personal Best

Marathon: 2:44 (46)

Age-Graded Personal Bests

- 5K (road): Five over 90% at age 76, best 92%
- 10K (road): Two over 89% at ages 70 and 76
- 15K (road): One at 91.99% at age 73
- Half marathon: Three over 89%, best 90.96% at age 73

Cathy Utzschneider: How did you get into training and competition?

William Riley: A routine stress test indicated a high $\dot{V}O_2$max and my doctor suggested I take up endurance running.

Cathy: How do you explain your success?

Courtesy of D. McSorley

(continued)

William Riley *(continued)*

William: Good genes (my mother lived to 100), good luck healthwise, remaining injury free until about five years ago when I had meniscus surgery, and being a late starter.

Cathy: How often do you race?

William: About every three weeks but more often in the fall's shorter races.

Cathy: What is your most memorable win and why?

William: In 1988 when I was 52 I entered the Bud Light Endurance Triathlon, an Ironman Triathlon on Cape Cod in September. It was my first race at this distance. This qualified me for the Hawaii Ironman World Championships, which was only six weeks later. I did go and won my age group and set an age-group record in 11:04.51, just 15 minutes off the course record. That was my most memorable win.

Cathy: In a peak training week for a marathon, what is your mileage and how much weekly speed work do you do?

William: I am no longer doing marathons. My last marathon was in Boston at age 66, when I ran 3:21. Then I averaged 25 to 30 miles (40-48 km) a week with a track or tempo run.

Cathy: What is the greatest challenge as a masters runner?

William: Continuing motivation and keeping speed without getting injured.

Cathy: How do you maintain motivation?

William: I enjoy the competition and camaraderie more than the training. My nerves are still on edge before every race.

Cathy: What has been the greatest surprise?

William: I am still challenged and motivated despite my slower times.

Cathy: Have you had injuries and how have you dealt with them?

William: I have had three arthroscopic knee surgeries that kept me from running, but I bike and swim a great deal, especially in winter.

Cathy: What advice do you have for other masters?

William: Vary your training regimen, course, and races and stay with the healthy lifestyle as long as you can.

Cathy: What is a sample training week?

William:

- January to May: Run 26-28 miles (42-45 km), bike 70 miles (113 km), swim 2-3 miles (3-5 km)
- May to December: Run 26-30 miles (42-48 km), swim 2-3 miles (3-5 km)

You may say, having read this chapter, "It's hard to motivate myself to stretch!" I understand. But stretching is important. It enhances range of motion and that enhances speed, and it becomes more important as we age. If you're cramped for time—who isn't?—reserve at least five minutes before and after your run for this miniroutine: the three leg swings described in this chapter and the A march, A skip, B march, B skip, and the side slides described in chapter 4 before your run. After you run, perform the standing calf, hamstring, quadriceps, hip flexor, and IT band stretches.

Part II

Training

Chapter 7

Goal Setting for Fitness and Competition

Runners of all ages need goals, the right goals. *Right* is the loaded word. It depends on so much: your fitness, experience, interests, work, everything in your life. The word *goal* itself stirs up mixed feelings: excitement, fear, and questions. Will you meet it? Do you really want it? Why not another race or distance over this one? Should you try something new or improve on a familiar course?

If you find choosing the right goals challenging, you're in good company. Post-collegiate and Olympic Trials runners have sought my help precisely because it's difficult to set goals outside a structured setting where the main focus is running, one where the coach and culture dictate daily schedules. Having graduated from a collegiate team or professional running, these "in-between" runners are unfamiliar with balancing running with work and maybe family. It can be hard to figure out goals that feel new and exciting, with personal bests most likely behind them. Matt Kerr, 38, director of Boston College men's track and field team, understands the challenges as a runner himself, husband and father of two, and also a coach. A 3:43 1,500-meter runner in high school and later a two-time NCAA steeplechase champion and four-time steeplechaser for the Canadian national team, Kerr stopped competing at age 31. The next year he became a coach at Boston College.

Now, focused on coaching, he said he might consider masters running sometime, if he finds the "right" (motivating) goal that fits with work and family. He reflected on the fact that many postcollegiate and professional runners stop running competitively at 24 or 25. "There's an endpoint," he said. "A time when they enter the normal, real world and don't know how to translate their experience running into their everyday life. In college, for example, they're either studying or running. To go from being a full-time athlete to being competitive and a regular person is hard. You don't know how to set goals or how to fit running into your life. You're used to a system where everything is fairly rigid—with a coach who oversees everything on a competitive basis. There's a huge gap afterward," Kerr told me.

As you consider your own goals, it's helpful to think about them as an experiment, particularly at first. There is no one "right" goal anyway. That's the fun and challenge. It's up to you, unlike preset running goals in school or college. If it's a particularly stressful time (you have a new job or you've just moved, for example) you might decide it's the year to set a fitness goal, one based on consistency and not performance. Maybe this year your goal is to run consistently, an average of 30 miles (48 km) a week for at least 45 weeks of the year. Or maybe you want a performance goal, one focused on doing your best. If so, the options may feel infinite. You can pick from many events. A performance goal encourages you to plan carefully and periodize your training. Periodization means you divide your overall training into periods, each with its own focus, such as endurance, strength, or speed (explained in more detail in chapter 8); incorporate specific workouts to meet each focus; and rest occasionally for recovery. A performance goal also rewards you for your efforts with a result and time. There's nothing like applause from the clock—a personal best!

SETTING GOALS AND WRITING THEM DOWN

The mere act of setting a goal is powerful. That alone can boost your mood. A goal provides a sense of purpose, focuses your energies in areas of your interests, reinforces persistence through tough times, and punctuates the rhythm of your life so there's an ending and a time to sit back, assess your achievement, celebrate, and recover. According to the fathers of goal-setting research in business, Edwin Locke and Gary Latham (2002; 1990), the most challenging goals produce the highest levels of effort and performance; they're better than moderate goals. The following story speaks for many runners. I encouraged a locally competitive runner and doctor in her 60s to enter the World Masters Track and Field Championships. Anyone can enter. She was petrified, knowing she'd be competing with some national- and world-class runners. Despite finishing last, she competed and loved the experience. She ran a personal age-graded best. A most challenging goal inspired her best training.

When mulling over goals, it's helpful to keep in mind the acronym SMART. Goals are more effective if they meet the following criteria:

- **S**pecific. Strive for a certain time over a certain distance by a particular date.
- **M**easurable. If a goal is measurable, it can be controlled.
- **A**ttainable. High goals are worth setting, but you should be able to reach them.

- **R**elevant. Pick a goal that you care about.
- **T**ime bound. Give yourself enough, but not too much, time. A deadline helps you focus and commit.

Setting "A" (highest), "B" (higher), and "C" (high) goals in terms of ranges and levels helps you set SMART goals. Say, for example, that you have run a 41:15 10K and your goal might be to run a 10K in 39:30 to 40:00 minutes. An 'A' goal might be to run a 10K in 39:30 to 40 minutes. A 'B' goal might be to run it in 40 to 40:30 minutes, and a 'C' goal might be to run it in 40:30 to 41. The faster you are, the narrower the ranges of your goals.

Goals are meaningful if you write them down. (Also, if you're like many, you may forget your goals after a few weeks.) In research for my doctoral dissertation on over 100 national- and world-class female masters runners, I learned that 100 percent of them set goals (Utzschneider 2002). Ninety-six percent of them wrote them down. Writing down goals—even if you eventually have to change them—raises the level of commitment that will carry you through the inevitable hurdles and tough times. You're more likely not only to focus on goal-related activities, but you're also more likely to avoid distractions (Locke and Latham 2002).

KEEPING YOUR GOALS FLEXIBLE

Not everything goes according to plan, either in your training or in a race. Keeping goals and plans flexible is par for the course. Whatever goals you set, feel free to reset them if circumstances suggest the timing isn't right. If, for example, your goal has been a half marathon that's a month away but you've recently been feeling tired and run down, reset and postpone that goal to later in the year. If you can adapt your goals to your circumstances, they'll work for you, not against you.

INTEGRATING RUNNING GOALS INTO YOUR LIFE

In our hectic world where most masters runners juggle multiple demands, goals provide a sense of perspective and control. Figure 7.1 is a pyramid completed by a runner to give you an example of how you might use it, and a blank goal pyramid is provided in figure 7.3 later in this chapter. However, when you set them, you need to keep in mind all your life commitments. Kids have graduations, parents have anniversaries, you have conferences and family vacations, and your house may need to be painted. If you don't consider energies needed for them, your goals may disappear into thin air, as fleeting as many New Year's resolutions. My first book, *MOVE! How Women Can Achieve Athletic Goals at Any Age*, focuses on the four stages of achieving goals: preparing for goals, setting goals, managing goals, and then assessing goal achievement. Preparing for goals is critical and often not considered. Use a calendar or the big-picture calendar (see figure 7.2) to note all your upcoming obligations around which you can plan your running workouts and events. Keep these three questions in mind as you fill out your big-picture calendar:

1. What is my long-term goal?
2. How will the commitments listed affect my pursuit of that goal?
3. How will I handle distractions so they're compatible with my life as a whole?

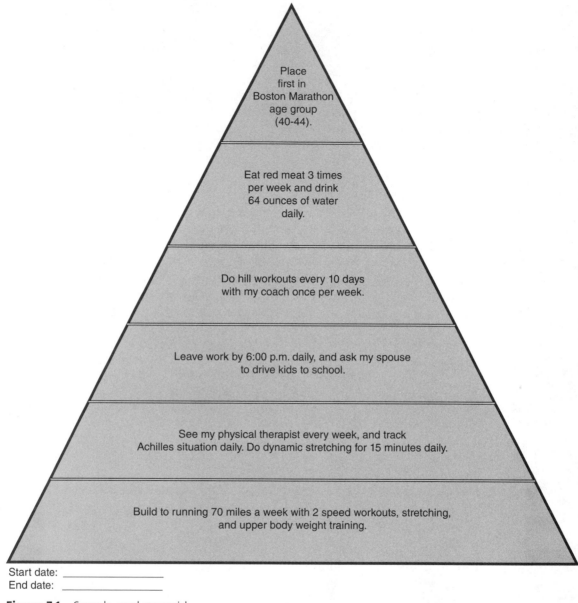

Start date: _____
End date: _____

Figure 7.1 Sample goal pyramid.

Adapted, by permission, from C. Utzschneider, 2011, *Move! How women can achieve athletic goals at any age* (Natick, MA: Cedar Crest Books).

Assess Your Fitness

If you're an experienced runner, you know your fitness level. You have recent race results. It's more challenging to determine your fitness if you are new to running or coming back after a long absence. Fitness depends on many factors, including your recent activity, medical history, genetics, and body weight (the leaner you are, generally the more fit you are). If you haven't been active recently, seeing your physician is a wise first step. After confirming your health, figure out your fitness

Responsibilities	January	February	March	April	May	June
Family and friends						
Personal						
Work						
Home						
Athletic						

Responsibilities	July	August	September	October	November	December
Family and friends						
Personal						
Work						
Home						
Athletic						

Figure 7.2 Big-picture calendar.

From C. Utzschneider, 2014, *Mastering running* (Champaign, IL: Human Kinetics). Adapted, by permission, from C. Utzschneider, 2011, *Move! How women can achieve athletic goals at any age* (Natick, MA: Cedar Crest Books).

baseline. Go to an outdoor track and see how long it takes you to walk and jog—or just walk, if you can't jog—12 laps. That's three miles (4.8 km). Or you might enter a 5K road race, which you can either walk and jog or jog easily. You'll have a time for a 5K and a starting point.

Guidelines for Progress

If you are starting or coming back to running after a layoff or injury, moderately increase your mileage and effort. A useful guideline for increasing mileage is the 10 percent rule. Increase your weekly mileage by no more than 10 percent over the previous week. Following that rule, you'll likely get stronger and more fit, while minimizing the chances of injury and overtraining.

I encourage the runners I coach to incorporate cutback weeks, reducing mileage by 15 to 25 percent every fourth week. Say you want to increase your weekly mileage from 20 to 30 miles (32-48 km) while including cutback weeks. Here's a sample of a 10-week schedule:

Week 1 – 20 miles (32 km)

Week 2 – 22 miles (35 km)

Week 3 – 24 miles (39 km)

Week 4 – 20 miles (32 km)

Week 5 – 24 miles (39 km)

Week 6 – 26 miles (42 km)

Week 7 – 28 miles (45 km)

Week 8 – 24 miles (39 km)

Week 9 – 28 miles (45 km)

Week 10 – 30 miles (48 km)

Tracking your resting heart rate (RHR) as you become more fit can help you measure progress. While RHR stays fairly constant with aging, if your level of activity stays the same, your RHR slows as your fitness improves. Good places to measure your heart rate are the radial artery in your wrist or the carotid artery in your neck. If you take your pulse at the radial artery, use the tips of your index and middle fingers to locate your pulse. First feel for the wrist bone at the base of the thumb and then slowly move toward your wrist. Start the watch and begin counting your pulse. After a minute you should have an accurate reading. (Know also that such factors as hot weather, too little sleep, caffeine, and over-the-counter medicines may increase heart rate.) As a rule of thumb, a normal resting heart rate for average adults ranges from 60 to 100 beats per minute. For an experienced runner or an athlete in training, however, resting heart rate may decline to an average of 40 to 60 beats per minute. The trained athlete's heart and cardiovascular system are so efficient that the heart beats fewer times per minute to achieve sufficient blood flow to the body.

TRACKING GOALS AND PROGRESS

You can't evaluate your goals without tracking your training, whether in a journal, on your smart phone, with a GPS watch or foot pod, or an infinite assortment of online computer programs. No one I've ever met remembers his or her training without recording it somewhere. How much you track in terms of details is up to you. At the very least, note your mileage goals and speed workouts. If you experience pains or soreness, note that too. The runners I coach note pains on a scale of 1 to 5, with 0 representing no pain, 1 representing awareness, 2 representing mild soreness, 3 representing intermittent pain, 4 representing pain, and 5 representing pain too great for running. Consult an expert if you've felt mild soreness for more than a week of running. As a final note, beware of writing down so much you get lost in the details. Records should be brief.

TYPES OF GOALS

The five kinds of goals are performance, outcome, and process goals on the one hand and short- and long-term goals on the other. Because all goals are flexible and because successive short-term goals lead to long-term goals, medium-term goals are unnecessary. If you familiarize yourself with these goals, you'll know what kind you are ready to set.

Performance Goals

Guidelines are helpful, but goals are more specific and will motivate you more. Always set performance (or mastery) goals, goals based on your results, independent of other runners' goals. A performance goal might be to achieve a certain time in a distance you've run before or to run a new distance, a half marathon or marathon, for example. Of course, unless you're racing on a track with a consistent surface, you'll need to adjust performance goals related to time according to how challenging the course is (the number of hills and turns), the weather (allow more time for extreme cold, heat, and humidity), footing (grass is slower than asphalt), and your recent training.

You can use several tools, all of which will produce similar results, to help you set a performance goal: a race time predictor, an age-grading calculator, or a $\dot{V}O_2$max predictor chart. A race time predictor, found online at various websites (www. runnersworld.com/tools/race-times-predictor, www.mcmillanrunning.com, and www.runningahead.com/tools/calculators/race), estimates what you might achieve if you trained appropriately for the distance. These estimates are based on an average reduction of speed as the race distance increases.

The age-grading calculator found at www.usatf.org/statistics/calculators/agegrading and used by World Masters Athletics, the official international governing body for masters runners, can help you set a goal based on an age-graded percentage for the distance and your age and gender. If you know you have run a 5K in an age-graded percentage of 80 percent, you can insert different values for a 10K race to find the pace that equates to an 80 percent.

My favorite $\dot{V}O_2$max predictor chart was developed by exercise physiologist, Olympian, author, and coach Jack Daniels, who popularized the concept of $\dot{V}O_2$max in his book *Daniels' Running Formula*, first published in 1998 with the third and latest edition published in 2014. I include a few pages from his book in the appendix. Know that a margin of error exists in all tools, varying by person and training. That margin of error is also greater the larger the gap between the distance you know and the distance you're aiming for. For example, a time for a half marathon will typically better predict your marathon time than a time for a one-mile (1.6 km) race. If you have trained for a 5K and achieved a good race time, you will achieve the corresponding time in a marathon if you train appropriately. In any case, together the three prediction tools can give you a good idea of how to set your goal.

So let's set a sample performance goal using the three tools: the *Runner's World/ Running Times* race time predictor, the USATF age-grading calculator, and Jack Daniels' $\dot{V}O_2$max prediction chart. All give similar results in terms of setting reasonable goals. Say you're a 55-year-old man who has run a 10K in 40 minutes and you want to set a goal for a half marathon.

- *A race time predictor* shows that if you run a 10K in 40 minutes, 6:26 per mile pace, you will run a half marathon in 1:28:15 (6:44 per mile pace).

- *The USATF age-grading calculator* asks you to input not only the distance but also the time, your age, and gender. Age and gender also affect this calculation. After inserting the data that you are 55 years old, a man, that the distance is a 10K, and that your recent time is 40:00, you click on "age-grade" and learn that your age-graded performance for the 10K is 79.95 percent. That's 79.95 percent of the world record speed for your age and sex. The age-grading concept assumes that you would run, if correctly trained, 79.95 percent for all distances, including a half marathon. If you insert "half marathon" in the calculator's distance box and insert various times, you will find that the time of 1:27:28 is closest to an age grading of 79.95 percent.

- *A $\dot{V}O_2max$ prediction chart* estimates your times based on $\dot{V}O_2max$ levels associated with different distances. I have found Daniels' charts reliable, having used them since his book was first published in 1998. See the appendix for these $\dot{V}O_2max$ prediction charts.

  Let's say you've just run a 40-minute 10K, or 10,000 meters. Using the Jack Daniels' chart, look under the 10,000 column and find the time closest to 40 minutes. You'll find 39:59 and you can look to the left to find the value closest to your actual $\dot{V}O_2max$ (without having to have it tested in a lab on a treadmill and hooked up to tubes with a face mask). That value in the chart is VDOT, your effective $\dot{V}O_2max$. The VDOT value corresponding to a 39:59 10,000 is 52. To see the half marathon time you are capable of, look to the half marathon time listed for a VDOT of 52 under half marathon. It is 1:28:31.

There is not a great deal of difference between the three times: 1:28:15 (race time predictor chart), 1:27:28 (age-grading calculator), and 1:28:31 ($\dot{V}O_2max$ predictor chart).

Outcome Goals

Under certain circumstances, you may also want to set outcome goals. Unlike performance goals, outcome goals are focused on winning or performance relative to others. Maybe you've placed in the top three of a local race and want to place second. Or you've won a regional race and want to take a shot at a national or even world age-group championship.

Outcome goals can be motivating in the long term, but they're not as much under your own control so it's wise to set process and performance goals as well. While you can set outcome goals in any event, many use them in events like cross country, trail, or mountain competitions where the terrain is uneven and the course distances sometimes irregular, making time goals difficult to set. If you set outcome goals, know your competition. Search online for competitors' past performances on the track or in road races to compare their relative times, if they're available, to yours.

Process Goals

Always set process goals, critical to achieving both performance and outcome goals. They are short-term, often weekly tasks, that you have to complete to meet your performance goal and over which you have control. Process goals for a half marathon might include the number of peak weekly miles you plan to reach and the number of miles of speed work you hope to run each week. A 55-year-old man who wants to improve his 40-minute 10K might include process goals of peaking at 48 to 52 miles (77-84 km) a week, distributing mileage over six days of running so there's a day of rest, drinking 64 ounces (2 L) of water daily, getting to bed by 10:30 p.m., and so on. Process goals are often personal. "No more Triscuits and Havarti cheese for midnight snacks!" was a process goal one runner recently noted.

Successive Short-Term Goals

Successive short-term goals of 6 to 12 weeks are the key to long-term success, whether you're a beginner or an elite runner. Short-term goals help you focus on immediate details and then measure and evaluate your results before too long. That span of time allows for several levels of improvements in fitness and in your habits. Physiological adaptations occur generally in 21 to 28 days and new habits of various kinds can usually be adopted within two months. After achieving your first short-term goal, you can build on that to set another short-term goal, and you may also have an idea of a long-term goal as well.

If you're setting a running goal for the first time, it helps to consider it as an experiment. Let's say you haven't run for a few years and you've just tested yourself by alternating minutes of walking and jogging over three miles (4.8 km). You covered the distance in 35 minutes, faster than you would have just walking it. Setting a 10-week performance goal of running a 5K in 32 to 33 minutes and a process goal of jogging and walking for 35 to 45 minutes five days a week gives you a sense of immediacy so you can focus on the details. Ten weeks is soon enough that you know you will feel a sense of accomplishment before too long.

Because diagrams are often more powerful than words, many of the runners I coach record their short-term goals in a goal pyramid that they can put on their refrigerator, bathroom mirror, or desk. It's simple and powerful visually. It captures in one place both a performance or outcome goal and process goals and reflects their relative order of importance. Write your performance or outcome goal in the pyramid's top triangle and the process goals in the layers below it. In the bottom strip, which is the widest strip of the pyramid, write the most important process goal, with goals of descending importance written in strips of descending width. Figure 7.3 provides a blank pyramid for your use.

Long-Term Goals

Sometimes you know your long-term goal from the start. Sometimes you don't. Long-term goals, major goals you aim to achieve over six months to a few years, are worth setting along with successive short-term goals. Having both a short- and long-term goal allows you to keep both goals in perspective and to stay on track as you move toward your major goal. Writing down your long-term goal on an index card, noting the event and time goal and the date by which you want to achieve it is powerful. Tape it to anywhere you will see it daily.

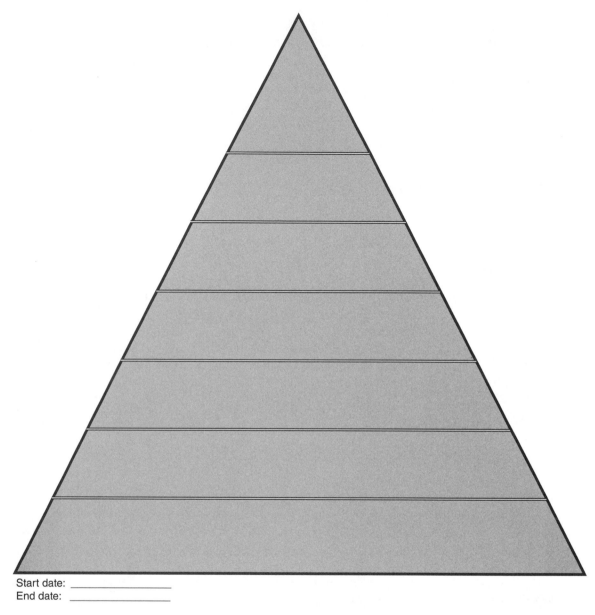

Start date: _____
End date: _____

Figure 7.3 Blank goal pyramid.

From C. Utzschneider, 2014, *Mastering running* (Champaign, IL: Human Kinetics).

POSTGOAL ANALYSIS

After meeting most important short- or long-term goals, my runners find evaluating them enormously helpful. Postgoal analysis provides a snapshot of your experience that can be used as an invaluable resource for improving your training for your next goal. Use your own judgment to determine how many of the questions you find helpful to answer. This is for you, so use it as you like.

Postgoal Analysis

If the question is not applicable, note N/A after the question.

1. What was your event goal and date? _____

   _____

2. What was your actual result? _____

   _____

3. On a scale of 1 to 10, with 10 representing highest and 1 representing lowest, how would you rate the following?

   • Physical readiness before the race: _____

   • Mental readiness before the race: _____

4. Recall circumstances on the day of the event that affected your results (e.g., logistics, heat, humidity, cold), if any._____

   _____

   _____

5. When did you start training for this event and how many weeks of training did you complete? _____

   _____

   _____

6. In how many races did you participate to prepare for this goal and were they helpful? _____

   _____

   _____

7. Describe the volume and intensity of a sample week of your peak training; include speed workouts:

   Monday: _____

   _____

   Tuesday: _____

   _____

   Wednesday: _____

   _____

   Thursday: _____

   _____

Friday: _____

_____

Saturday: _____

_____

Sunday: _____

_____

Did you take periodic rest days, and how often did you take them? _____

_____

8. Summarize your weekly strength training and stretching routine; include yoga, Pilates, and other classes: _____

_____

_____

_____

9. What other life events (e.g., work, personal life) have helped or hindered your training? _____

_____

_____

_____

10. Did you have injuries or pain while training, and if so, how did this affect it? _____

_____

_____

_____

11. What did you learn during the training process and race that you might incorporate into your next training plan and race? _____

_____

_____

12. Other comments: _____

_____

_____

From C. Utzschneider, 2014, *Mastering running* (Champaign, IL: Human Kinetics). Adapted, by permission, from C. Utzschneider, 2011, *Move! How women can achieve athletic goals at any age* (Natick, MA: Cedar Crest Books).

FINDING RUNNING FRIENDS OR OTHERS WHO SUPPORT YOU

Surrounding yourself with people who believe in your goals, both runners and nonrunners, will help you meet your goals and have fun along the way. While you may sometimes want to run alone, running with others is motivating and interesting. Sweat and trust go together. You'll make some of the best friendships of your life training with others. You'll hear their stories and share yours. You'll double the pleasure and halve the pain on the challenging runs. Friends who aren't runners but who are interested in your goals can be important supporters, too. An Olympian client of mine has always said one of her best supporters is her elderly neighbor who uses a wheelchair. The importance of emotional support for all athletes was documented in a study with 170 Division I college athletes on the value of emotional support. They reported that emotional support from friends and family was more important than technical support from coaches or teammates (Rosenfeld et al. 1989).

Take time to find these friends. Like developing other friendships, finding running friends can take time. Running is not just about running. It may take a while to find kindred spirits.

Finding a Coach

A coach will help you meet challenging goals by supporting you along the way and steering you in the most efficient direction to avoid overtraining and injury. A coach can help you maximize your potential and achieve your goals sooner than you could without one. Your challenge may be to figure out how to find the best coach for you. Begin by asking yourself what you are looking for. Do you want a group or individual setting? Do you want to meet with someone, and if so, do you want to talk and strategize or run with that person? Do you want a coach who watches you run? Or do you want to be coached online? Do you want a younger or an older coach? A male or female coach? Do you want someone who understands the pressures of the business world? Your needs are individual. Find someone with whom you click. No one can quantify that.

Once you know the answers to some of those questions, the following checklist of considerations may help your search:

- Credentials. Is the coach certified by organizations like USA Track & Field and the Road Runners Club of America? Is the person certified in CPR and first aid?

- Education. Does the coach have at least an undergraduate education in physical education, exercise physiology, health and wellness, or an allied health field such as nursing or physical therapy? What is the highest degree the coach holds?

- Experience. How many years has he or she been a coach? Does he or she have a history of coaching a club, high school, or college team? Can you check? In what distances has the coach trained runners to compete? What is the coach's experience as a runner?

Running and Discipline

You can't be a strong runner without discipline. Running is a discipline in itself, as are the healthy habits that support it. If you want to be a good runner, you have to get out the door, regularly. You have to be disciplined just to fit it in. Sometimes you have to run when you don't feel like it. If you want to run at an optimal weight, you have to eat and drink healthily. Ninety-six percent of the masters female runners I studied were happy with their weight, far more than most women their age. More than half said that improved self-discipline helped them break bad eating or drinking habits (Utzschneider 2002).

The discipline of running increases discipline in other areas of life as well. (Discipline is contagious!) It helps you to manage your time, set goals in other areas, and endure discomfort. Eighty-eight percent of the women in the study for my dissertation reported that running increased their ability to focus. Seventy percent reported an improved ability to handle hardships, and 67 percent said running helped them organize their time. Forty-nine percent reported that running success improved their career progress (Utzschneider 2002). This discipline affects the rest of life from daily activities to things that occur over a long span of time. "During my morning run, I reorganize all my thoughts, set priorities, and strategize how to solve issues. I'm calm when I get home," Francesca Dominici, Harvard University senior associate dean of public health told me. "My brain is refreshed and I am ready to hit the ground with a highly packed day with meetings and strategic decisions." Speaking at a Harvard University panel on tenure, she said that mental "marathon" habits such as skills persisting toward a long-term goal and having a vision are the same as those required for securing tenure. Another runner who applied the discipline of setting and achieving goals in running to other areas of life is internist Barbara Stewart, MD, who said, "Goal setting in running supported my courage to conceptualize and thus revise and improve my entire medical practice." Still another runner who told me about how she transferred the discipline needed for running to other aspects of her life is entrepreneur Felice Shapiro, who found that setting short- and long-term goals for her first Boston Marathon at age 55 led to what she called an inconceivable success. After completing the marathon, Shapiro used the same goal-setting technique to launch www.betterafter50.com, an online magazine for women over 50.

- Services and cost. What does he or she charge? Will you be training with a group or alone? Will the coach provide a training schedule? If you become injured and cannot complete the terms of your contract, is the money refundable if you opt out?

- Communication. Will you communicate in person, by e-mail, phone, Skype, or all of these? Does it cost extra if you need to contact the coach outside a scheduled training session?

- Insurance. Does the coach carry liability insurance? Do you have to sign a contract or waiver? If so, make sure you read the fine print regarding terms and conditions.

- Logistics. If you're meeting with a coach, or even if you're e-mailing, Skyping, or talking on the phone, find a coach whose schedule fits yours.

- Coaching style. Running coaches have different personalities and styles. Some are more authoritarian, making decisions for you, and others are more cooperative, allowing you to share in the decision-making process. Find a coach who is interested in coaching your event, and someone who listens well.

Once you know what you're looking for, ask runners in your area for names of coaches, or check out local running clubs and associations through USA Track & Field. Ask local middle school, high school, and college coaches for suggestions. Many local running stores have groups and coaches. USA Track & Field (www.usatf.org/Resources-for---/Coaches/Coaches-Registry/Coaches-Registry.aspx) and the Road Runners Club of America (www.rrca.org/find-a-coach) also list coaches throughout the country.

Runner Profile: Carmen Troncoso

Date of birth: April 2, 1959

Personal Information

- Coach of Rogue Running, a running club in Austin, Texas
- Bachelor's degrees in community development and in sports management
- Master's degree in exercise physiology
- Married for 30 years, no children
- Started focused training at 27, started running at 20

Open Personal Bests

- 1,500 meters 4:21 (35)
- 3,000 meters 9:12 (35)
- 5,000 meters 15:50 (36)
- 5K (road) 16:00 (37)
- 10K (road) 33:25 (36)

© Adolfo Isassi

Personal Bests at 40 to 49

- 1,500 meters 4:27 at 40
- 1,500 meters 4:46 (46, masters national record)
- 3,000 meters 9:27 (41, masters national record)
- 5,000 meters 16:02 (41, masters national record)
- 10,000 meters 33:50 (41)
- 5K (road) 16:09 (40), 16:50 (46)
- 8K (road) 27:45 (46, record)
- 10K (road) 34:46 (44), 35:26 (46)
- Half marathon 1:14:46 (44)

Personal Bests at 50 to 59

- 800 meters 2:29 (50)
- 1,500 meters 4:57 (51)
- 3,000 meters 10:05 (51, record)
- 5,000 meters 17:29 (50)
- 5K (road) 17:36 (50)
- 10K (road) 36:50 (50)

Age-Graded Personal Bests

- 3,000 meters 98.49% (10:05 at age 51)
- 5,000 meters 96.83% (17:29 at age 51)
- 5K (road) 95.23% (16:50 at age 46)
- 10K (road) 93.20% (36:52 at age 50)

(continued)

Cathy Utzschneider: What do you think has made you such a successful runner?

Carmen Troncoso: I think it is my patience to see a goal through. I also have a very narrow set of goals that involve only running (good or bad?), so I have been able to focus on that for many years. A little bit of luck and a little bit of good genes help. I have never been in a hurry to check anything off a list and move on. I like running. I like competing, so I see no point in hurrying the process. I might as well enjoy all of it and for as long as I can. In summary, I love it, and I don't think I can quit at this point in my life. It is a good addiction.

Cathy: Having run at elite levels in your 20s, 30s, 40s, and now in your 50s, what changes have you noticed in your training and racing?

Carmen: The recovery time increases. So in order to train as hard as you did in your 30s on any given week, month, and year, you need to rest a lot longer between hard days. I also learned that injuries take a lot longer to heal, so patience becomes much more important as you get older. Up to my 40s I could train hard two or three days per week. In my late 40s I was doing a solid twice-a-week hard workouts. Now in my 50s I can do about one and a half workouts per week. I haven't change the way I race, but in my 50s I race much less. I need about three weeks to recover well. If I have two races back-to-back, I train for them, but in general I race less. I also started to do some cross-training in my 50s. As far as weight training, I have always done that two or three times per week, and I believe it is much more important as I get older to keep doing that.

Cathy: How has your motivation changed over the decades?

Carmen: Luckily, my motivation has been constant throughout. But an important aspect of staying motivated has been to adjust my goals a little bit as I get older. If my goals fit the energy I put in (or can put in), I can stay motivated just like when I was younger. My husband, Ricardo, also runs so we motivate and support each other during the good and bad periods. We do a lot of the training together and know each other well as runners.

Cathy: What has surprised you most about performance and aging?

Carmen: In all honesty, not much has surprised me. I believe that if you are going to try to do something well, you need to be informed, and the more knowledge you have about the subject, the fewer the surprises. In this case, the more you know about your own body and how it responds to training, the easier it is to be flexible to make the right decisions. But having said all that, in my 50s I have had a very hard time predicting performances based on workouts. It could be the fact that it is harder to put together a string of good workouts that can predict an outcome; thus, the data might be insufficient. It could also be attributed to the menopause changes. Purely hormonal? I will know more about this in a couple of years.

Cathy: You recently had an injury. Can you describe it briefly, and have you learned anything from it?

Carmen: It was more an accident than an injury. I fell during an 800 race on the track. I broke my right wrist, but amazingly for as bad as that was, it was the only thing I had to deal with. Everything else was intact. I was able to do all the leg weights, most of the core work, and some minimal cardio on a stationary bike. What I learned is that accidents happen when you least expect them. (I find that funny, because if you are expecting it, it is not really an accident, I suppose.) I try to deal with it as quickly as possible, get through the "why me," figure out how quickly I can get over this to resume my life, and move on. I also try to find the positive in the situation as soon as I can and just hold on to that. Otherwise the negative starts to sneak in and you lose focus.

Cathy: As a coach of Rogue Running, how do you motivate masters runners?

Carmen: I'm very lucky to coach a bunch of very self-motivated runners (masters or open). I'm not a very vocal coach and not very good at cheerleading, but I try to motivate them by example. So I stay in shape to race well. I have been surprised throughout the years by how much my experience helps me coach runners, especially my age or younger. I have gone through all of it, so I can pass it along. Trust and communication are the key to keeping my runners motivated. My first goal is to keep them healthy. My second goal is getting them to run as fast as they can given their set of circumstances. If I stay true to those principles, we can usually succeed together.

Cathy: As a coach, do you have words of wisdom for masters runners?

Carmen: Age grading is a beautiful thing. Accept that we get slower with age, but don't give in to it completely. You need to be twice as smart when you plan your season and make sure you follow that plan through. We need to listen to our bodies, because our injuries will set us back a lot longer than when we were in our 30s. We are the pioneers of this thing called masters running, so we need to be good role models.

Cathy: What is a sample training week for a 5K these days?

Carmen: I am training for cross country at the moment, so most of this is run on grass.

> Monday: a.m. weight session (mostly legs and core); p.m. spin for 40-60 minutes, depending on energy or jog easy for 40 minutes
>
> Tuesday: 60 minutes easy on the road or trail; p.m. light core and upper-body weights
>
> Wednesday: a.m. overall weight session; p.m. 3 × 7 minutes of running 30 seconds fast and 30 seconds easy (average pace is 10K pace), two-minute recovery between sets
>
> Thursday: stretching and core-work session
>
> Friday: rest or 65-minute run (This will build to 90 minutes later in the season.)
>
> Saturday: 4 miles (6.4 km) easy plus strides
>
> Sunday: 3 × 2K at 5K pace, jog 2 minutes, 200 meters at 3K pace, jog 4 minutes.

This workout is done after I have finished with a few weeks of base, hill work, tempos and progressive downtype workouts (workouts that involve running faster as distance progresses). I usually do this sequence for about six weeks in preparation for a season's goal.

I will of course vary the intensity workouts, and hopefully the pace will get a little faster as I go along.

Join a Running Club

A running club provides a chance to meet other runners, get motivated, find training partners, learn training and racing strategies, and obtain at least general feedback from a coach. USA Track & Field and the Road Runners Club of America are established organizations that provide lists of clubs. Clubs have unique personalities. Some are more focused on competition, others on recreation, some on younger age groups, some on older age groups, some on all age groups, some on track, some on trail and mountain running, and some on men and some on women. Most clubs will let you try a few meetings before committing to membership. If you don't find a club in one of those categories that appeals to you, you may want to join a group focused on a cause like the Team to End Aids or the Team in Training for the Leukemia and Lymphoma Society.

In conclusion, because setting goals increases your chances of achieving them, and because achieving goals is a catalyst for achieving more goals, why not set them? And why not write them down and find a coach or at least a friend who can help hold you accountable? If your experience is like that of others, your accomplishments will probably end up being those you previously thought, as Felice said, "inconceivable."

Chapter 8

Getting Faster

You enjoy running, and now you have a goal. You want to get faster, test yourself in a race, and organize your training for best results. How should you start? Without playing fields, opponents, and rule books (and with little equipment), running is easy. It should be as simple as just run and run more. But don't do that. You need a plan to run faster and avoid injury. It's helpful to understand speed and periodization and principles of training. The more you know, the more you're in the driver's seat.

BUILDING A MILEAGE BASE

If you are not running now, start by building a mileage base. That's easiest to do if you think of running as part of an overall healthy lifestyle, not just running but also eating, drinking, sleeping, and of socializing with others who value exercise, especially running occasionally with other runners. A base of weekly miles allows you to focus on a goal from a solid foundation.

How do you build a base if you don't have one now? As long as you are in good health, start by walking for at least 5 minutes and then by alternating minutes of walking and minutes of jogging for 30 to 40 minutes. For example, after a warm-up walk, see if you can maintain a pattern of jogging for 3 minutes and then walking for 2 minutes. Repeat the process six times so that you've held the pattern for 30 minutes after the warm-up. If you can't do that, try a pattern of alternating 2 minutes of running with 1 minute of walking over a 30-minute period. Following is an eight-week program that has worked for many beginners. It entails running for four days each week, say, Mondays, Wednesdays, Fridays, and Sundays. Or pick days that work for you as long as you allow a few rest days.

Week 1: Walk 2 minutes, jog 1 minute 10 times

Week 2: Walk 1 minute, jog 2 minutes 10 times

Week 3: Walk 1 minute, jog 4 minutes 6 times

Week 4: Walk 2 minutes, jog 6 minutes 4-5 times

Week 5: Walk 2 minutes, jog 8 minutes 4 times

Week 6: Walk 2 minutes, run 10 minutes 3 times

Week 7: Walk 2 minutes, jog 15 minutes 2 times

Week 8: Jog 30 minutes

Once you can jog for 30 consecutive minutes, begin measuring your running in miles rather than minutes and work up to running at least 20 miles (32 km) a week. Whether you're starting with minutes or miles, don't increase your running by more than 10 percent a week to avoid injury.

PERIODIZING YOUR TRAINING

Once you have a short-term goal, perhaps your first mile, 5K, or even 10K race, and once you have built up a base of 20 miles (32 km) of running, the next step is to periodize your training.

So what is periodization? Periodization is a progressive training method that divides your training into phases that build on each other to achieve peak fitness. Each phase has a particular focus, such as to incorporate long, moderately intense efforts for strength or short, very intense efforts for speed. Together, all phases improve the three main determinants of speed:

- $\dot{V}O_2max$, your maximum level of oxygen consumption
- *Lactate threshold*, the point during moderately intense exercise at which lactic acid is produced faster than the body can absorb it, causing fatigue and muscle soreness (In most athletes, that is generally between 60 and 85 percent of $\dot{V}O_2max$.)
- *Running economy*, a measure of how efficiently you use oxygen at a given pace (Two runners may have the same $\dot{V}O_2max$, but if one uses less of the $\dot{V}O_2max$ than the other, the pace feels easier so the first can run faster before feeling tired.)

Periodization depends on age, fitness level, current mileage, your goal race, and also on the philosophy of your coach. (Coaches, like teachers, have their own perspectives and approaches. A variety of periodization methods work.) Periodization may involve macrocycles of three months to one year, mesocycles of two to four weeks, and microcycles of 4 to 10 days. The simplicity of my periodization method makes it easy to adjust to your own circumstances. No one size fits all.

Periodization plans incorporate the following training principles that help you tailor any plan to your own needs:

- *Specificity* is the training that most closely simulates the speed and movement of your goal event. It offers the greatest gains. Runs of five or six miles (8 or 9.6 km) and 200-meter sprints alone may improve your performance in the half-mile or mile, but not in the marathon. Your training for that needs to include long runs.

- *Overload* produces a greater than normal stress or load on your body and is needed to run faster.

- *Adaptation* is your body's ability to adapt to new levels of training through repeated practice.

- *Rest and recovery* help you adapt to higher levels of fitness. Take off a day from running every week. After building mileage for three weeks, incorporate a week of lower mileage.

- *Hard–easy rule* dictates that a day of hard running should be followed by at least two days of easy running to prevent injury and help recovery.

- *Variety and flexibility* should be built into your workouts to prevent boredom and injury. Don't force the miles if you don't feel well.

- *Individualism* should be taken into account because everyone responds to training differently. Respect your own rate of progress.

Four Phases of Periodization

My periodization plans outlined in chapters 11, 12, and 13 are meant to begin after you have established a routine of running 20, 30, or 40 miles (32, 48, 64 km) a week. You can adjust them to bases of less than 20 miles or more than 45 miles (72 km). Periodization plans are longer as the race distance increases. The plan for the mile is 8 weeks, and the marathon plan takes 16 weeks to complete.

The plans for each distance are the same length no matter what your baseline mileage is. For example, a periodization plan for the half marathon is 12 weeks, whether you are running 20, 30, or 40 miles a week.

Generally, the plans reflect four phases regardless of whether you are aiming for a mile or a marathon (see figure 8.1):

- Endurance
- Strengthening
- Sharpening
- Tapering

The two plans that are exceptions are for runners who are already running 40 miles and aiming to race the mile. These plans begin with the strengthening phase because those runners have already built the necessary endurance.

Focus of the Four Phases

The *endurance phase* focuses on building mileage through easy runs according to the 10 percent rule (increase weekly mileage by no more than 10 percent over the previous week's mileage) and also building the length of the long run. Long runs should be no more than about 25 percent of your weekly mileage. If you run

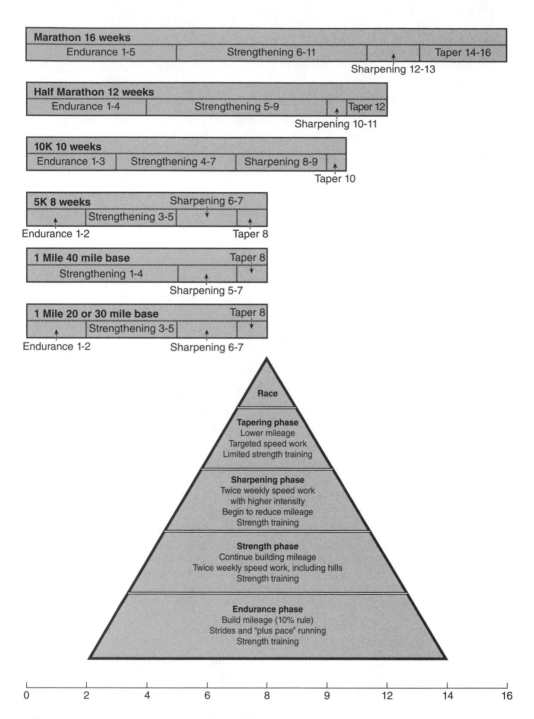

Figure 8.1 Periodization plans for specific distances.

40 miles (64 km) a week, for example, your long run should be no more than 10 miles (16 km). During the endurance phase begin building strength with weight training, as discussed in chapter 9. Light, casual speed work called strides—short, fast runs focused on form—should be included twice a week.

The *strengthening phase* focuses on building mileage, except in the case of the plans for the mile. It incorporates two speed workouts a week, including intermittent hill workouts; lengthens the long run depending on the race distance; substitutes a race for a speed workout; and continues weight training and strides.

The *sharpening phase* focuses on reducing mileage slightly; continuing the two speed workouts a week, including one of more intense speed work; and entering a race to prepare for the goal race. Weight training and twice weekly strides are continued.

The *tapering phase* focuses on limited short, intense speed work, a significant reduction in mileage, and rest. Figure 8.1 shows the focus of each phase.

GETTING FASTER: IT'S NOT JUST ABOUT SPEED

While you need to train fast to race fast, know that all kinds of running—fast and slow as well as days of complete rest—are part of an effective weekly training plan. Running fast every day, for example, leads to injury. Respecting the hard–easy rule, you need a few days of easy running before and after hard running. A rest day once a week gives you a chance to recover, which will help you run better on your "on" days. Understanding the different kinds of runs now helps you better understand speed workouts later.

For the sake of simplicity, running can be divided into two categories: running that's less intense and speed training, which is more intense. In the less intense category are easy short runs, long runs, plus-pace runs, and recovery jogs. Easy short runs—runs during which you can carry on a conversation—allow for recovery and still strengthen your cardiovascular and muscular systems. Long runs strengthen these systems, too, and also teach your body to metabolize and spare glycogen. Consider a long run anything over 10 miles (16 km), unless you are an elite half marathoner or marathoner, and limit those to once a week. Plus-pace runs are performed at a slightly faster pace than your usual easy runs. While plus-pace runs don't have a quantified physiological benefit and they are not difficult, they add mental variety and encourage you to speed up a bit more than on easy-run days. Recovery jogs are run more slowly than your usual runs and are good for cooling down at the end of a workout or getting back into running after extended time off.

Speed Training

More intense, or speed, training includes threshold runs, intervals, sprints, repetitions, hill repeats, fartlek, and strides. As shown in table 8.1, threshold runs are comfortably hard to raise the level at which lactic acid builds up so you can hold a faster speed over a longer distance. While threshold runs are less intense than intervals, for example, many runners feel they are more challenging because they last longer. A threshold run might last 20 to 40 minutes or as long as 60 minutes compared to the 14 to 20 minutes of intense running broken up by rest intervals, for example. Threshold runs include tempo workouts held for a continuous stretch of time and cruise intervals, which are 4- to 8-minute efforts interspersed with a minute of easy jogging.

Table 8.1 Getting Faster

Type of running	Goal	$\dot{V}O_2$max	RRPE*
Short	Enable recovery. Maintain conversational pace.	70%	5-6 (easy)
Long	Maintain conversational pace. Build confidence. Improve blood supply. Teach body to metabolize and spare glycogen. Strengthen heart and legs.	70%	5-6 (easy)
Plus pace	Add mental variety. Focus on form and pace. Increase pace of easy runs. Take as little recovery as needed.	75%	6-7 (slightly faster than easy)
Threshold: Runs of 20 to 40 min and sometimes as long as 60 min that include the following: 1. Tempo workouts, continuous runs at threshold pace 2. Cruise intervals, repeats of 4 to 8 threshold-pace min interspersed with a min of easy jogging	Improve running economy, strength, and anaerobic capacity. Boost lactic threshold for faster, longer runs without lactic acid build-up and fatigue. Recovery periods of 1 min or less keep blood lactate levels fairly constant.	86-88%	7 to 8.5 (comfortably hard)
Intervals: Repeated runs over 200 m to one-half to three-quarters of a mile or 30 sec to three to five minutes.	Increase $\dot{V}O_2$max and endurance. Develop sense of pace. Rest between intervals can be one-third to equal the time of the interval.	95-98%	8.5 to 9 (hard)
Sprints or repetitions: Very fast running of 20 sec to 1 min	Improve power, speed, and endurance. Reinforce good form. Rest between sprints should be a full recovery or up to five times the time in effort.	98-100%	9 to 9.8 (very hard)
Hill repeats: Runs of 10 sec to 3 min	Build strength and speed. Encourage proper form. Recovery should be equal to the efforts.	95-100%	8.5 to 9.8 (hard or very hard)
Fartlek: Swedish word for "speed play," informal speed work of 20–30 min run off the track and at different intensities	Build endurance and speed. Add variety. Improve running economy and strength by running over hills. Recovery varies depending on effort.	86-88%	7 to 8.5 (comfortably hard or hard)
Strides: Short, fast runs of 20 sec to 1 minute	Focus on form and quick leg turnover. Recovery should be at least equal in time or distance to the efforts.	95-100%	8.5 to 9 (hard)
Easy jog	Warm up before or cool down after a workout or recover between harder efforts.	<70%	3–5 (very easy)

Adapted from J. Daniels, 1998, *Daniels' running formula* (Champaign, IL: Human Kinetics), 51, 53, 94.

*RRPE=running rate of perceived exertion

Fartlek running is informal speed work at a comfortably hard or hard pace. It takes place wherever you are, roads, trails, fields, or hills. Workouts generally last 20 to 30 minutes and are broken into segments that you determine depending on what you feel like doing. Fartlek runs build endurance and speed and offer variety.

Interval training improves your VDOT maximum and endurance. Intervals are run at hard effort for 30 seconds to 3 or at most 5 minutes. Sprints repetitions are very fast running and build power, speed, and endurance and also reinforce good form. Because they are so intense, they should be run at most once a week and only after drills, leg swings, and a 20-minute warm-up to prevent injury.

Hill repeats are hard or very hard efforts of 30 seconds to three minutes and should also be limited to once a week at most. They help build strength and speed and encourage you to practice good form. Strides are hard, not very hard, runs of 20 seconds to one minute that help you focus on form and speed. They are run 20 to 30 minutes before a race or at the end of an easy day of running. Strides can be run up to three days a week.

Masters and Speed Training

For masters runners, speed training can be more challenging physically, psychologically, and logistically than for open runners. Unless you are a masters runner who is new to running, you're probably running slower times than you were 10 years ago. That can be disheartening, until you judge your workouts according to age grading. Finding other masters runners who are able to train at your pace and where and when you can is not easy.

If you are focusing on speed for the first time, check with your physician first and be sure you have built a base of 20 miles (32 km) a week. Then consult a coach in addition to this or other books before incorporating one speed session a week. After three to four weeks of one speed session you may add a second, allowing at least two recovery days between them. (While some the open runners I coach incorporate three speed sessions a week, with the exception of strides, masters should include no more than two each week.) As an example, if you run intervals on Tuesday, run fartlek on Friday. Even a few runners in their 70s try to fit in two speed workouts, cutting out a few easy days of running if they're tired.

Master's Method: A Mix of Measures

The method my masters use for speed work is a combination of two measures: the quantitative, or objective, testing system of monitoring timed distances on the track and a qualitative, or subjective, testing system of monitoring effort, or perceived exertion, for units of time you can use on a business trip, in your neighborhood, in a park, on a trail, or anywhere. My method, which you can alter, suggests two speed sessions a week with one timed track session and another perceived exertion session. During particularly hectic weeks, you can skip the track altogether, running both speed sessions based on perceived exertion, and then, when life settles down, return to the track to check your progress. The perceived exertion session gives you control and challenge. Life's pressures can be overwhelming, making more than once-a-week track workouts impractical. Also, you may only have one group workout on a track a week (unlike school, college, or professional runners who train with a group and coach two to five times a week). As a master, you may not even have a group, track, or coach. (Or the coach is Mr., Ms., or Mrs. Garmin.)

Speed sessions based on effort allow you to be creative, relieve stress, and offer flexibility, variety, and fun without the pressure of the track. Current Liberty Athletic Club president Dru Pratt-Otto achieved her personal best in the 5K at the North American, Central American and Caribbean World Masters Athletics Championships with speed sessions at least once a week based on perceived exertion. "It

Runner Profile: Libby James

Date of birth: July 12, 1936

Personal Information

- Widow since November 1991
- Two sons and two daughters
- Six granddaughters and six grandsons ages 8 to 24
- Taught in a program for low-income single mothers for 15 years, also taught sixth grade and community college
- Newspaper and magazine feature writer and editor, currently reporter for a small monthly newspaper serving north Fort Collins, Colorado, and the surrounding mountain communities
- Hold the doubtful distinction of never having held a job that offered benefits (but I'm not complaining)
- Started focused training at 40

Personal Bests at 40 to 49

- 5K (road) 21:11 (age 41)
- 10K (road) 42:06 (45)
- Half marathon 1:32:33 (49)
- Marathon 3:24:18 (47)

Personal Bests at 50 to 59

- 5K (road) 22:10 (58)
- 10K (road) 47:10 (58)
- Half marathon 1:46:17 (58)

Personal Bests at 60 to 69

- 5K (road) 23:50 (69)
- 10K (road) 47:53 (64)
- Half marathon 1:50:44 (61)
- Marathon 4:05 (63)

Courtesy of Don Hajicek

Personal Bests at 70 to 79

- 5K (road) 23:30 (75)
- 10K (road) 48:54 (72)
- Half marathon 1:45:52 (76)
- Marathon 4:23 (75)

Age-Graded Personal Bests

- 5K (road) 103.24% (23:53 at age 76)
- 10K (road) 100.2% (50:15 at age 75)
- Half marathon 103.75% (1:45:52 at age 76)
- Marathon 90.55% (4:23 at age 75)

Cathy Utzschneider: Having started to focus on running and racing at 40, you've raced for nearly four decades now and had your greatest success in your 70s. How do you explain that?

Libby James: It's a bit of a puzzle. Maybe over time, I've learned how to race smarter, to pace myself better, and to avoid injuries by training fewer miles and mixing it up with biking. I think I pay a bit more attention to diet as well.

Cathy: How is your training different today, in your late 70s, from what it was in your 40s? Can you give an example?

Libby: I train fewer miles a week, but run more frequently. My preference is to run every day, though I end up taking a day off every 10 days or so. My training pace is pretty slow, somewhat under 10-minute miles.

Cathy: You have said that your approach to running is rather informal.

Libby: Yes, I don't do things like RunKeeper and I don't use a Garmin. As another example, I don't go to the track regularly. I'll take a half-mile (800 meters) road near my house and run as fast as I can, nothing planned or formal. I prefer to run from home rather than driving somewhere to run, though I do that occasionally to run with friends. I don't do any specific strength training or stretching in a gym or with a trainer. I do a brief Pilates session at home several times a week. I get some upper-body workout from doing home maintenance such as putting up storm windows and gardening.

Cathy: How has your motivation changed over the decades?

Libby: I do remember being pretty obsessed during the first few years that I competed. I ran two marathons every year. I really don't think my motivation has changed a great deal since those first few years. I enjoy competition and trying to do my best, but I truly love running just for the joy of it. I'm so very grateful for the good things that have come my way because of running—the friendships, opportunities to travel, and the fun of writing a monthly column in our local paper about my favorite sport. Sharing runs with my children and grandchildren is always a special treat.

Cathy: What has surprised you most about performance and aging?

Libby: I guess I'm surprised and delighted that I can still run. I'm beating some people at races who wonder what in the world I'm doing there, but most people are supportive and encouraging and say things like, "I want to be like you when I'm older."

Cathy: Through the inevitable ups and downs of life, including the death of your husband, how has running helped you?

Libby: A few days after my husband's open heart surgery in 1982, I remember getting up at 4:30 a.m. to do a 19-mile run in the foothills near our home. It must have been my way to release tension. The morning after he died, nine years later, my brother called and said, "How about a run?" I remember exactly where we went. I so appreciated that. My husband was a great supporter of my running and regularly checked the finishing board before I got there. He always encouraged me and never resented my running time, something I didn't fully appreciate until many years later. Running has always been good "thinking time" for me. Maybe that is why I so often run alone.

Cathy: At 40, would you have predicted that you would still be running in your late 70s?

Libby: Probably not. I remember making a plan to quit when I turned 70, but when that day came, I changed my mind. I was having fun and could find no good reason to stop. I'm thankful, because the last seven years have been a blast!

Cathy: What has been your experience with injuries?

Libby: In 2004 I was having some knee issues until I spent nine months in Africa where it was so hot that I regularly ran two miles (3.2 km) and then swam a kilometer every day. No knee troubles since then. The rest cure, I guess. I did have an Achilles problem that took a full year to get over completely, but it is fine now. Long ago I pulled a hamstring water skiing that kept me from running any distance for about six months.

Cathy: Do you plan to run forever?

Libby: I'm not good at planning ahead.

Cathy: What is a sample peak training week for a half marathon these days?

Libby: For me, these days, training for a half marathon includes maintaining my four miles (6.4 km) a day and getting serious about adding miles—up to 12 (19.3 km)—on my weekend long run. When I was younger, I figured if I did my regular mileage and made sure I cut my toenails, I was ready to go.

takes the pressure and stress out of speed work," she told me. "For some workouts focused on a particular time, the experience can be negative if you don't achieve that time. PE [perceived exertion] is a wonderful way to relax into effort, to work on relaxing in the intensity." Commenting on the fact that speed based on perceived exertion is flexible and within your control, Liberty Athletic Club runner Pam Linov —told me that "if you are training to a pace it can be frustrating when you can't make the splits you usually can due to weather, terrain, or how you feel on that day. While your literal speed might change from one day to the next, you can still determine the level of effort. To run a PE of 8 might be slower on a day when I'm tight, or faster on a day that I'm loose, but it can still be 80 percent of my effort either way."

RUNNING RATING OF PERCEIVED EXERTION

To give masters guidelines for runs based on perceived exertion, I created a 10-point running rating of perceived exertion (RRPE) scale. Unlike Gunnar Borg's (1982) 10-point rating of perceived exertion scale, which is based on exertion in any activity, my scale is based on perceived exertion in running only. Perceived exertion (PE) reflects your own judgment of how hard you are running based on heart rate, breathing rate, sweating, and muscle fatigue. Because training based on PE reflects your judgment, it changes as you age. A pace that you feel is hard at age 75 is different from a pace you felt was hard at age 40.

Here's an example of how it works. Say you are asked to run five sets of three minutes at a hard pace: a PE of 8. After warming up for 20 minutes at a PE of 5, a pace that you feel is your average conversational pace, run three minutes at a pace that you feel is hard, your PE of 8. After three minutes, jog for two minutes at your easy recovery pace, your PE of 3. You have then run your first set. Repeat that four more times.

10-Point Running Rating of Perceived Exertion Scale

1 = brisk walk

3 = recovery jog between or after intense efforts, run easier than your average conversational pace

5 = average conversational pace

6 to 7 = plus pace, a little faster than usual

7 to 8.5 = comfortably hard efforts for threshold runs with jog recovery from one to two minutes

8.5 to 9 = hard efforts for intervals that last from 30 seconds to 3 or at most 5 minutes, interspersed with periods of rest or slow jogging that may last as long as the effort

9 to 9.8 = very hard efforts (particularly for sprints and occasional hill workouts) lasting from 20 seconds to two minutes and followed by a walk or slow jog three or four times as long as the exertion in duration

Trusting Perceived Exertion

Runners like numbers, their ultimate and objective rewards. Trusting the effectiveness of perceived exertion, a subjective measure, takes time to try it out and experience positive results. Give yourself at least three or four weeks of running perceived exertion workouts to feel comfortable with them. At first it will be hard to gauge the difference between your comfortably hard, hard, and very hard paces, for example. (If you want objective feedback, you can always run perceived exertion workouts on a track or known distance to check your pace until you develop confidence in your judgment.) Of course, perceived exertion paces will vary according to how you feel that day, the terrain, and the weather, for example.

Perceived exertion workouts have comprised at least 50 percent of speed training for personal bests for many elite open and masters times. Boston College track and field and cross country assistant coach Tim Ritchie, 26, ran a personal best marathon at the 2013 Twin Cities Marathon (2:14:50) using perceived exertion as a major part of his training mix and also during the marathon itself. "The perceived exertion system is ideal because it removes expectations so you can run freely," he recently told me in an e-mail. Perceived exertion workouts have helped Jan Holmquist, now 70, run her fastest age-graded workouts ever (over 100 percent). Several of the runners I coach have won national masters age group championships for 5K and longer, having run speed workouts based only on perceived exertion.

Daniels' $\dot{V}O_2$max Charts

Jack Daniels' $\dot{V}O_2$max pace charts provide exact times to aim for in speed workouts or the track. Having used them with runners for the past 20 years, I've found them particularly helpful for intervals when we're checking for progress and want to ascertain readiness to run at goal race pace. Daniels' charts, which appear in the appendix, have helped thousands of runners. Daniels has found that a runner's time can determine his or her approximate $\dot{V}O_2$max. He assigns what he calls a VDOT number to that time. His charts show a VDOT number that corresponds to times for many distances, including the mile, 5K, 10K, half marathon, and marathon. Say you have recently run a 5K in 20:00. Looking at the chart, you'll find your VDOT is a 50. (If you feel discouraged scanning the chart, remembering that you used to run a 5K in 17:20, remember that age grading is more important than actual time.) Daniels' charts tell you not only your VDOT, but also exact times that you should run for different kinds of speed work. So you ran a 5K in 20:00? Daniels' charts say you should be running about 8:14 per mile pace for your easy long runs, threshold 1,000s at 4:15, interval 400s at 93 seconds, and repetition 400s at 87 seconds.

The science of Daniels' pace charts and the art of PE provide a combination of flexibility, fun, and exactitude. (Other methods for measuring speed are paces based on a percentage of heart rate, either maximum or working heart rate, and speed as a percentage of race pace. I don't use heart rate because it varies person to person and according to weather, dehydration, blood sugar, and excitement, and basing speed work on pace requires making mental calculations that sometimes feel cumbersome.)

Table 8.1 explains the different kinds of running as defined by both running rating of perceived exertion and Jack Daniels' chart, though some of his definitions have been adapted for masters runners.

FINAL NOTES ON SPEED

Intense training should be treated with respect by all runners. Key points to remember are the following:

- Before you begin speed training consult not just your physician, if you have medical issues, but also a coach. A coach is helpful for beginners and can help experienced runners maintain perspective (since we often lose that).

- Periodize your training, particularly for major races, so you can peak for race day, and don't rush speed. I'll never forget the advice an experienced runner gave me when I first started running: Be patient.

- Speed and recovery (through an easy run or rest) are both important.

- Balanced, effective plans include running at different intensities, which challenge you in different ways.

- Use your head as well as your heart. Masters runners often want to do more speed work than they should.

- Speed training is often hard, but fun and rewarding, too. Consider running fast using perceived exertion. It may take a while to get used to and trust, but it offers flexibility and a feeling of control. And it has helped runners achieve world-class age-graded results.

Chapter 9

Getting Stronger

As a masters distance runner, building strength—whether it's through resistance training or hill running—will help you run faster. Remember that beginning at about age 30, most of us lose about 1 percent, or a third of a pound (.15 kg), of muscle every year. A study of age-related decline in track and field, swimming, rowing, cycling, triathlon, and weight-lifting performance found the fastest and greatest decline in weight lifting. Comparing weight-lifting records for masters with the world best by lifters 30 to 35 years old, the researchers found that weight-lifting performances dropped to 75 percent of the world best by age 49 in women and by age 60 in men (Baker and Tang 2010). A stronger body overall—core, upper, and lower body—not only staves off muscle loss but also improves running economy, time to exhaustion, stride length and frequency, and neuromuscular coordination. Finally, stronger muscles reduce your chances of injury.

WEEKLY STRENGTH WORK

There's no doubt that strength training is essential for masters runners and no doubt that it's challenging to schedule. If pressed for time (which most masters are) and given the choice of either running or strength training, 10 out of 10 runners from milers to marathoners will choose running over strength training. "Strength training is hard for a lot of runners," said Ben Shersten, 35, a marathoner whose personal best is 2:33:48. "We came to running because of the running part, not getting to lift. Training that is actual running (hills, tempo, intervals, and so on) is fun; it's what we signed up for. Even if it's hard, it's fun. But weights are different. They represent the part of training we don't like, so it's easy to ignore it. It's easy to say we don't have time for it. For many runners, the same is true for stretching. But it's vital. As we get older, we need to support all areas of our bodies. I always tell people, strength training probably won't make you faster, but it will keep you from getting hurt, and if you're healthy you can run more miles and harder workouts and that will make you faster," he recently told me.

This chapter reviews how strength training helps runners, the strength-training debate about using machines vs. your own body weight, and scheduling so you can fit strength training into your day. It also outlines two strength-training options. The first is a 45-minute routine consisting of 13 exercises that use body weight, free weights, and isometric exercises. The second is the 10 minutes of strength circuit for which you need only a chair, rock, or bench. The chapter also explains how to run hills to build strength.

Signs That You Need Strength Training

"I'm running well," you might think. "How might I know whether strength training can help my running?" Here are a few signs that you would benefit.

- Running up a slight hill affects the rhythm and length of your stride. (All runners feel an increase in effort on a hill, but strong ones are able to maintain their rhythm.)
- You are frequently outkicked in races.
- You end long runs at an uncomfortable shuffle because of discomfort in your thighs and around your knees (stronger quads are needed).
- You regularly get hip or leg injuries.
- You have an unusual running style, suggesting a muscle imbalance.
- You've hit a plateau in your running.

Strength-Training Debate

For years experts have debated how athletes should best build strength: whether with machines or functional strength exercises that use just body weight. Machines isolate one muscle group working in one plane of motion. Functional exercises focus on several muscles and require balance and coordination, sometimes mimicking specific movements in sport or daily life. Often these exercises work in several planes of motion. The leg curl machine, for example, focuses on strengthening the hamstring alone. On the other hand, the lunge, a functional exercise, strengthens the gluteal muscles, hamstrings, quadriceps, and hip flexors, requiring balance and coordination. When you run up a hill you are performing modified lunges. Machines are considered safer than functional exercises performed with free weights, although that is mainly true if you are lifting heavy weights without a spotter present.

Because masters runners find scheduling strength training a greater challenge than the lifting itself, I recommend functional training because you can do it more easily at home. This makes it more convenient and flexible and easier to work into a busy schedule.

Fitting It In

Scheduling strength training can be a challenge, even functional weight training. Here are suggestions that might help you.

- Weight train year-round. It's good for general health as well as performance, particularly as you age. Weight training year-round will help it become habit.

- A program of strength training for 45 minutes twice a week or at most three times a week is plenty for masters to peak in distance racing. Allow at least a day of rest for each muscle group.

- To integrate weight training most effectively into training that also includes speed work, plan your strength training on the days after speed workouts or later in the same day of a speed workout. For example, if you do speed work on Tuesdays and Fridays and run long on Sundays, strength train on Wednesdays and Fridays.

- Following are two sample schedules showing how you might balance speed work and strength training. As always, use your judgment. Are you too tired to strength train after a long run? Postpone it for another day. Alter the schedule to your needs.

Strength Schedule: Twice a Week	Strength Schedule: Three Times a Week
Monday – Off	Monday – Off
Tuesday – Speed work	Tuesday – Speed work
Wednesday – Easy run and strength train	Wednesday – Easy run and strength train
Thursday – Easy run	Thursday – Easy run
Friday – Speed work	Friday – Speed work and strength train afterward
Saturday – Easy run and strength train	Saturday – Easy run
Sunday – Long run	Sunday – Long run and strength train afterward

EXERCISES FOR MASTERS RUNNERS: 45-MINUTE PROGRAM

The weight training exercises listed here will strengthen your entire body. Completing all 13 exercises takes about 45 minutes. (If you have a weakness in a joint or muscle, such as the knee or hamstring, consult a physical therapist before beginning a weight-training program.) You can do these exercises at home with free weights. A few of them, such as the bench press and the bent-over row are best done on a weight bench. As with any strength-training exercise, if you feel an intense or sudden unexpected pain in your chest or shoulders, stop immediately. Remember to exhale on exertions and inhale during the easy part of the lifting or lowering.

The exercises are organized into three types:

- A exercises. These require just your body weight: lunge, squat, straight- and bent-leg donkey kick, push-up, dip with a chair, seated running arms, heel raise, and toe raise.

- B exercises. These require free weights: bench press and bent-over row.
- C exercises. These do not require visible movement and are also known as isometric exercises: front and side plank.

For A and B exercises, begin with one set of 12 repetitions. While there is no absolute rule about when to increase repetitions and sets, my masters runners of all ages add a second set, or at least half a second set, within two or three weeks of being able to perform one set of 12 repetitions. While two sets of 12 repetitions with a one-minute rest between sets are plenty, if you want to add a third set, consider adding that after you've performed two sets for three weeks.

For B exercises, choose a weight you can only lift 12 times. Once you have been lifting a weight for four to six weeks, add enough weight that you can only do one set of 10 to 12 repetitions. Continue to progress by adding a few repetitions each week until you can lift two sets of 12 repetitions. Control the dumbbells during the lift and recovery, and don't allow gravity to take over.

For the planks, begin by trying to hold a position once for at least 20 seconds. Build up to holding each plank three times for one minute, taking up to a minute of rest between holds. Breathe normally.

A: Body Weight Exercises

SQUAT

1. Stand upright, facing forward. Place your feet shoulder-width apart or slightly wider. Extend your hands straight out in front of you to help keep your balance.
2. Sit back and down as if you're sitting into an imaginary chair. Keep your head facing forward as your upper body bends forward a bit. Rather than allowing your back to round, let your low back arch slightly as you descend.
3. Lower so your thighs are as parallel to the floor as possible, with your knees over your ankles. Press your weight back into your heels.
4. Keep your body tight and push through your heels to bring yourself back to the starting position.
5. You may prefer a single-leg variation as shown in figure c.

LUNGE

1. Stand with hands on your hips. Lunge forward on one leg, keeping the front knee aligned with the foot. Land on the heel first, and then the forefoot.

2. Lower your body by flexing the knee and hip of the front leg until the knee of the rear leg is almost in contact with floor. Don't lean forward, and do not allow the front knee to go in front of that foot's toes.

3. Return to standing position by forcibly extending the hip and knee of the forward leg. Repeat with the opposite leg.

➕ *Safety tip: If you have knee pain, try taking smaller steps as you lunge or seek another leg-strengthening exercise.*

STRAIGHT-LEG DONKEY KICK

1. Kneel on all fours.
2. With your foot flexed, extend one leg back so that only the toes touch the floor. Maintaining that angle, slowly raise your leg as high as you can directly upward. Keep your torso flat so it doesn't twist in the direction of the lift.
3. Lower your leg until your toes touch the floor and repeat. Repeat on the opposite leg.

BENT-LEG DONKEY KICK

1. Kneel on all fours, with your hands directly below your shoulders and your arms straight.
2. Bend one knee to 90 degrees. Maintaining that angle, slowly raise your leg as high as you can directly upward. Keep your torso flat so it doesn't twist in the direction of the lift.
3. Lower your leg until your thigh is parallel with the floor and repeat. Repeat on the opposite leg.

PUSH-UP (FULL OR BENT KNEE)

1. Assume a prone position on the floor, with palms on the floor, approximately shoulder-width apart. Extend your thumbs toward each other. For full push-ups, support your weight on your hands and the balls of your feet. For bent-knee push-ups support your body weight on your hands and knees. Make a straight line from your head to your heels. This is the beginning and the ending position of a single push-up.

2. Without swaying your hips, raise yourself with your arms by pushing away from the ground. Continue the push until your arms are straight but not locked. Think of keeping your body in a straight line from your head to your ankles so your rear end, head, and neck don't sag.

3. Slowly lower your body to the ground until your elbows form a 90-degree angle. Keep your elbows close to your body and your nose pointed at the floor. Draw a breath as you lower yourself.

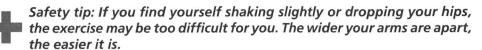 *Safety tip: If you find yourself shaking slightly or dropping your hips, the exercise may be too difficult for you. The wider your arms are apart, the easier it is.*

CHAIR DIP

1. Sit on the edge of a chair with your hands on the edge and close to your sides. Place your feet together with your legs straight in front of you.

2. With your heels on the floor and your hands on the chair's edge, lower yourself toward the floor until your elbows form a 90-degree angle.

3. Slowly raise yourself so your arms are straight. Your arms and not your legs do the work.

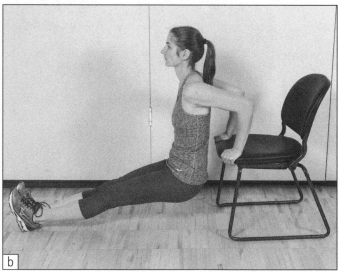

SEATED RUNNING ARMS

1. Sit on the ground with your legs extended straight in front of you. Bend your elbows to 90 degrees.

2. Drive your arms back and forth vigorously as if you are running. Keep your elbows close to your body. As they swing back and forth, your hands should pass just above the level of the ground.

ONE- OR TWO-LEG HEEL RAISE

1. Stand on a box or step with your weight on the balls of the feet. You may also do this exercise on one leg, putting all your weight on one foot.
2. Raise your heels as high as you can, then lower your heels back down to starting position.

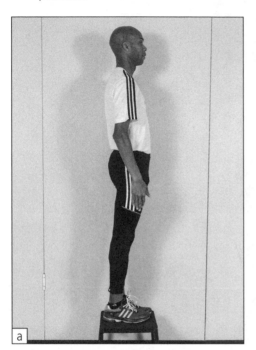
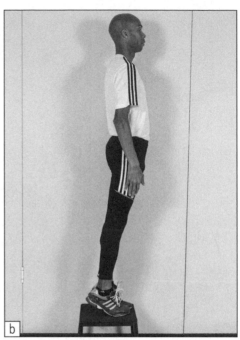

TOE RAISE

1. Sit on a chair with your knees bent and feet on the floor. With a towel holding a light weight just on top of your toes, lift your toes and forefoot of either one or both feet off the ground, keeping your heels on the ground.
2. Return to the starting position.
3. Switch feet.

B: Free Weight Exercises

BENCH PRESS

1. Lie back on the bench and use your thighs to help you push the dumbbells up to your chest. Straighten your arms over your chest (keeping a slight bend in elbows), palms facing forward. Keep your feet flat on the floor and your back in a neutral position (no more than a slight arch).

2. Lower the dumbbells by bending your elbows out to the sides until they are just below your shoulders and your biceps are parallel with the ground.

3. Press the dumbbells back up, bringing them close together at the top but not touching, and angled slightly inward. Keep a slight bend in your elbows so they don't lock.

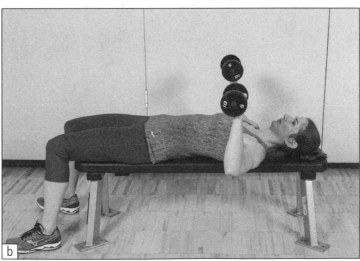

BENT-OVER ROW

1. Kneeling over the end of a bench, place the right knee and right hand on the bench for support. Your back should be parallel to the floor. Position the left foot on the ground and slightly back. The left hand should hang straight down, perpendicular to your body. Grasp a dumbbell in the left hand.

2. Keeping your torso horizontal—and without rotating it—pull the dumbbell up to your side until it is parallel with your rib area or until the upper arm is just beyond horizontal. Keep your elbow in and pointed up.

3. Extend the arm and stretch the shoulder downward. Repeat the exercise on the other arm.

C: Isometric Exercises

FRONT PLANK

1. Lie facedown on a mat, resting your forearms on the mat. Keep legs straight and together with the toes on the floor. Keep your eyes focused on the floor.
2. Raise your body and hold it in a straight line.

SIDE PLANK

1. Lie on your side on a mat, resting the lower forearm on the mat under you and perpendicular to your body. Your top arm should be parallel to your torso with your elbow bent with your hand at your waist. Place your upper leg directly on top of your lower leg and straighten your knees and hips.

2. Raise the body by straightening your waist so the body is rigid from head to toes. Hold this position. Repeat on the other side. (You can also begin performing the side plank with your legs bent at the knees. Support yourself on your forearm and knee instead of forearm and feet.)

Runner Profile: Sheri Piers

Date of birth: May 15, 1971

Personal Information

- Nurse practitioner
- Divorced, now lives with boyfriend
- Three children: Conner, 12; Noah, 11; Karley, 9
- Started focused training at age 35

Personal Bests

- 5K (road) 16: 46 (41)
- 10K (road) 34:17 (38)
- Half marathon 1:14:16 (41)
- Marathon 2:36:59 (41)

Age-Graded Personal Bests

- 5K (road) 92.07% (16:46 at age 41)
- 10K (road) 92.02% (34:23 at age 41)
- Half marathon 93.12% (1:14:16 at age 41)
- Marathon 91.43% (2:36:59 at age 41)

© www.kevinmorris.com

Cathy Utzschneider: How did you get into training and competition?

Sheri Piers: I ran cross country and track throughout high school (Westbrook High) and was actually a state champion my junior year and runner-up my sophomore and senior years. Because of pressure I put on myself to succeed during that time, I decided to play basketball (my first love) in college. I participated all four years at Saint Joseph's College. However, I continued running three to five miles (5-8 km) daily for exercise and peace of mind. Later, I got married and had three children, each 18 months apart. I continued running for peace of mind and entered a few fun local races as my children grew older. In 2005, I attended a local turkey trot in Cape Elizabeth where I met my current training partner Kristin Barry. Although she was a few years younger and attended South Portland High, she remembered me and the success of our high school team. We talked about running and racing and in May of 2006 we attended the Freihofer's 5K. Then we began training together and racing. It was her idea to try and qualify for the Olympic Trials in the marathon for 2008. The training began and it hasn't stopped!

Cathy: How do you explain your success?

Sheri: Success is difficult to define. I am very driven (to a fault I would say) and goal oriented. I have individual goals that I have never shared with anyone. I don't or won't ever feel success until I am able to check them off as complete. They motivate me to be the best I know I can and want to be. I put in whatever needs to be done to succeed. If I have to get up at 2:30 a.m. to run or work out, then that's what I do. I want to be the best at everything I do. I want to win. For me, winning doesn't mean crossing the finish line first. It's checking off my own individual goals.

Meeting Kristin has been the best thing that has ever happened. As we train together and race against each other, it doesn't matter who wins. You can feel successful in running through training and seeing your partner perform well.

Cathy: How often do you race?

Sheri: I typically have three goal races for which I taper throughout the year. Other races are just stepping stones to get to the goal race. Some races are "workouts," and some I race full throttle but are typically on tired legs. My three goal races are usually a spring marathon (usually Boston), Beach to Beacon, and a fall marathon (the Medtronics Twin Cities Marathon the last few years). During the Olympic Trial years there were a couple extra marathons squeezed in.

(continued)

Cathy: What is your most memorable win and why?

Sheri: My most memorable race was the 2007 Philadelphia Marathon when Kristin and I qualified for the 2008 Olympic Trials. We ran the entire thing together and finished in 2:45:37. I will never forget how happy we both were and the happiness lasted for more than a day. Typically, if I race well, I am happy for a very short period because my mind starts drifting to the file of "reach goals." I have attainable goals and then, of course, "reach" goals that are a little more difficult to attain.

Cathy: In a peak training week for a marathon, what is your mileage and how much weekly speed work do you do?

Sheri: Marathon peak weekly training has been anywhere from 120 to 130 miles (193-209 km) for five to seven weeks. Recently my peak mileage has been 100 to 110 miles (161-177 km) per week. Speed work usually consists of two days a week followed by a weekly long run.

Cathy: What is the greatest challenge as a masters runner?

Sheri: My greatest challenge is to stay focused on masters runners. Most of the races I attend include most of the best runners in the country, young and old. I constantly say to myself, focus on your own age group and let the young group go. When you're as competitive as I am, it's tough to settle.

Cathy: What has been the greatest surprise?

Sheri: When I started running competitively again I didn't realize that I would be competing with some the greatest runners in the country or the world for that matter.

Cathy: Have you had injuries and how have you dealt with them?

Sheri: I have been extremely blessed to have never been injured. A lot of that has to do with my mind-set. I don't have the time to be injured, and I believe positive thoughts will always bring positive outcomes. In marathon training I walk the fine line between injury and just fatigue, but I believe I have worked so hard that it just can't happen. I also believe that never taking a break from running helps. Even after a marathon, though I take a break from speed workouts, my running itself never stops. I take maybe one day off. When I look back at my logs, I have more than one year in which I have had one or two days off in a calendar year. I believe if I stop, I won't get started again!

Cathy: What advice do you have for other masters?

Sheri: Age is only a number. You can run at any age. Everyone can create his or her own destiny by creating goals for themselves. I have been blessed to have attained some of my goals. Anyone who attains his or her goal is a winner. A PR (personal record) is a PR. It doesn't matter how old you are, and it doesn't matter if it's by a minute or half a second. Keep running if your body allows. It's an amazing sport with amazing outcomes. Success will come if you put everything you've got into the preparation phase (the training): You will always get out what you put into something.

Cathy: What is a sample training week?

Sheri: This was what I did the week of March 5 (six weeks out from Boston).

> March 5 – a.m. 16 miles (26 km), p.m. 4 miles (6.4 km)
>
> March 6 – a.m. 11 miles (17.7 km), p.m. 4 miles (6.4 km)
>
> March 7 (quality day) – a.m. 3-mile (4.8 km) warm-up, 4 × 3-mile (4.8 km) tempo, with 4 minutes between sets at 6:40 pace, (6:00, 5:56, 5:52) (5:56, 5:52, 5:49) (5:52, 5:49, 5:46) (5:46, 5:39, 5:36), 2-mile (3.2 km) cool-down, total 18 miles (29 km); p.m. 6 miles (9.6 km)
>
> March 8 – 14 miles (22 km)
>
> March 9 – a.m. 8 miles (13 km), p.m. 5 miles (8 km)
>
> March 10 (quality day) – 6-mile (9.6 km) warm-up, 12-mile (19 km) cutdown (3 miles [4.8 km] at 6:20 pace, 3 miles at 6:05, 3 miles at 6:00, 3 miles at 5:50)
>
> March 11 – 10 miles (16 km) easy
>
> Total for the week: 120 miles (193 km)

10 Minutes of Strength Circuit

Whoa, you might think. There's no way I'm fitting in all those exercises in addition to running, at least not now at this stage in my life. Then try the 10 minutes of strength circuit. It's simple. Cut 10 minutes off your run four to six times a week and perform each of the following exercises for the length of time indicated:

1. Squat – 1 minute
2. Lunge – 2 minutes (1 minute leading with each leg)
3. Bent-leg donkey kick – 1 minute (working each leg for 30 seconds)
4. Straight-leg donkey kick – 1 minute (working each leg for 30 seconds)
5. Front plank – 1 minute
6. Side plank – 1 minute (on each side for 30 seconds)
7. Push-up – 1 minute
8. Dip with a bench or chair – 1 minute
9. Seated running arms – 1 minute

"I've added this quick 10-minute strength circuit to my training. No matter how busy my day is, I know I can always find 10 minutes to do something positive for myself," said Mary Kate Shea, one of the Liberty Athletic Club runners. A mother of four whose full-time work in sports sponsorship involves frequent travel (including trips to the Olympics, major world marathons, and the World Championships) and who has also run the past 17 Boston Marathons as a qualifier. "Whether I add the circuit after a run or fit it into a rest day, it's an immediate and tangible activity that makes me feel stronger while also providing me confidence that I can achieve the big goals," she told me recently.

HILL RUNNING

Hills are runners' friends, as long as you treat them with respect and as long as you don't have calf or Achilles injuries. Running hills is the best way to combine getting stronger with practicing good form. They are nature's form of plyometrics, exercises that involve jumping to exert maximum force quickly for increased speed and power. Hill running improves not just speed and endurance (by increasing leg strength and turnover) but also ankle flexibility. Ultimately, running on hills improves your ability to shift gears in races. Hill running also offers the variety of a different venue for training and prepares you for cross country and hill racing.

Form

Running hills—up and down them—requires correct running form, and hills offer an excellent opportunity to practice it. Because all runners tend to get tired and lose their form on hills, it is helpful to focus on form when you're running on them.

Running Uphill

- Lean into the hill from your hips, with your head and chest up. The steeper the hill the more you should lean forward (see figure 9.1).

- Shorten your stride and lift your knees. Push your legs off and up the hill rather than into it. Drive off your back foot and think of springing up the hill.

- If you think of running on eggshells without breaking them or on hot coals, you'll keep your contact time as short as possible.

- Pump your arms but do not exaggerate the action. Keep your hands loose.

- Look straight ahead and visualize the top of the hill as being about 20 meters above where it is to help maintain your pace.

- Maintain the same breathing rate as you would on level ground.

Figure 9.1 When running uphill, pump your arms and look straight ahead.

Running Downhill

- Look down the hill, not at your feet. Let gravity pull you down the hill (see figure 9.2).

- Try to maintain an upright body posture, keeping your torso perpendicular to the horizontal.

- Emphasize quicker turnover rather than longer strides, though they will be slightly longer than normal. Running downhill increases leg turnover and speed.

- Think of running on eggshells or hot coals.

- Try to land on the middle of your foot, not on your heels. Maintain a bend in your knee when landing to absorb the shock and think about landing lightly.

- Control your arms to maintain balance. Don't throw them around.

Figure 9.2 When running downhill, keep your body posture upright and your head up.

You can gain the benefits of hill training by doing one hill session per week for five to seven weeks. You can do hill training *in place of* speed training or a track workout in the strengthening and sharpening phases of race preparation. You can choose one of these types of hill workouts:

- Hill repeats are strenuous efforts of 10 seconds to three minutes on a moderate hill (4 to 5 percent grade) at a perceived exertion of 8.5 to 9.8 (hard or very hard; see chapter 8). Given masters runners' increased susceptibility to calf or Achilles injuries, avoid repeats on steep hills (8 to 10 percent grade).
- Hill fartlek consists of informal runs at a perceived exertion of 7.0 to 8.5 (comfortably hard to hard) on gradual hills (2 to 3 percent grade).

Six-Week Progression for Hill Repeats

As noted earlier, it's safest for masters to run hill repeats on gradual or moderate hills to avoid calf or Achilles tendon strains. A warm-up of at least 15 minutes with a few 20-second strides and dynamic stretching before the repeats help prevent injury as well. Hill repeats run at a running rating of perceived exertion (RRPE) of 8.5 should total no more than 5 percent of your weekly mileage and allow for recoveries at least equal in length to your efforts. Take more time if you need it. Hill repeats run at a RRPE of 9.5 (very hard) build your anaerobic capacity and muscle strength, although I don't recommend more than six 10-second repeats with jog recoveries of 1 minute or more. You can also judge when you're ready for the next repeat by your heart rate. Generally speaking, if your heart rate is at 120 beats per minute or lower, you are ready for the next hill repeat.

Following is a six-week progression for hill repeats run at a hard, not at a very hard, perceived exertion.

Week 1: 8 × 30 seconds

Week 2: 6 × 45 seconds, 4 × 30 seconds

Week 3: 6 × 45 seconds, 6 × 30 seconds

Week 4: 3 × 1 minute, 4 × 45 seconds, 4 × 30 seconds

Week 5: 4 × 1 minute, 4 × 45 seconds, 4 × 30 seconds

Week 6: 5 × 1 minute, 4 × 45 seconds, 4 × 30 seconds

Six-Week Progression for Hill Fartlek

As an alternative to hill repeats, you may prefer running hill fartleks. First, find a course with frequent rolling hills. Then, after a 20-minute easy run warm-up, when you find a moderate uphill, pick up the pace to an RRPE of 7.5 (comfortably hard). When you choose to ease up, whether it's after 30 seconds or 3 minutes, begin running easy again. Take as much recovery as you need before the next effort on the next gradual hill. Table 9.1 suggests approximate minutes of hill fartleks based on mileage of 20, 30, and 40 miles (32, 48, 64 km) a week. (Don't worry if you lose track of the exact number of fartlek minutes.) Because these runs combine hills with comfortably hard efforts, limit them to no more than 8 percent of your weekly mileage.

Table 9.1 Approximate Minutes of Hill Fartlek

Weekly mileage	20	30	40
Week 1	8-10	10-12	14-16
Week 2	8-10	10-12	14-16
Week 3	10-12	12-14	16-18
Week 4	10-12	12-14	16-18
Week 5	12-14	14-16	18-20
Week 6	12-14	14-16	18-20

Building strength is an important component of masters training, and you can build and maintain strength in various ways. As one example, a few of my runners combine the 10 minutes of strength circuit with an Ashtanga (power) yoga practice twice a week. When you plan your hill sessions, choose different hills to run. The best training plan that combines strength training and hill running is the one you actually do, one that fits your unique schedule. Whatever keeps you motivated works, whether that's lifting weights during the news hour or your favorite television series, lifting with a friend, or changing your routine every three to six months for variety.

Event-Specific Training Programs

Back to Basics

The best runners—like the best in any field—go back to basics. Before focusing on training plans for specific race distances such as the mile or the 5K (chapter 11), the 10K or half marathon (chapter 12), or the marathon (chapter 13), you can gain a greater understanding of your own running times and of the training plans by reviewing the fundamentals of masters performance, advantageous attitudes, guidelines for training, and characteristics of the plans.

MASTERS PERFORMANCE: DOING YOUR BEST AS A RUNNER

While age grading—the best measure of masters performance—puts your results in a universal perspective, knowing when your times will increase with aging is impossible. Decline through the decades is hard to predict; it's more individual than growth. "Why am I suddenly getting slower?" one runner might ask at 47, having raced at the same pace for the past four years, and then, plunk! Another 47-year-old runner with a similar history may slow gradually. Although I've coached and researched performance of masters runners of all levels for more than 20 years—and watched runners of all ages continuously compete for several decades—I can't predict when a runner's times will slow down. Masters performance depends on several factors besides chronological age, which varies widely from the 30s to 50s to 70s and up. It also depends on variables that are hard to quantify: genetics (your parents), physiology, the process of aging, the culture and environment, and training load, including cumulative mileage. No simple formula determines performance. Some world champions have parents who were smokers or sedentary. The contribution of genetics to performance is tough to pinpoint.

Also, the process of aging is individual and difficult to predict. Biological aging, determined by changes in physiology and the physical structure of the body, is different from chronological aging, the number of years a person has lived. For example, take two women as they age from 62 to 65. During this period, both age three years, but one feels the onset of arthritis while the other does not. Just as runners make sudden improvements through training, signs of decline may be unpredictable as well. It is heartening to note, however, that since I began masters running in 1995 at 40, I've learned that masters runners can handle a greater volume of speed work than I thought back then. (As an example, when I started at age 40 training for the mile, one interval workout in a strengthening phase might consist of six to eight 200-meter repeats, up to one mile of speed. Today I give some milers of the same age and level three times that workload.)

Furthermore, masters runners have diverse training histories. Take two 55-year-olds. One may have been running competitively since his teens while the other may have taken up running two years ago. The former has the advantage of experience, while the latter has the advantage of fresh legs. Many who have been running for decades speak about tired or stale legs.

With so many variables, genetics included, our best performance years in age-graded terms and most appropriate mileage vary widely. Joan Benoit Samuelson has been running superbly for almost four decades. Some others are not so fortunate. I've coached several runners who ran the Olympic Trials in their 20s and now in their mid-40s are unable to compete, mainly because of injury. Although some masters runners race as often as every other weekend (or more frequently), picking just a few main competitions each year—and a few training races along the way—increases the chances of preserving the body for a longer running lifespan. It's also impossible to prescribe the most appropriate mileage for maximizing race performance by age groups. Aging and running history vary. Runners in their 60s who train for 25 miles (40 km), 35 miles (56 km), and 50 miles (80 km) a week for a 5K may run times similar to those of runners in their 40s who train for 45 miles (72 km), 55 miles (88 km), and 70 miles (113 km) for a marathon. Clearly this represents a wide range of mileage.

FIVE ADVANTAGEOUS ATTITUDES

While it is impossible to say that one training plan fits all masters runners (or runners of any age, for that matter), adopting an advantageous attitude can help any runner. The following five general attitudes will help ensure your success as a masters runner.

1. **Reframe once a year or at least every few years.** If you refresh your running annually with new running goals, training venues, and training partners

Performance Running and Aging:
Michael J. Joyner, MD

The physiology and performance of elite aging runners, including world record holders, is a major area of interest of physician and researcher Michael J. Joyner, MD. An anesthesiologist and the Frank R. and Shari Caywood Professor of Anesthesiology at the Mayo Clinic and consultant to the National Institutes of Health and NASA, Dr. Joyner is one of the world's leading experts on human performance and exercise physiology. He was named a Distinguished Investigator by the Mayo Clinic in 2010. Dr. Joyner knows running, having been a member of his college track team at the University of Arizona, a 2:25 marathoner, and a triathlete.

Courtesy of Teri Joyner

Cathy Utzschneider: In 1993 you wrote an article called the "Physiological Limiting Factors and Distance Running: Influence of Gender and Age on Record Performances" in which you studied race results of 10,000-meter runners to marathoners over 40, analyzing world age group records and performance records from USA Road Running rankings, *Track & Field News,* and *Runner's World.* That was 20 years ago and I'd like to address some of the same questions you raised then to get an update on the answers. *Mastering Running* focuses on training for the mile to the marathon. Related to different distances, how do you summarize the difference between age-related decline in a sprint, like the 400 meters, and the mile, the 10K, and the marathon? Should runners expect more decline in sprint or endurance events, and if it's one or the other, why?

Michael J. Joyner, MD: The first thing that everyone has to realize is that there are a lot more competitive opportunities from 5K up in distance running. This is primarily because there are just so many more road races than track races. However, when you look at the really elite times, there are a limited number of sprinters who have continued to run fast over many years. One person who comes to mind is Bill Collins. To do well in masters distance running you have to do some higher-intensity training. To do well at distances of a mile or less you have to do hardcore speed work and for whatever reason fewer people continue to do this type of training as they age. An interesting contrast is with swimming where almost all of the training is interval based and you don't have the pounding factor associated with running. In general sprint times for elite older swimmers are pretty fast. The key in running is how to train hard and fast and avoid injury.

Cathy: What is the difference in decline in performance between men and women?

Dr. Joyner: For the top male performances it is about 6 percent per decade until people are in their 70s, and there are some impressive outliers in their 70s. For women it looked like the decline was more dramatic, but as the "girls of Title IX" age and become the women of Title IX, the rates of decline are looking pretty similar. I expect a wave of women's records in the

(continued)

60-plus age groups in the coming 10 to 15 years. Joan Benoit is a good example of a person on the leading edge of this trend. Joani, as she is popularly called, was a gold medalist in the 1984 women's Olympic marathon, the first marathon for women ever in the Olympics. She has continued to compete and in 2011 at age 53 participated again in the Boston Marathon, placing first in her age group (women 50 to 54) and completing the course in 2:51:29.

Cathy: Is the decline in performance consistent or does it drop in certain decades? Do you know why that decline stays fairly constant for years and then drops suddenly?

Dr. Joyner: The decline in records is pretty constant into the 70s. However, estimating the decline using records means that you are using snapshots of gifted people at times when they were very fit. When runners are considered over many decades, only a very few people are close to 6 percent, and for most people it is more like 8 to 10 percent per decade. My guess is that there are different factors for different runners. People may develop other interests, they may have an injury and never bounce back after the injury, the motivation to push it every day might change, and weight gain is always a challenge. Things might change for us all at some point in our 70s and certainly in our 80s. For people in these age groups, the basic biology of maintaining muscle mass becomes a challenge even for the most motivated person.

Cathy: Can men and women do anything specific to offset that decline? Are specific kinds of speed work for distance runners more valuable? Do you recommend threshold workouts over sprint workouts, for example?

Dr. Joyner: There are a couple of studies and all sorts of anecdotal reports. For men, the studies show that people who keep their intensity up with traditional longer (3- to 5-minute) intervals and speed work (fast 200s) seem to lose the least over time. Total volume is not that critical. There is less information for women, but examples like Kathy Martin, who has set multiple American and world records in her 40s and 50s (see profile in chapter 12) would suggest that the same principles apply. The other key is to keep your lean muscle mass up, watch what you eat, and avoid weight gain.

Cathy: If you were 30 and planning a career as a masters runner, would you start focusing on shorter or longer events?

Dr. Joyner: I would try to keep my 3K (2 miles) and 5K times as fast as I could. To do your best at these distances you have to train in a way that keeps your $\dot{V}O_2$max at its upper limit. Running economy (efficiency) and the lactate threshold seem to change less with aging than $\dot{V}O_2$max. I think this is also a general principle for all distance runners who stay fast at the shorter races and then do enough mileage to prepare for the longer races. People forget that 1972 Olympic marathon champion Frank Shorter used to compete in a number of indoor two-mile races and was in fact very good at distances from two miles up.

Cathy: Knowing what you know and being a masters athlete yourself, how do you maintain your performance?

Dr. Joyner: I mostly do Olympic distance triathlons now. I was born in 1958. I had some hamstring problems in the late 1990s and switched almost exclusively to swimming for about 10 years. Now I am running, cycling, and swimming. Essentially, I do 5 × four-minute intervals on the trainer followed by 20 minutes of minute-on, minute-off running two or three times per week. On alternate days I swim 1,000 to 2,000 meters and do a lot of push-ups, dips, and burpees. On the weekends I might do a bit more, and one or two days a week I do some active rest which might be 30 minutes of spinning. My focus is mostly about health and keeping my exercise capacity and lean muscle mass high. As I have gotten older our family has made a concerted effort to get the junk food (chips, soft drinks, sweets) out of the house.

Cathy: What has helped you maintain motivation?

Dr. Joyner: I probably have exercised an average of 360 days per year or more since the late 1970s. Motivation has never been an issue for me. I get it done first thing in the morning before the day catches up with me. I also try to plan my life so that the healthy choice is the default choice and save the decision making for other things. When I was younger my motivation had a major competitive element. Now it is more about being fit and robust as I age. The data are pretty clear that physical activity, watching your weight, eating a healthy diet, never smoking, and not drinking too much are the keys to healthy aging. Almost everyone knows of a "crazy" aunt or uncle who is in their 80s and fit enough to instigate with the teenagers at family events. My goal is to be the crazy uncle.

and practices, you'll reenergize your training for better results, variety, and more fun. How about the steeplechase, a mountain run, or a trail race, for example? Find different running routes. If you haven't already, why not add pool running, biking, or yoga or try an elliptical bike, for example?

Reframing each year can help training feel like a new game. Some of my runners give new training years names like Mountain Year to help them focus. One of my runners in her 60s, Leni Webber, has been training seriously since age 49. Reframing each year has helped her improve her training so that more than 15 years after starting running she is more competitive than ever. While her age-graded race result percentages used to be in the low 70s, they are now in the 80s. In 2013, her 16th year of training, she reframed by gradually adding hill repeats, trail runs, and twice-a-week workouts on an Arc Trainer into her training mix. "Tweaking my training to reach a new level is my focus and it's more fun," she told me. "It's amazing how little changes can make a big difference in your results." Her name for this year is the Tweaking Year.

2. **Plan your race year ahead, to a reasonable degree, given everything going on in your life.** Who doesn't have many obligations to family, friends, work, and community, who depend on you to support their priorities? My runners like the big picture calendar, found in chapter 7, because they can note all their obligations in one place and plan around it.

3. **Be flexible.** Don't worry if your best-laid plans are interrupted. They're rarely followed exactly. Life happens. Unexpected work obligations postpone a long run. You feel a slight pain so you decide to take off a few days.

4. **Trust your body.** No matter what an expert or plan suggests, if you're feeling dog tired or not up to it, trust your judgment. If a plan calls for a nine-mile (14 km) run on a Saturday, and you are not feeling well, don't do it. Dump the guilties and pick up the plan on Sunday. Don't try to make up for lost mileage.

5. **Be patient.** If you are patient, your best times will come to you. Impatience can lead to disappointment or injury.

GUIDELINES FOR MASTERS TRAINING

The following training guidelines form the foundation of plans from the mile to the marathon. They address specific elements such as speed and weight training.

1. Although there is an inevitable decline in performance over the decades, a combination of both volume and intensity can significantly slow that decline. It's possible for the best runners in their 40s and even 50s to compete with the best open runners.

2. Incorporating intensity each week into your running—at a minimum of threshold level or at 85 percent or more of $\dot{V}O_2max$—is a better recipe for improved performance than running more easy miles.

3. If you have gained weight or been inactive or are ill, expect a decline in performance until you are healthy again and have lost the weight and resumed training.

4. Focus on building muscle with some form of strength training, particularly after age 40. Many age group champions find the 10 minutes of strength routine, mentioned in chapter 9, sufficient to maintain muscle mass.

5. Rest and be consistent in your training. While my plans suggest taking off just one day before a race, if you're in your 50s or older, consider taking off two days before a race. Many masters over 50 have run personal bests after taking off two days. Consistency generally leads to more focused training over time. You get to know what works and what doesn't.

6. Consider decreasing your weekly mileage every 5 to 10 years if you are consistently feeling tired. (If you are a vegetarian, and even if you are not, ask your physician to check your blood chemistry, including your ferritin, hematocrit, and hemoglobin levels. If those are low, you may have iron deficiency anemia.) Many runners decrease their weekly mileage as they age. A runner who ran 60 to 70 miles (97-113 km) a week when in the 30s may run 45 to 60 miles (72-97 km) in the 40s, 35 to 50 miles (56-80 km) in the 50s, 20 to 50 miles (32-80 km) in the 60s, and 15 to 35 miles (24-56 km) or less in the 70s. Those ranges are of course broad; everyone is different. Many successful runners also decrease their number of weekly running days as they age, particularly in their 60s and older. Running three or four days a week is enough for some in their 70s and older. They lift weights, cross-train, or rest on alternate days. By contrast, some runners in their 70s run six or seven days a week.

MY TRAINING PLANS

My training plans for all distances, mile through the marathon, are based on principles of training and tried-and-true strategies. While there are many excellent training plans, these have worked well for beginner to elite masters runners. The plans reflect a combination of art and science and are similar in the following respects:

- To accommodate the diversity of masters ages, levels, and running backgrounds, they are based on three common mileage bases: 20, 30, and 40 miles (32, 48, 64 km) a week. (If you're not running 20 miles yet, you can build to that by following the eight-week plan suggested in chapter 8.)

- Most all the training plans are divided into endurance, strengthening, sharpening, and tapering phases. The only exception is the mile plan for those with a 40-mile (64-km) base that starts with a strengthening phase because there's no need for runners to build more endurance.

- Mileage does not increase weekly by more than 10 percent, give or take a mile or two, and there are occasional cutback weeks to allow for recovery.

- Generally, weeks include one longish run and after the endurance phase, two speed workouts a week (strides do not count as speed workouts), one track workout based on Jack Daniels' $\dot{V}O_2$max charts, and a second off-track workout based on perceived exertion. I schedule at least two easy days between speed workouts. I've also introduced plus-pace running both on easy days and after sprints or repetitions because it adds variety and interest, encourages focus on form and pace, and increases the pace of easy runs.

- While my plans recommend running six days a week, if you run only four days—and therefore less mileage—cut out two easy days, leaving two speed workouts, one long run, and one easy day. You won't build up to the same weekly mileage, but you will be in your best shape to race the distance.

- All the plans recommend at least one race midway through the schedule to give you a chance to see your progress and learn from race experience. If you like to race more frequently, feel free to substitute a race for a speed workout. In general, unless you can run a race as a workout and not as a peak performance, I don't recommend racing a mile more than once every two weeks, a 5K more than once every three weeks, a 10K more than once a month, a half marathon more than once every six weeks, and a marathon more than once every three months. To repeat, those are generalizations.

- These plans are guidelines that you can adjust to your own needs. Your schedule most likely varies more than that of runners on school or professional teams. (I suggest mileage for each day rather than recommend a weekly total because, more often than not, people want specific suggestions.) If you feel stressed or if you've been feeling rundown, take a day or several days off, cross-train, or repeat an earlier week. Depending on your recent training, you can begin a plan in the middle of it. If you are not close to a track, exchange a track workout for equivalent intervals or repeats on the roads or level trails instead. Use your VDOT number to find the time you should run for an interval or repetition. Then run that amount of time *plus five seconds* at the corresponding intensity. If, for example, your VDOT is 48 and training calls for four 800-meter intervals, instead of running them in 3:12 on the track, run for 3:17 on the roads, allowing yourself up to 3:17 for an easy jog or brisk walk recovery because intervals call for a 1:1 exertion-to-recovery ratio. Using the treadmill chart, you can also do your running on a treadmill. See the treadmill pace conversion chart in the appendix. The point is, you are in control.

- Warm-ups and cool-downs are essential, particularly on days with speed work. On those days warm up and cool down for at least 10 to 15 minutes at a perceived exertion of 5.

READING THE PLANS

As you read the plans, you may want to review chapters 6, 8, and 9 to refresh your understanding of stretching, types of training, and strengthening. A key that appears below each plan reminds you of different recovery lengths for different kinds of runs.

One main difference between the plans for your goal race is their length: while the mile and 5K plans both last 8 weeks, the plans for the 10K, half marathon, and marathon last 10 weeks, 12 weeks, and 16 weeks respectively. Once again, if you are already training and have been racing regularly, you don't have to begin the plan at week one. As an example, you may want to cut the first two weeks of a plan and begin with the third week.

A FEW WHAT IFS?

What if, for example, you want to add more miles? You can add an early-morning or late afternoon run for a double on one or two days a week. Or maybe you know you can handle running seven days a week.

What if, on the other hand, you find yourself too tired to run six days a week? Cross-train at least one day a week: swim, bicycle, work out on the elliptical, or row. Just allow the same amount of time for cross-training that you would spend running that day. If the plan calls for five miles (8 km) of running that takes 50 minutes, combine rowing with cycling so your total activity lasts for 50 minutes. An excellent day for cross-training is generally Wednesdays, the day after the Tuesday speed workout.

Perspective, perspective, perspective. I could repeat that again. You can't get enough of it. Having returned to the basics and reviewed the fundamentals of masters performance, advantageous attitudes, guidelines for training, and characteristics of the plans, you are in the driver's seat. Peruse the next chapters. What event are you considering?

Chapter 11

Mile and 5K

In this and the next two chapters, you'll find training plans. This chapter is focused on plans for the middle-distance races, the mile (1,609 meters) and the 5K. They offer challenges different from the longer distances. You're not going to run out of endurance if you've trained at least moderately. "Running at the edge" refers to the experience during both the mile and the 5K. Joe Navas, 43, has run 14 marathons and has a personal best of 2:33:18 at 40. He has run close to 100 5Ks and has a personal best of 15:29 at 41. He has run the mile just twice, including the New Balance Indoor Grand Prix masters mile, where he ran 4:33 at 40. For Joe, the mile is the most difficult, tougher than the marathon. "With the mile you go beyond the edge," he told me. "It's this desperate speed, no matter how fast you're running, you feel as if you can't possibly keep that and you're trying to go faster at the same time. With the 5K it's a balance of going close to the edge. In both races, though, you may risk running too fast too soon."

Runner Profile: Brian Pilcher

Date of birth: August 23, 1956

Personal Information

- Earned an MBA in 1979 from Tuck School of Business at Dartmouth University
- Served as options market maker on the floor of the Pacific Options Exchange
- Worked on Wall Street as a Co-CEO of Nomura's Commercial Real Estate Finance Co.
- Married with three children
- Started focused training at age 50

Courtesy of Dave Waco, Editor, Tamalpa Gazette

Personal Bests and Age-Graded Bests

- 5K (road) 15:46 (52)
- 5K (road) 94.5% (16:24 at age 56)
- 10K (road) 97.12% (32:56 at age 55)
- 10 mile (road) 96.16% (54:42 at age 55)
- Half marathon 95.98% (1:12:52 at age 55)
- Marathon 94.22% (2:34:57 at age 55)

Cathy Utzschneider: How did you get into training and competition?

Brian Pilcher: I had run some in high school. I started running again when I was 50 and my youngest went out for cross country and I ran once with the team. Then I raced three weeks later and found out about masters competition in the Pacific Association. I have always been more about racing than just running.

Cathy: How do you explain your success?

Brian: My success comes from 1) good genetics, particularly lean muscles and virtually no calves, 2) fresh legs from not running until I was 50, and 3) aging well compared to my peers.

Cathy: How often do you race?

Brian: I run 20 to 25 races a year.

Cathy: What is your most memorable win and why?

Brian: I care more about times than wins. My best race was the 32:56 10K because it is on my local course and I was able to go out fast and keep it going even with some wind. The next best race was the 10 mile (16 km) in 54:42. Both were just real good times, and I felt like I got all I could get out of myself.

Cathy: In a peak training week for a marathon, what is your mileage and how much weekly speed work do you do?

Brian: 80 to 90 miles (129-145 km). When I am training for a marathon I do three or four × 2 miles (3.2 km) at 5:27 to 5:30 pace only once a week. I might have another workout that would include doing something like this: 8 miles (13 km) easy, 1 mile (1.6 km) tempo pace (5:32), 2 miles (3.2 km) marathon pace (5:50), 1 mile tempo pace, 2 miles marathon pace, 1 easy, for a total of 15 miles (24 km). When I do track once a week, I am probably doing a 3-mile (4.8 km) warm-up, 4 to 6 miles (6.4-9.6 km) of work, depending on whether it is shorter stuff or miles, and a 3-mile cool-down.

Cathy: What is the greatest challenge as a masters runner?

Brian: Staying healthy. There is always something going on and it is tough deciding when to let injuries heal and when to keep running.

Cathy: What has been the greatest surprise?

Brian: I thought I could be this good. The surprise was that I actually got the chance to do it.

Cathy: Have you had injuries and how have you dealt with them?

Brian: My biggest injury was my hips in 2010. I was told that I had a torn labrum and had lost all my cartilage in the left hip. I found a doctor who did arthroscopic surgery on both hips, and I was going up two stairs at a time a day or so after surgery. I still had knee tendinitis that kept me out for the rest of 2010.

Cathy: What advice do you have for other masters?

Brian: A race is the best workout.

Cathy: What is a sample training week?

Brian:

> Sunday: long run
> Monday: easy or elliptiGO
> Tuesday: track: 5 × 1,200, 3 × 400, 6 ×200
> Wednesday: 10-12 miles (16-19 km)
> Thursday: 10-12 miles
> Friday: 3 × 2 mile at threshold pace
> Saturday: 10-12 miles

MILE

The gold standard of track events, the mile is considered the shortest of the middle-distance indoor events. (The 800 meters or half mile is usually considered the longest sprint.) The mile is generally featured at indoor events on the track in the United States and outdoors on the roads, while its cousin, the 1,500 meters—just about 109 meters shy of the mile—is featured at outdoor track meets in the United States and at indoor and outdoor track meets in Europe and in world masters championships. The mile and 1,500 are so similar that you can follow the same plans for either. No matter how fast you run the mile, more than 50 percent of the energy required is aerobic—more than from anaerobic energy pathways, so you need not only strength and speed but also considerable aerobic endurance. Training for the mile therefore requires strength, speed, and endurance.

Why run the mile? Why not? First, with age grading, you're never too old for the mile. You may be in your 50s, 60s, or 70s and it's never too late to run your fastest mile time. One of the Liberty Athletic Club runners, Mary Harada, set a world record in the mile in her age group at 70 and 75, running her fastest age-graded mile times ever. While a distance runner in earlier decades, she had never set a world record before. If you're a sprinter, you can use your speed to help you in the mile and also work on your endurance as well. If you're a distance runner, racing the mile or 1,500 meters will help you to improve your ability to handle speed in the 5K, 10K, half marathon, and even marathon. The mile is getting more popular with masters who run the distance on the track or on the roads. If you're a beginner, you can find many mile races with 5- and 10-year age divisions for masters. Why not see what you can do? You might surprise yourself, and no time is too slow. You're out there and in the game.

If you're an elite masters runner, you can find mile and 1,500-meter races at state, regional, national, and international masters track and field championships, including state and national senior games. The Hartshorne Memorial Masters Mile at Cornell University, held each year in January, attracts top-caliber masters. In 2013, the top 10 male masters competitors, age 40 to 52, finished under 5:00, clocking

Mile Training From a 20-Mile (32 km) Base*

Phase	Week	Monday	Tuesday	Wednesday	Thursday	
Endurance	1	Off	3 miles**, 5 × 30-sec strides (PE 8.5)	3 miles easy***	2-4 miles easy	
Endurance	2	Off	4 miles, 5 × 30-sec strides (PE 8.5)	3 miles easy	3-5 miles easy	
Strengthening	3	Off	5 miles, 6 or 7 × 400 meter intervals (PE 8.5-9)	4 miles easy	2-4 miles easy	
Strengthening	4	5 miles, 6 or 7 × 400 meters intervals (PE 8.5-9)	4 miles easy	4 miles, 5 × 30-sec strides (PE 8.5)	3-5 miles easy	
Strengthening	5	Off	4 miles easy	4 miles easy	3-5 miles, 5 × 20-sec strides (PE 8.5)	
Sharpening	6	Off	4 miles, 2 × 800 meters plus 4 × 400 meters (PE 8.5-9)	4 miles easy	2-4 miles easy	
Sharpening	7	Off	4 miles, 2 sets: 800, 400, 200 meter intervals (PE 8.5 to 9), 3-5 min between sets	3 miles easy	2-4 miles easy	
Tapering	8	5 miles, 4-6 × 200-meter reps (PE 9.5)	3 miles easy	3 miles easy	2-4 miles, 5 × 30-sec strides (PE 8.5)	

* Use a site such as www.worldwidemetric.com/measurements.html to calculate metric conversions.
** Daily mileage totals **include** recommended speed work.
*** All easy running should be done at a PE of 5.

times from 4:23:39 to 4:55.31. The top 10 women masters, age 44 to 55, finished in 5:17:55 to 6:03:68. The top age-graded performances were scored by a man and woman, not in their 40s or 50s, but their 60s: Nolan Shaheed, 63, ran 5:07:54, for an age-graded time of 92.41 percent (the equivalent of running a 4:00 open mile) and Coreen Steinbach, 61, ran 6:15:73, for an age-graded time of 92.5 percent (the equivalent of running a 4:32 open mile).

I suggest that before you start the training plan, you run the mile on a track, if possible, as fast as you can, to obtain a baseline time. You can then find your VDOT on Jack Daniels' charts in the appendix for the paces at which you should run for track intervals and repetitions in the strengthening, sharpening, and tapering training phases. You'll also notice that a 5K race is recommended at the end of the fourth week. While a 5K will feel long compared to a mile, it will help you build endurance, making you feel a mile is short. If you can't find a race, you can time yourself for one to three miles (1.6-4.8 km) just to check on your progress.

	Friday	Saturday	Sunday	Total weekly mileage
	4 miles, 6 × 2 min plus pace (PE 6.5)	3 miles easy	5 miles, 5 × 30-sec strides (PE 8.5)	20-22 miles
	4 miles, 5 × 3 min plus pace (PE 6.5)	4 miles easy	6 miles	23-25 miles
	5 miles, 10-12 min of hill fartlek (PE 7.5)	3 miles easy	7 miles, 5 × 30-sec strides (PE 8.5)	26-28 miles
	3 miles easy	Off	5K race, 7 miles total	26-28 miles
	4 miles easy	7 miles, 5 × 4-min cruise intervals (PE 7.5)	4 miles easy	26-28 miles
	5 miles, 8 × 30-sec hill repeats (PE 8.5)	4 miles easy	7 miles, 5 × 30-sec strides (PE 8.5)	26-28 miles
	3 miles, 5 × 30-sec sprints (PE 9.5)	3 miles easy	7 miles	22-24 miles
	3 miles easy	Off	Mile race	16-18 miles before race

Length of easy jog or walk recovery:
Cruise intervals: one to two minutes
Intervals: one-third to equal the interval
Repetitions and sprints: up to five times length of the repetition

Hill repeats: equal the effort (PE of 8.5 to 9) or up to four times the effort (PE of 9 to 9.8)
Fartlek, including hill fartlek: one to four minutes
Strides: equal the effort

Mile Training From a 30-Mile (48 km) Base*

Phase	Week	Monday	Tuesday	Wednesday	Thursday	
Endurance	1	Off	5 miles**, 5 × 30-sec strides (PE 8.5)	5 miles easy***	4-6 miles easy	
Endurance	2	Off	5 miles, 5 × 30-sec strides (PE 8.5)	5 miles easy	4-6 miles easy	
Strengthening	3	Off	5 miles, 2 × 800 meter, 4-6 × 400 meter intervals (PE 8.5)	5 miles easy	4-6 miles easy	
Strengthening	4	6 miles, 4 or 5 × 800 meter intervals (PE 8.5- 9)	6 miles easy	5 miles easy	4-6 miles, 5 × 30-sec sprints (PE 9.5)	
Strengthening	5	Off	5 miles easy	5 miles easy	4-6 miles, 5 × 30-sec strides (PE 8.5)	
Sharpening	6	Off	5 miles, 3 × 800 meter, 4 or 5 × 400 meter intervals (PE 8.5-9)	4 miles easy	3-5 miles easy	
Sharpening	7	Off	4 miles, 2-3 sets: 2 × 400 meter, 4 × 200 meter intervals (PE 8.5-9), 3-5 min between sets	4 miles easy	3-5 miles easy	
Tapering	8	4 miles 2 sets: 600, 400, 200 meter intervals (PE 8.5-9), 3-5 min between sets	4 miles easy	4 miles, 4-6 × 200-meter reps (PE 9.5)	3-5 miles easy	

* Use a site such as www.worldwidemetric.com/measurements.html to calculate metric conversions.
** Daily mileage totals **include** recommended speed work.
*** All easy running should be done at a PE of 5.

Mile Training From a 40-Mile (64 km) Base*

Phase	Week	Monday	Tuesday	Wednesday	Thursday	
Strengthening	1	Off	6 miles**, 4 × 800 meter, 2-6 × 200 meter intervals (PE 8.5)	6 miles easy***	5-7 miles easy	
Strengthening	2	Off	6 miles, 5 or 6 × 800 meter intervals (PE 8.5)	6 miles easy	5-7 miles easy	
Strengthening	3	Off	6 miles, 3 or 4 sets: 600, 400, 200 meter intervals (PE 8.5-9), 3-5 min between sets	6 miles easy	5-7 miles easy	
Strengthening	4	6 miles, 6-8 × 400 meter intervals (PE 8.5-9)	6 miles easy	6 miles easy	5-7 miles, 5 × 30-sec sprints (PE 9.5)	
Sharpening	5	Off	5 miles easy	8 miles easy	4-6 miles, 5 × 30-sec strides (PE 8.5)	
Sharpening	6	Off	5 miles, 4 × 800 meter, 4-6 × 400 meter intervals (PE 8.5-9)	7 miles easy	4-6 miles easy	
Sharpening	7	Off	5 miles, 4 sets: 600, 400, 200 meter intervals (PE 8.5-9)	7 miles easy	4-6 miles easy	
Tapering	8	5 miles, 6 × 400 meter intervals (PE 8.5-9)	5 miles easy	4 miles, 5 or 6 × 200-meter reps (PE 9.5)	3-5 miles easy	

* Use a site such as www.worldwidemetric.com/measurements.html to calculate metric conversions.
** Daily mileage totals **include** recommended speed work.
*** All easy running should be done at a PE of 5.

Friday	Saturday	Sunday	Total weekly mileage
5 miles, 7 × 2 min plus pace (PE 6.5)	5 miles easy	7 miles, 5 × 30-sec strides (PE 8.5)	31-33 miles
6 miles easy, 6 × 3 min plus pace (PE 6.5)	5 miles easy	8 miles	33-35 miles
6 miles, 14-16 min of hill fartlek (PE 7.5)	5 miles easy	8 miles, 5 × 30-sec strides (PE 8.5)	33-35 miles
4 miles easy	Off	5K race, 8 miles total	33-35 miles
4 miles easy	8 miles, 6-7 × 4-min cruise intervals (PE 7.5)	5 miles easy	33-35 miles
4 miles, 4 × 45-sec, 2 × 30-sec hill repeats (PE 8.5), 2 × 10-sec hill repeats (PE 9.5)	3 miles easy	8 miles, 5 × 30-sec strides (PE 8.5)	31-33 miles
4 miles, 3 × 400-meter reps plus 2 × 200-meter reps (PE 9.5)	4 miles easy	8 miles	31-33 miles
3 miles easy		Mile race	18-20 miles before race

Length of easy jog or walk recovery:
Cruise intervals: one to two minutes
Intervals: one-third to equal the interval
Repetitions and sprints: up to five times the length of the repetition

Hill repeats: equal the effort (PE of 8.5 to 9) or up to four times the effort (PE of 9 to 9.8)
Fartlek, including hill fartlek: one to four minutes
Strides: equal the effort

Friday	Saturday	Sunday	Total weekly mileage
7 miles, 7-8 × 4-min cruise intervals (PE 7.5)	6 miles easy	8 miles, 5 × 30-sec strides (PE 8.5)	38-40 miles
7 miles, 16-18 min of hill fartlek (PE 7.5)	5 miles easy	9 miles easy	38-40 miles
7 miles, 18- to 20-min. hill fartlek (PE 7.5)	5 miles easy	9 miles, 5 × 30-sec strides (PE 8.5)	38-40 miles
6 miles easy	Off	5K race, 9 miles total	38-40 miles
6 miles easy	9 mile, 8 or 9 × 4-min cruise intervals (PE 7.5)	6 miles easy	38-40 miles
5 miles, 4 × 45-sec, 2 × 30-sec hill repeats (PE 8.5), 2 × 10-sec hill repeats (PE 9.5)	6 miles easy	9 miles, 5 × 30-sec strides (PE 8.5)	36-38 miles
5 miles, 4 × 400-meter reps (PE 9.5), 5 × 5 min plus pace (PE 6.5)	5 miles easy	8 miles	34-36 miles
3 miles easy		Mile race	20-22 miles before race

Length of easy jog or walk recovery:
Cruise intervals: one to two minutes
Intervals: one-third to equal the interval
Repetitions and sprints: up to five times the length of the repetition

Hill repeats: equal the effort (PE of 8.5 to 9) or up to four times the effort (PE of 9 times 9.8)
Fartlek, including hill fartlek: one to four minutes
Strides: equal the effort

5K

The 5K is run on the roads. When it is run on the track, mostly outdoors, it is designated as a 5,000-meter run. One of the most popular race distances today, you can find a 5K almost every weekend not too far from you. Most races have 5- or at least 10-year age divisions. The popularity of the 5K means that you can follow your progress easily. State, regional, national, and international track meets offer competitive 5,000 meters for masters only. Several well-known road 5K races offer elite masters divisions. These include the Freihofers 5K race for women, held in early June each year in Albany, New York, and the Carlsbad 5000, held in April most years. The top Carlsbad male and female masters finishers in 2012 were two outstanding runners, Kevin Castille, who ran the course in 14:57, and Dorota Gruca, who ran the course in 16:58.

5K Training From a 20-Mile (32 km) Base*

Phase	Week	Monday	Tuesday	Wednesday	Thursday	
Endurance	1	Off	4 miles**, 5 × 30-sec strides (PE 8.5)	3 miles easy***	2-4 miles easy	
Endurance	2	Off	4 miles, 5 × 30-sec strides (PE 8.5)	3 miles easy	2-4 miles easy	
Strengthening	3	Off	4 miles, 6 or 7 × 400 meter intervals (PE 8.5)	4 miles easy	2-4 miles easy	
Strengthening	4	4 miles easy	5 miles, 4 × 45-sec, 4 × 30-sec hill repeats (PE 8.5)	4 miles easy	2-4 miles, 5 × 30-sec strides (PE 8.5)	
Strengthening	5	Off	3 miles easy	4 miles easy	2-4 miles, 5 × 30-sec strides (PE 8.5)	
Sharpening	6	Off	4 miles, 3 × 800 meter intervals (PE 8.5 to 9), 3 or 4 × 200 meter repetitions (PE 9-9.8)	4 miles easy	2-4 miles easy	
Sharpening	7	Off	4 miles easy, 2 × 800, 2 × 400, 2 × 200 meter intervals (PE 8.5)	3 miles easy	2-4 miles easy	
Tapering	8	5 miles easy	3 miles, 4 × 200-meter reps (PE 9.5)	3 miles easy	2-4 miles, 5 × 30-sec strides (PE 8.5)	

* Use a site such as www.worldwidemetric.com/measurements.html to calculate metric conversions.

** Daily mileage totals **include** recommended speed work.

*** All easy running should be done at a PE of 5.

As mentioned, the 5K programs are 8 weeks long, whether based on weekly mileage of 20, 30, or 40 miles (32, 48, 64 km). The endurance phase is two weeks, the strengthening phase three weeks, the sharpening phase two weeks, and the tapering phase one week. You'll see that over those weeks are suggestions for two 5K to 8K training races on the way to your goal race: one at the end of the fourth and the other at the end of the eighth week. A 5K competition can help you practice racing for your goal event, and a longer race of 5 miles (8 km) can help build your race endurance, making your ultimate 5K race feel short.

As with the mile, time yourself over a 5K before beginning training so you have a baseline.

	Friday	Saturday	Sunday	Total weekly mileage
	4 miles, 6 × 2 min plus pace (PE 6.5)	3 miles easy	5 miles, 5 × 30-sec strides (PE 8.5)	21-23 miles
	5 miles, one set: 5, 4, 3, 2, 1 min plus pace (PE 6.5), with a 1-min jog recovery	3 miles easy	6 miles easy	23-25 miles
	5 miles, 4 or 5 × 5-min cruise intervals (PE 7.5)	4 miles easy	7 miles, 5 × 30-sec strides (PE 8.5)	26-28 miles
	4 miles easy	Off	5K to 5-mile race, 7 miles total	26-28 miles
	4 miles easy	5 miles, 12-14 min of hill fartlek (PE 7.5)	8 miles easy	26-28 miles
	5 miles, 4 or 5 × 5-min cruise intervals (PE 7.5)	3 miles easy	8 miles, 5 × 30-sec strides (PE 8.5)	26-28 miles
	4 miles, 5 × 30-sec sprints (PE 9.5)	3 miles easy	7 miles easy	23-25 miles
	3 miles easy	Off	5K race	16-18 miles before race

Length of easy jog or walk recovery:
Cruise intervals: one to two minutes
Intervals: one-third to equal the interval
Repetitions and sprints: up to five times the length of the repetition

Hill repeats: equal the effort (PE of 8.5 to 9) or up to four times the effort (PE of 9 to 9.8)
Fartlek, including hill fartlek: one to four minutes
Strides: equal the effort

5K Training From a 30-Mile (48 km) Base*

Phase	Week	Monday	Tuesday	Wednesday	Thursday	
Endurance	1	Off	5 miles**, 6 × 30-sec strides (PE 8.5)	6 miles easy***	3-5 miles easy	
Endurance	2	Off	6 miles, 6 × 30-sec strides (PE 8.5)	5 miles easy	4-6 miles easy	
Strengthening	3	Off	6 miles, 8 × 400 meter intervals (PE 8.5)	5 miles easy	5-7 miles easy	
Strengthening	4	6 miles easy	6 miles, 4 × 45-sec, 5 × 30-sec hill repeats (PE 8.5)	7 miles easy	4-6 miles, 6 × 30-sec strides (PE 8.5)	
Strengthening	5	Off	6 miles easy	5 miles easy	5-7 miles, 5 × 30-sec strides (PE 8.5)	
Sharpening	6	Off	6 miles, 2 or 3 × 800 and 400 meter intervals (PE 8.5 to 9), 3 or 4 × 200 meter repetitions (PE 9.5)	5 miles easy	5-7 miles easy	
Sharpening	7	Off	6 miles easy, 5 × 1,000 meter cruise intervals (PE 7.5)	5 miles easy	4-6 miles easy	
Tapering	8	4 miles easy	4 miles, 1 set: 400 meters, 3 × 200 meter repetitions (PE 9.5)	4 miles easy	3-5 miles, 5 × 30-sec strides (PE 8.5)	

* Use a site such as www.worldwidemetric.com/measurements.html to calculate metric conversions.
** Daily mileage totals **include** recommended speed work.
*** All easy running should be done at a PE of 5.

5K Training From a 40-Mile (64 km) Base*

Phase	Week	Monday	Tuesday	Wednesday	Thursday	
Endurance	1	Off	7 miles**, 5 × 30-sec strides (PE 8.5)	6 miles easy***	5-7 miles easy	
Endurance	2	Off	7 miles, 5 × 30-sec strides (PE 8.5)	7 miles easy	6-8 miles easy	
Strengthening	3	Off	7 miles, 2 × 800 meters, 4 × 400 meter intervals (PE 8.5)	7 miles easy	6-8 miles easy	
Strengthening	4	7 miles easy	7 miles, 4 × 45-sec, 6 × 30-sec hill repeats (PE 8.5)	6 miles easy	5-7 miles, 5 × 30-sec strides (PE 8.5)	
Strengthening	5	Off	7 miles easy	8 miles easy	5-7 miles, 5 × 30-sec strides (PE 8.5)	
Sharpening	6	Off	6 miles, 6 or 7 × 5-min cruise intervals (PE 7.5)	7 miles easy	5-7 miles easy	
Sharpening	7	Off	6 miles easy, 5 or 6 × 800 meters (PE 7.5)	5 miles easy	4-6 miles easy	
Tapering	8	4 miles easy	5 miles, 1 × 400 meters, 3 × 200 meter repetitions (PE 9.5)	4 miles easy	4-6 miles, 5 × 30-sec strides (PE 8.5)	

* Use a site such as www.worldwidemetric.com/measurements.html to calculate metric conversions.
** Daily mileage totals **include** recommended speed work.
*** All easy running should be done at a PE of 5.

	Friday	Saturday	Sunday	Total weekly mileage
	5 miles, 7 × 2 min plus pace (PE 6.5)	5 miles easy	7 miles, 5 × 30-sec strides (PE 8.5)	31-33 miles
	6 miles, 8 or 9 × 2 min plus pace (PE 6.5)	6 miles easy	7 miles	34-36 miles
	6 miles, 5 or 6 × 5-min cruise intervals (PE 7.5)	6 miles easy	8 miles, 5 × 30-sec strides (PE 8.5)	36-38 miles
	5 miles easy	Off	5K to 5-mile race, 8 miles total	36-38 miles
	6 miles easy	6 miles, 14-16 min of hill fartlek (PE 7.5)	8 miles easy	36-38 miles
	6 miles, 5 or 6 × 5-min cruise intervals (PE 7.5)	6 miles easy	8 miles, 5 × 30-sec strides (PE 8.5)	36-38 miles
	5 miles, 5 × 30-sec sprints (PE 9.5)	5 miles easy	8 miles easy	33-35 miles
	3 miles easy	Off	5K race	18-20 miles before race

Length of easy jog or walk recovery:
Cruise intervals: one to two minutes easy jog
Intervals: one-third to equal the interval
Repetitions and sprints: up to five times the length of the repetition

Hill repeats: equal the effort (PE of 8.5 to 9) or up to four times the effort (PE of 9 to 9.8)
Fartlek, including hill fartlek: one to four minutes
Strides: equal the effort

	Friday	Saturday	Sunday	Total weekly mileage
	7 miles, 10 × 2 min at plus pace (PE 6.5)	6 miles easy	9 miles, 5 × 30-sec strides (PE 8.5)	40-42 miles
	7 miles 12 × 2 min at plus pace (PE 6.5)	7 miles easy	9 miles	43-45 miles
	7 miles, 6 or 7 × 5-min cruise intervals (PE 7.5)	7 miles easy	9 miles, 5 × 30-sec strides (PE 8.5)	43-45 miles
	5 miles easy	Off	5K to 5 mile race, 8 miles total	38-40 miles
	7 miles easy	7 miles, 16-18 min of hill fartlek (PE 7.5)	9 miles easy	43-45 miles
	6 miles, 4 × 45-sec, 2 × 30-sec hill repeats (PE 8.5), 4 × 10-sec hill repeats (PE 9.5)	7 miles easy	9 miles, 5 × 30-sec strides (PE 8.5)	40-42 miles
	5 miles, 7 × 30-sec sprints (PE 9.5)	6 miles easy	9 miles easy	36-38 miles
	3 miles easy	Off	5K race	20-22 miles before race

Length of easy jog or walk recovery:
Cruise intervals: one to two minutes easy jog
Intervals: one-third to equal the interval
Repetitions and sprints: up to five times the length of the repetition

Hill repeats: equal the effort (PE of 8.5 to 9) or up to four times the effort (PE of 9 to 9.8)
Fartlek, including hill fartlek: one to four minutes
Strides: equal the effort

ONE LAST THOUGHT

Because the mile and 5K are relatively short distances, whether you are a beginner or experienced runner, you don't need as many weeks to train for them. And it's easier to jump in a mile or 5K than it is a 10K or longer race. The more you run them, the better you'll race them. There's hardly a weekend in most areas when you can't find at least a local, casual 5K event for your first race ever or to use as a tune-up for a 10K, half-marathon, or marathon. You can also use it to replace a workout if you missed a track session during the week, enjoy a weekend event with your kids, run off your Thanksgiving dinner, or raise money for a charity.

Chapter 12

10K and Half Marathon

As with the mile and 5K, three plans are outlined for the 10K and half marathon, based on a foundation of 20, 30, and 40 miles (32, 48, 64 km). As you look through both the 10K and the half marathon programs, keep in mind that they are guidelines. No one plan fits all. For example, the number of ideal training miles for a particular distance varies with the runner. A 10K runner of mine who logs 35 miles (56 km) a week may run the same time as another who logs 55 miles (88 km) a week. As with the mile and 5K plans, a day of rest once a week is built into every plan. In the first phase, the endurance phase, running is almost all easy with the exception of 30-second strides run at a comfortably hard pace and plus-pace running. It takes a while to get used to running at a plus pace, a pace just a tiny bit faster than your usual pace. The tendency is to run too hard. Resist that temptation.

You may be surprised that the weekly mileage, expressed as ranges, is not a great deal higher for the 10K and half marathon than it is for the mile and 5K. The training plans in this chapter show how little weekly mileage increases in preparation for longer race distances. As an example, the plan for someone who runs a base of 30 miles (48 km) a week peaks for the half marathon at 46 miles (74 km) a week compared to 42 miles (68 km) for the 10K, 38 miles (61 km) for the 5K, and 35 miles (56 km) for the mile.

Weekly mileage is just one component of building. The long run is another. For example, whereas the long run for the mile for runners beginning from a 30-mile (48 km) base builds to 8 miles (13 km), the long runs for the 5K, 10K, and half marathon plans build to 9, 10, and 14 miles (15, 16, 22 km) respectively. Speed workouts and tempo runs increase in length. A moderate increase in overall mileage along with an increase in the long run of the week, increased speed work, strength training, and a day of rest (with the exception of two weeks in the half marathon plan for those with a 40-mile [64 km] base) allow for the building and recovery needed for best performance. Some masters runners log unnecessary junk miles that hurt rather than help performance. A few longitudinal studies of masters athletes have shown that in general better performance with aging occurs through a combination of volume and intensity than through too many easy miles. Some rest keeps your legs springy!

10K

The 10K is a great option for masters, whether you're moving up from the 5K or 5 mile (8K) distance or down from the 10 mile (16 km) or half marathon. The longest standard racing distance on the track for the Olympic Games (referred to as the 10,000 meters when it's run on the track), the 10K is a very popular road race distance, although it is also contested on the track at some masters meets.

10K Training From a 20-Mile (32 km) Base*

Phase	Week	Monday	Tuesday	Wednesday	Thursday	
Endurance	1	Off	4 miles**, 5 × 30-sec strides (PE 8.5)	3 miles easy***	2-4 miles easy	
Endurance	2	Off	3 miles, 5 × 30-sec strides (PE 8.5)	3 miles easy	2-4 miles easy	
Endurance	3	Off	4 miles, 5 × 30-sec strides (PE 8.5)	4 miles easy	2-4 miles easy	
Strengthening	4	Off	5 miles, 2 × 800, 3 or 4 × 400 meter intervals (PE 8.5)	4 miles easy	2-4 miles easy	
Strengthening	5	6 miles easy	4 miles easy, 4 × 45-sec, 4 × 30-sec hill repeats (PE 8.5)	4 miles easy	3-5 miles, 5 × 30-sec strides (PE 8.5)	
Strengthening	6	Off	4 miles easy	4 miles easy	4-6 miles easy	
Strengthening	7	Off	5 miles easy, 25-30 min tempo run (PE 7.5)	4 miles easy	3-5 miles easy	
Sharpening	8	Off	4 miles, 4 × 45-sec, 2 × 30-sec hill repeats (PE 8.5), 2 × 10-sec hill repeats (PE 9.5)	3 miles easy	3-5 miles easy	
Sharpening	9	Off	5 miles, 4 × 5-min cruise intervals (PE 7.5)	3 miles easy	2-4 miles easy	
Tapering	10	4 miles easy	4 miles, 6 × 200-meter reps (PE 9.5)	4 miles easy	3-5 miles, 5 × 30-sec strides (PE 8.5)	

* Use a site such as www.worldwidemetric.com/measurements.html to calculate metric conversions.
** Daily mileage totals **include** recommended speed work.
*** All easy running should be done at a PE of 5.

Among the 10 largest U.S. races in 2012 were four 10Ks. The Peachtree Road Race in Atlanta, Georgia, was largest, with 50,918 finishers. The other most popular 10Ks in 2012 were the Bolder Boulder 10K in Boulder, Colorado; the Cooper River Bridge Run in Charleston, South Carolina; and the Monument Avenue 10K in Richmond, Virginia. If you compete in a national masters 10K road race championship, awards are given not only to individuals and teams based on absolute results but also to individuals based on age grading. Of the 186 entrants in the 2013 U.S. national 10K road race championships held in Dedham, MA, Liberty Athletic Club runner Jan Holmquist, 68, placed first in the age grading, covering the distance in 46:06 for an age-graded percentage of 95.87 percent.

The 10K plans that follow are 10 weeks long, with a 3-week endurance phase, 4-week strengthening phase, 2-week sharpening phase, and a week of tapering. A 5K race is suggested for the end of week five.

	Friday	Saturday	Sunday	Total weekly mileage
	4 miles, 6 × 2 min plus pace (PE 6.5)	3 miles easy	5 miles, 5 × 30-sec strides (PE 8.5)	21-23 miles
	5 miles, 1 set: 5, 4, 3, 2, 1 min plus pace (PE 6.5)	3 miles easy	6 miles easy	23-25 miles
	5 miles, 8 × 2 min plus pace (PE 6.5)	4 miles easy	7 miles, 5 × 30-sec strides (PE 8.5)	26-28 miles
	5 miles easy, 5 × 5-min cruise intervals (PE 7.5)	4 miles easy	8 miles easy	28-30 miles
	3 miles easy	Off	5K race, 8 miles total	28-30 miles
	4 miles easy	5 miles, 3 × 800 meters, 4 × 400 meter intervals (PE 8.5)	9 miles easy	30-32 miles
	4 miles, 1 set: 400, 800, 1,200. 800, 400 meter intervals (PE 8.5-9)	5 miles easy	9 miles, 5 × 30-sec strides (PE 8.5)	30-32 miles
	5 miles, 2 × 1,000 meter, 2 × 800 meter, 2 × 400 meter intervals (PE 8.5-9)	4 miles easy	9 miles easy	28-30 miles
	4 miles easy, 3 × 400-meter reps (PE 9.5), 2 × 5-min plus pace (PE 6.5)	4 miles easy	8 miles easy, 5 × 30-sec strides (PE 8.5)	26-28 miles
	3 miles easy	Off	10K race	18-20 miles before race

Length of easy jog or walk recovery:
Cruise intervals: one to two minutes
Intervals: one-third to equal the interval
Repetitions and sprints: up to five times the length of the repetition

Hill repeats: equal the effort (PE of 8.5 to 9) or up to four times the effort (PE of 9 to 9.8)
Fartlek, including hill fartlek: one to four minutes
Strides: equal the effort

10K Training From a 30-Mile (48 km) Base*

Phase	Week	Monday	Tuesday	Wednesday	Thursday	
Endurance	1	Off	6 miles**, 5 × 30-sec strides (PE 8.5)	4 miles easy***	4-6 miles easy	
Endurance	2	Off	6 miles, 5 × 30-sec strides, (PE 8.5)	5 miles easy	5-7 miles easy	
Endurance	3	Off	6 miles, 5 × 30-sec strides (PE 8.5)	5 miles easy	5-7 miles easy	
Strengthening	4	Off	7 miles, 4 × 800 meter, 2-4 × 400 meter intervals (PE 8.5)	6 miles easy	4-6 miles easy	
Strengthening	5	7 miles easy	6 miles, 4 × 45-sec, 5 × 30-sec hill repeats (PE 8.5)	6 miles easy	5-7 miles, 5 × 30-sec strides (PE 8.5)	
Strengthening	6	Off	7 miles easy	6 miles easy	4-6 miles easy	
Strengthening	7	Off	7 miles easy, 30-35 min tempo run (PE 7.5)	6 miles easy	4-6 miles easy	
Sharpening	8	Off	6 miles, 3 × 1-min, 4 × 30-sec hill repeats (PE 8.5), 2-4 × 10-sec hill repeats (PE 9.5)	5 miles easy	4-6 miles easy	
Sharpening	9	Off	7 miles, 4 × 6-min cruise intervals (PE 7.5)	5 miles easy	4-6 miles easy	
Tapering	10	4 miles easy	4 miles, 6 or 7 × 200-meter reps (PE 9.5)	5 miles easy	4-6 miles, 5 × 30-sec strides (PE 8.5)	

* Use a site such as www.worldwidemetric.com/measurements.html to calculate metric conversions.
** Daily mileage totals **include** recommended speed work.
*** All easy running should be done at a PE of 5.

10K Training From a 40-Mile (64 km) Base*

Phase	Week	Monday	Tuesday	Wednesday	Thursday	
Endurance	1	Off	7 miles**, 5 × 30-sec strides (PE 8.5)	8 miles easy***	5-7 miles easy	
Endurance	2	Off	7 miles, 5 × 30-sec strides (PE 8.5)	9 miles easy	5-7 miles easy	
Endurance	3	Off	7 miles, 5 × 30-sec strides (PE 8.5)	9 miles easy	5-7 miles easy	
Strengthening	4	Off	7 miles, 4 × 800 meters, 2-4 × 400 meters (PE 8.5-9)	7 miles easy	5-7 miles easy	
Strengthening	5	7 miles easy	7 miles, 4 × 45-sec, 5 × 30-sec hills (PE 8.5)	8 miles easy	6-8 miles, 5 × 30-sec strides (PE 8.5)	
Strengthening	6	Off	8 miles easy	7 miles easy	6-8 miles easy	
Strengthening	7	Off	7 miles easy, 35-40 min tempo run (PE 7.5)	7 miles easy	5-7 miles easy	
Sharpening	8	Off	7 miles, 4 × 1-min, 4 × 30-sec hill repeats (PE 8.5), 2-4 × 10-sec hill repeats (PE 9.5)	5 miles easy	5-7 miles easy	
Sharpening	9	Off	8 miles, 5 × 6-min cruise intervals (PE 7.5)	5 miles easy	4-6 miles easy	
Tapering	10	4 miles easy	4 miles, 6 or 7 × 200-meter reps (PE 9.5)	5 miles easy	4-6 miles, 5 × 30-sec strides (PE 8.5)	

* Use a site such as www.worldwidemetric.com/measurements.html to calculate metric conversions.
** Daily mileage totals **include** recommended speed work.
*** All easy running should be done at a PE of 5.

Friday	Saturday	Sunday	Total weekly mileage
5 miles, 7 × 2 min plus pace (PE 6.5)	5 miles easy	7 miles, 5 × 30-sec strides (PE 8.5)	31-33 miles
5 miles, 9 × 2 min plus pace (PE 6.5)	5 miles easy	8 miles easy	34-36 miles
5 miles, 10 × 2 min plus pace (PE 6.5)	5 miles easy	8 miles, 5 × 30-sec strides (PE 8.5)	34-36 miles
7 miles easy, 5 × 6-min cruise intervals (PE 7.5)	5 miles easy	9 miles easy	38-40 miles
5 miles easy	Off	5K race, 9 miles total	38-40 miles
7 miles easy	6 miles, 2 × 1,200 meter, 2 × 800 meter, 2 × 400 meter intervals (PE 8.5)	10 miles easy	40-42 miles
7 miles, 1 set: 400 meter, 800 meter, 1,200 meter, 800 meter, 400 meter intervals (PE 8.5-9)	6 miles easy	10 miles, 5 × 30-sec strides (PE 8.5)	40-42 miles
7 miles, 3 × 800 meter, 6 × 400 meter intervals (PE 8.5-9)	4 miles easy	10 miles easy	36-38 miles
6 miles easy, 3 × 400 meters (PE 9.5), 2 × 5 min plus pace (PE 6.5)	5 miles easy	9 miles easy, 5 × 30-sec strides (PE 8.5)	36-38 miles
3 miles easy	Off	10K race	20-22 before race

Length of easy jog or walk recovery:
Cruise intervals: one to two minutes
Intervals: one-third to equal the interval
Repetitions and sprints: up to five times the length of the repetition

Hill repeats: equal the effort (PE of 8.5 to 9) or up to four times the effort (PE of 9 to 9.8)
Fartlek, including hill fartlek: one to four minutes
Strides: equal the effort

Friday	Saturday	Sunday	Total weekly mileage
7 miles, 7 × 2 min plus pace (PE 6.5)	6 miles easy	9 miles, 5 × 30-sec strides (PE 8.5)	42-44 miles
8 miles, 9 × 2 min plus pace (PE 6.5)	7 miles easy	10 miles easy	46-48 miles
8 miles, 10 × 2 min plus pace (PE 6.5)	7 miles easy	10 miles, 5 × 30-sec strides (PE 8.5)	46-48 miles
6 miles easy, 5 or 6 × 6-min cruise intervals (PE 7.5)	5 miles easy	12 miles easy	42-44 miles
8 miles easy	Off	5K race, 10 miles total	46-48 miles, race
7 miles easy	6 miles, 2 × 1,200 meters, 3 × 800 meters (PE 8.5)	12 miles easy	46-48 miles
7 miles, 1 set: 400, 800, 1,200, 800, 400 meter intervals (PE 8.5-9)	6 miles easy	10 miles, 5 × 30-sec strides (PE 8.5)	42-44 miles
6 miles, 3 × 1,200 meter, 3 × 400 meter intervals (PE 8.5-9)	5 miles easy	10 miles easy	38-40 miles
5 miles easy, 3 × 400 meters (PE 9.5), 2 × 5-min plus pace (PE 6.5)	5 miles easy	9 miles easy, 5 × 30-sec strides (PE 8.5)	36-38 miles
3 miles easy	Off	10K race	20-22 before race

Length of easy jog or walk recovery:
Cruise intervals: one to two minutes
Intervals: one-third to equal the interval
Repetitions and sprints: up to five times the length of the repetition

Hill repeats: equal the effort (PE of 8.5 to 9) or up to four times the effort (PE of 9 to 9.8)
Fartlek, including hill fartlek: one to four minutes
Strides: equal the effort

HALF MARATHON

Since 2003, the half marathon has become the fastest growing race distance in the United States, both in terms of number of finishers and in the number of new races, according to Running USA. For seven consecutive years (2006-2012), the number of 13.1-mile finishers has grown by 10 percent or more each year. From 2011 to 2012 alone, the number of half marathon finishers increased by 14.9 percent, from 1.61 million to 1.85 million finishers. For the first time, 60 percent of U.S. half marathon finishers were women (approximately 1.11 million). According to Running USA's 2013 National Runner Survey, the half marathon is the favorite distance among both men and women (38% men, 43% women).

If you're competitively minded, USA Track & Field also offers a half marathon national masters championship every year. Like the USATF 10K road race national championships, the half marathon national championships awards prizes based on absolute performances and age-graded results. In the 2013 championships, 9 of the top 10 finishers completed the race in age-graded times of 90 percent or higher.

Half Marathon Training From a 20-Mile (32 km) Base*

Phase	Week	Monday	Tuesday	Wednesday	Thursday	
Endurance	1	Off	4 miles**, 5 × 30-sec strides (PE 8.5)	3 miles easy***	2-4 miles easy	
Endurance	2	Off	4 miles, 5 × 30-sec strides, (PE 8.5)	3 miles easy	3-5 miles easy	
Endurance	3	Off	5 miles, 5 × 30-sec strides (PE 8.5)	3 miles easy	3-5 miles easy	
Endurance	4	4 miles easy	5 miles, 7 × 2 min plus pace (PE 6.5)	4 miles easy	3-5 miles easy, 5 × 30-sec strides (PE 8.5)	
Strengthening	5	Off	5 miles easy	4 miles easy	5-7 miles easy	
Strengthening	6	Off	8 miles easy, 7 or 8 × 5-min cruise intervals (PE 7.5)	4 miles easy	4-6 miles easy	
Strengthening	7	Off	7 miles easy, 35-40 min tempo run (PE 7.5)	4 miles easy	4-6 miles easy	
Strengthening	8	5 miles easy	7 miles, 4 × 45-sec, 4 × 30-sec hill repeats (PE 8.5), 2 × 10-sec hill repeats (PE 9.5)	4 miles easy	4-6 miles easy, 5 × 30-sec strides (PE 8.5)	
Strengthening	9	Off	4 miles easy	7 miles easy	4-6 miles easy	
Sharpening	10	Off	5 miles, 2 × 800 meters, 4 × 400 meter intervals (PE 8.5-9), 2 × 100-meter sprints (PE 9.5)	4 miles easy	4-6 miles easy	
Sharpening	11	Off	5 miles, 4 × 6-min cruise intervals (PE 7.5)	5 miles easy	4-6 miles easy	
Tapering	12	3 miles easy	6 miles easy	3 miles easy	3-5 miles easy, 6 × 20-sec strides (PE 8.5)	

* Use a site such as www.worldwidemetric.com/measurements.html to calculate metric conversions.

** Daily mileage totals **include** recommended speed work.

*** All easy running should be done at a PE of 5.

Preparing for the half marathon is similar to preparing for a marathon. Chapter 13 includes valuable information about planning for a marathon that would also be helpful for a runner planning to participate in a half marathon. Chapter 13 also includes details on what to eat and how to plan your running in the days and weeks after a long race that would also apply to a half marathon race.

The half marathon training plans included here are 12 weeks long. They include a 4-week endurance phase, 5-week strengthening phase, 2-week sharpening phase, and a week of tapering.

Feel free to adapt these plans to your own interests. If you like to aqua run, substitute an easy-run day for a day in the pool. Or take a spinning class. Tailor these plans to your interests, listen to your body, and stay in the driver's seat. Having gotten to the end of this chapter, are you wondering whether you feel like taking on the marathon?

Friday	Saturday	Sunday	Total weekly mileage
4 miles, 6 × 2 min plus pace (PE 6.5)	3 miles easy	5 miles, 5 × 30-sec strides (PE 8.5)	21-23 miles
4 miles, 7 × 2 min plus pace (PE 6.5)	3 miles easy	6 miles easy	23-25 miles
5 miles, 8 × 2 min plus pace (PE 6.5)	3 miles easy	7 miles, 5 × 30-sec strides (PE 8.5)	26-28 miles
4 miles easy	Off	10K race, 8 miles total	28-30 miles
5 miles easy	4 miles easy, 5 × 800 meters (PE 8.5)	9 miles easy	32-34 miles
5 miles easy, 2 × 1,200 meter, 2 × 800 meter, 1 × 400 meter intervals (PE 8.5-9)	3 miles easy	10 miles easy, 5 × 30-sec strides (PE 8.5)	34-36 miles
6 miles, 5 × 1,000 meter intervals (PE 8.5)	3 miles easy	12 miles easy	36-38 miles
6 miles easy	Off	10K to 10-mile race, 10 miles total	36-38 miles
4 miles easy	4 miles easy, 6 × 30-sec strides (PE 8.5)	13 miles easy	36-38 miles
8 miles, 35-40 min tempo run (PE 7.5)	3 miles easy	10 miles easy, 5 × 30-sec strides (PE 8.5)	34-36 miles
6 miles easy, 4 × 45-sec, 2 × 30-sec hill repeats (PE 8.5), 2 × 10-sec hill repeats (PE 9.5)	3 miles easy	9 miles easy	32-34 miles
3 miles easy	Off	Half marathon	18-20 miles before race

Length of easy jog or walk recovery:
Cruise intervals: one to two minutes
Intervals: one-third to equal the interval
Repetitions and sprints: up to five times the length of the repetition

Hill repeats: equal the effort (PE of 8.5 to 9) or up to four times the effort (PE of 9 to 9.8)
Fartlek, including hill fartlek: one to four minutes
Strides: equal the effort

Half Marathon Training From a 30-Mile (48 km) Base*

Phase	Week	Monday	Tuesday	Wednesday	Thursday	
Endurance	1	Off	6 miles**, 6 × 30-sec strides (PE 8.5)	4 miles easy***	4- 6 miles easy	
Endurance	2	Off	6 miles, 6 × 30-sec strides (PE 8.5)	4 miles easy	5-7 miles easy	
Endurance	3	Off	6 miles, 6 × 30-sec strides (PE 8.5)	3 miles easy	5-7 miles easy	
Endurance	4	6 miles easy	8 miles, 8-9 × 2 min. plus pace (PE of 6.5)	4 miles easy	4-6 miles easy, 6 × 30-sec strides (PE 8.5)	
Strengthening	5	Off	8 miles easy	6 miles easy	5-7 miles easy	
Strengthening	6	Off	9 miles easy, 8 or 9 × 5-min cruise intervals (PE 7.5)	7 miles easy	4-6 miles easy	
Strengthening	7	Off	8 miles easy, 40-45 min tempo run (PE 7.5)	6 miles easy	5-7 miles easy	
Strengthening	8	6 miles easy	8 miles, 4 × 45-sec, 4 × 30-sec hills (PE 8.5), 2 × 10-sec hill repeats (PE 9.5)	6 miles easy	5-7 miles easy, 5 × 30-sec strides (PE 8.5)	
Strengthening	9	Off	8 miles easy	6 miles easy	5-7 miles easy	
Sharpening	10	Off	6 miles, 5 × 800 meter, 4 × 200 meter intervals (PE 8.5-9), 2 × 100-meter sprints (PE 9.5)	5 miles easy	5-7 miles easy	
Sharpening	11	Off	8 miles, 5 × 6-min cruise intervals (PE 7.5)	4 miles easy	3-5 miles easy	
Tapering	12	5 miles easy	6 miles easy, 4 × 400 meter intervals (PE 8.5-9)	5-7 miles easy	3 miles easy, 6 × 20-sec strides (PE 8.5)	

* Use a site such as www.worldwidemetric.com/measurements.html to calculate metric conversions.
** Daily mileage totals **include** recommended speed work.
*** All easy running should be done at a PE of 5.

Half Marathon Training From a 40-Mile (64 km) Base*

Phase	Week	Monday	Tuesday	Wednesday	Thursday	
Endurance	1	Off	7 miles**, 5 × 30-sec strides (PE 8.5)	6 miles easy***	6-8 miles easy	
Endurance	2	Off	7 miles, 5 × 30-sec strides (PE 8.5)	8 miles easy	7-9 miles easy	
Endurance	3	Off	7 miles, 5 × 30-sec strides (PE 8.5)	8 miles easy	6-8 miles easy	
Endurance	4	7 miles easy	7 miles, 9 or 10 × 2 min plus pace (PE 6.5)	7 miles easy	6-8 miles, 6 × 30-sec strides (PE 8.5)	
Strengthening	5	Off	8 miles easy, 4 × 45-sec, 5 × 30-sec hill repeats (PE 8.5)	7 miles easy	6-8 miles, 5 × 30-sec strides (PE 8.5)	
Strengthening	6	Off	8 miles easy, 9 or 10 × 5-min cruise intervals	8 miles easy	7-9 miles easy	
Strengthening	7	4 miles easy	8 miles easy, 45-50 min tempo run (PE 7.5)	7 miles easy	6-8 miles easy	
Strengthening	8	7 miles easy	7 miles, 6 × 1-min, 4 × 30-sec hill repeats (PE 8.5), 2 × 10-sec hill repeats (PE 9.5)	8 miles easy	6-8 miles easy, 5 × 30-sec strides (PE 8.5)	
Strengthening	9	5 miles easy	7 miles easy	7 miles easy	5-7 miles easy	
Sharpening	10	Off	7 miles, 6-8 × 800 meter intervals (PE 8.5-9.0), 2 × 100-meter sprints (PE 9.5)	8 miles easy	6-8 miles easy	
Sharpening	11	Off	8 miles easy, 6-7 × 6-min cruise intervals (PE 7.5)	5 miles easy	6-8 miles	
Tapering	12	5 miles easy	5 miles, 4 × 400 meter intervals (PE 8.5-9)	4 miles easy	5-7 miles, 6 × 20-sec strides (PE 8.5)	

* Use a site such as www.worldwidemetric.com/measurements.html to calculate metric conversions.
** Daily mileage totals **include** recommended speed work.
*** All easy running should be done at a PE of 5.

Friday	Saturday	Sunday	Total weekly mileage
5 miles, 7 × 2 min plus pace (PE 6.5)	5 miles easy	7 miles, 5 × 30-sec strides (PE 8.5)	31-33 miles
6 miles, 9 × 2 min plus pace (PE 6.5)	5 miles easy	8 miles easy	34-36 miles
7 miles, 10 × 2 min plus pace (PE 6.5)	7 miles easy	10 miles, 5 × 30-sec strides (PE 8.5)	38-40 miles
5 miles easy	Off	10K race, 11 miles total	38-40 miles
7 miles easy	6 miles easy, 6 × 800 meter intervals (PE 8.5- 9)	10 miles easy	42-44 miles
6 miles easy, 4 × 1,200 meter intervals (PE 8.5- 9)	6 miles easy	12 miles easy, 5 × 30-sec strides (PE 8.5)	44-46 miles
7 miles, 4 × 1,200 meter strides (PE 8.5)	5 miles easy	13 miles easy	44-46 miles
5 miles easy	Off	10K to 10-mile race, 12 miles total	42-44 miles
6 miles easy	5 miles easy, 5 × 30-sec strides (PE 8.5)	14 miles easy	44-46 miles
9 miles easy, 40-45 min tempo run (PE 7.5)	6 miles easy	11 miles easy, 5 × 30-sec strides (PE 8.5)	42-44 miles
5 miles easy, 4 × 1-min, 2 × 30-sec hill repeats (PE 8.5), 2-4 × 10-sec hills (PE 9.5)	3 miles easy	9 miles easy	38-40 miles
3 miles easy	Off	Half marathon	22-24 before race

Length of easy jog or walk recovery:
Cruise intervals: one to two minutes
Intervals: one-third to equal the interval
Repetitions and sprints: up to five times the length of the repetition

Hill repeats: equal the effort (PE of 8.5 to 9) or up to four times the effort (PE of 9 to 9.8)
Fartlek, including hill fartlek: one to four minutes
Strides: equal the effort

Friday	Saturday	Sunday	Total weekly mileage
7 miles, 7 × 2 min plus pace (PE 6.5)	6 miles easy	9 miles, 5 × 30-sec strides (PE 8.5)	42-44 miles
7 miles, 9 × 2 min plus pace (PE 6.5)	7 miles easy	10 miles easy	46-48 miles
7 miles, 10 × 2 min plus pace (PE 6.5)	6 miles easy	12 miles, 5 × 30-sec strides (PE 8.5)	46-48 miles
7 miles easy	Off	10K race, 10 miles total	44-46 miles
6 miles easy	5 miles easy	14 miles easy	46-48 miles
8 miles easy	7 miles, 5 × 1,000 meter intervals (PE 8.5-9)	12 miles easy	50-52 miles
7 miles, 1 set: 400, 800, 1,200, 1,200, 800, 400 meter intervals (PE 8.5-9)	5 miles easy	13 miles, 5 × 30-sec strides (PE 8.5)	50-52 miles
6 miles easy	Off	10K to 10-mile race, 12 miles total	46-48 miles
6 miles easy	5 miles easy, 5 × 30-sec strides (PE 8.5)	15 miles easy	50-52 miles
9 miles easy, 45-50 min tempo run (PE 7.5)	4 miles easy	12 miles easy, 5 × 30-sec strides (PE 8.5)	46-48 miles
6 miles easy, 4 × 30-sec hill repeats (PE 8.5), 4 × 10-sec hill repeats (PE 9.5)	7 miles easy	10 miles easy	42-44 miles
3 miles easy	Off	Half marathon	22-24 miles before half marathon

Length of easy jog or walk recovery:
Cruise intervals: one to two minutes
Intervals: one-third to equal the interval
Repetitions and sprints: up to five times the length of the repetition

Hill repeats: equal the effort (PE of 8.5 to 9) or up to four times the effort (PE of 9 to 9.8)
Fartlek, including hill fartlek: one to four minutes
Strides: equal the effort

Runner Profile: Kathy Martin

Date of birth: Sept. 30, 1951, in Ontario, Canada

Personal Information

- I served as a nurse in Ottawa and moved to United States in 1975.

- I met my husband, Chuck Gross, skiing in Canada and it was easier for me to relocate as a nurse. He had his own business on Long Island. He was divorced and had a 9-year-old son, Chris, who thought he had found a new playmate when I arrived.

- Worked as nurse and went to C.W. Post for a bachelor of science degree and then worked in the emergency room and intensive care unit. I was going to go to law school to become a patient ombudsman but could not face so many more years of school.

- In 1981, I began a real estate career and I am currently employed as broker. I just transferred listening and people skills from one profession to another.

John Keklak.

- I started running at age 30, having realized the lack of cardio even though I was not overweight.

Open Personal Bests

- 5K (road) 17:23 (38)
- 10K (road) 36:54

Personal Bests at 50 to 59

- 5,000 meters 17:49
- 5K (road) 17:43
- 10K (road) 36:31 (51)
- Half marathon 1:23:27

Age-Graded Personal Bests

- Syracuse at 60 yrs old 100+%; 5K (road): 100.35% (19:04 at age 60)
- Marathon: Set new American record for a 60-year-old woman in the Chicago 2011 marathon; Marathon: 97% (3:10:27 at age 60, American record)

Cathy Utzschneider: Can you list your American or world records and national masters titles?

Kathy Martin: 20 to 25 American and national records and five or six indoor world records.

Cathy: Were your parents runners and are there other runners in your family?

Kathy: There were no runners in my family. They are all smokers and couch potatoes. My husband always ran and I just thought I could run with him. He is the one who has been my biggest advocate. I don't think I would have discovered the hidden talent or passion if he had not led the charge. There are so many other athletes I admire, particularly masters athletes. I love the camaraderie and truly believe we are all so happy to see our friends and competitors at these events, to see them healthy and pursuing fitness for life. They are so inspiring.

Cathy: In a typical year, how often do you race?

Kathy: I race probably 12 to 15 times a year.

Cathy: What is your favorite race distance or event?

Kathy: I love the 5K. You run hard but not for long. I do not enjoy the long runs. I'm too impatient to get it done and get on with other events of the day. I guess you could say I have a short attention span.

Cathy: How has your training changed over the decades?

Kathy: My training has changed to include more stretching and cross-training. For years, I would just run and then you begin to notice changes—a little more stiff, a longer warm-up needed. I used to do back-to-back hard workouts but now recognize that I need an easy day between. Recovery time is noticeably longer. I include massage, chiropractic, and occasionally physical therapy as needed to ensure good running form and longevity. Stretching is crucial as is some form of cross-training.

Cathy: Can you give an example of a typical training week for a 5K?

Kathy: My typical week is about 35 to 40 miles (56-64 km) when I am in good running form. I am currently building up to that postinjury. Running the 10K in Dedham (national 10K masters championship), I recognized I had no business racing a 10K with so little mileage. Lesson learned.

> Monday: yoga
>
> Tuesday: speed of some sort, (e.g., repeat miles or 3:50 repeats)
>
> Wednesday: trail run
>
> Thursday: short speed workout (Went to the track for first time postinjury in one and half years. Oh my! Tough.)
>
> Friday: easy 5 miles (8 km)
>
> Saturday: 5-7 miles (8-11 km)
>
> Sunday: long run of 10-12 miles (16-19 km)

Cathy: What advice do you have for masters runners?

Kathy: Listen to your body! Do not try to run through injuries. You will be stronger and run longer if you take care of the assets. Remember the old adage that our mothers taught us about moderation in everything

Cathy: You recently had one of your first injuries. What was it and do you have any idea how you became injured?

Kathy: I had a fractured left femoral condyle and could not run for three months. I had just started to train hard and about six months later I had a fractured right femoral condyle. The only variable in my training over 30 years was the addition of a trainer for weight workouts. I truly believe too much weight lifting contributed to the fractures. After the second fracture, I was told absolutely not a step of running as the fracture was contained. If it broke through the capsule, I would be looking at a knee replacement. Yikes. That got my attention so absolutely, I didn't run a step. I had a lot of extra time on my hands but really felt as if life was out of sync. After the first fracture I was swimming at least three days per week and running in the pool. I

(continued)

was not allowed to do the same thing with the right leg so I gained a few pounds. Of course, the first thing everyone thought was osteoporosis, but I had always had the DEXA scans for bone density, and there were no changes, so that was not the cause.

Cathy: How long was your break from racing and running?

Kathy: Basically a year.

Cathy: How was life different, given that you were away from running and racing?

Kathy: It was a tough year mentally, but I just kept telling myself I was in it for longevity. I walked a lot. I had a lot more time, but I am not sure I used it constructively. I have run most mornings for over 30 years, so I felt out of sync and at odds for a while. I also believe that affected my business. As we all know our economy took a hit and the real estate business was anything but normal. So it all coincided with being able to work more and focus on business and family. My grandson is 11 so I got to spend more time with him.

Cathy: What advice do you have for other masters regarding bouncing back from injuries?

Kathy: Listen to your body. It tells you what it needs. Know your body. Incorporate other modalities into your training. Do not just run. Have patience. You will prevail. A year ago I thought I might not return to the previous level of fitness but now believe I am on my way. It truly is a long road back but we have time. Perhaps patience was the lesson to be learned.

Cathy: Do you have other thoughts to offer?

Kathy: Keep on keeping on. We are the role models for the upcoming generation. Continue to have fun and keep fit for life.

Chapter 13

Marathon

Is the marathon for you? It is a favorite race among masters runners for many reasons: performance, a test of endurance, a streak showing consistency over years, or contributing to a charity and cause larger than oneself. Running for charity has been a popular reason to run marathons for decades. According to a 2010 story in the *New York Times*, nearly 80 percent of the 36,550 participants in the 2010 London Marathon ran for charities, raising $81 million (Robbins). According to Running USA (2013), in 2012 46 percent of marathon finishers were over age 40. Fifty-nine percent of 2012 Boston Marathon finishers were over age 40.

As a young masters runner, it's possible to compete at elite levels. According to a 2011 story in *Running Times*, of the more than 300 men and women who qualified for the 2012 U.S. Olympic Marathon Trials, 22 were 40 or older, and 21 of them were women. Three—Colleen De Reuck, Linda Somers Smith, and Sheri Piers—surpassed the women's A standard of 2:39:00 (De Reuck also qualified at 49 for the 2016 Olympic Marathon Trials with a time of 2:39:22). The only male, Mbarak Hussein, qualified for his second straight U.S. Olympic Trials Marathon as a masters runner with a 2:16:58 in 2010, well under the men's A standard of 2:19:00 (Kissane 2011).

PLAN, BUT BE FLEXIBLE

Chapter 10 stressed the importance of planning and more planning. That is nowhere more true than in the case of the marathon, which because of its length, requires more planning and practice than the shorter races. Put it this way: you can't plan too much. You need to look months ahead and consider many factors beyond those related to running: work commitments, family obligations, community involvement. They may determine which marathon you choose.

Once you've picked your marathon, begin by planning dates for your long runs. Just sneaking in an 18 or 20 miler (29 or 32 km) doesn't usually work. You probably want to find others to run with. And you want to plan to back off just a bit before and after those long runs. In short, you need to plan, plan, plan. A form that can help you plan ahead is the big-picture calendar found in chapter 7.

Just as important as planning is flexibility. I've yet to see a marathon plan followed exactly. Over three or more months stuff happens. You pull a calf muscle. A parent falls ill. Work pressures mount unexpectedly. Like the plans for shorter distances, the marathon plans later in this chapter are guidelines for you to tailor to your needs. Like the other plans for shorter races, the marathon plans are guidelines based on a foundation of 20, 30, and 40 miles (32, 48, 64 km).

So what choices do you have? First, you might lengthen these 16-week plans, which include a 5-week endurance phase, 6-week strengthening phase, 2-week sharpening phase, and 3 weeks of tapering. Should you want more time to build to your marathon, repeat several weeks. Say you want 20 weeks to build to your marathon: repeat weeks 5 and 6 and then also 6 and 7, so you add 4 weeks to the existing 16. Second, you may want to add more mileage per week by adding, for example, 2 to 6 miles (3.2-9.6 km) in the middle of each week. While the three plans peak at 44, 54, and 64 miles (71, 87, 103 km) per week, you can add mileage for a higher peak. If you want to lower weekly mileage a bit, rest on a short or medium easy-run day or use it for cross-training.

PRACTICE, PRACTICE, PRACTICE

Practice for the marathon includes not just running but many other considerations as well. Focus on long and tempo runs and staying hydrated and fueled. Pay attention to recovery, learning how much rest you need before and after long runs and maintaining healthy sleep habits. Stretching and injury-prevention measures and continuing to say "no" to too many other life commitments so you can stay focused on your training are also important. Three weeks before your marathon consider a dress rehearsal of race logistics. Gather together and try on race accessories and clothing, including shoes, so you have time to buy and run in new ones. Also think about prerace meals to eliminate last minute questions. The less uncertainty before your race, the better.

LONG RUNS AND TEMPO RUNS

Long runs and tempo runs are essential for a strong marathon for a variety of reasons. Faster running, such as intervals at a perceived exertion (PE) of 8.5, is important, but long runs and tempo runs are essential and particularly challenging. It helps to know why they are so important. (Most runners would prefer to run shorter, more intense intervals at a PE of 8.5 or higher than shorter intervals at a comfortably hard pace, or perceived exertion of 7.5.)

First, the principle of specificity applies. Long runs at a moderately intense pace will prepare you to run 26.2 miles (42 km). Tempo runs, usually 15 to 20 seconds per mile faster than goal marathon pace, make marathon pace feel easier and more manageable.

Second, fat and carbohydrate are our two main sources of fuel for exercise. Fat provides an unlimited source of fuel for lower-intensity exercise while carbohydrate provides a limited source that fuels exercise at a moderate to high intensity, such as a 5K. Tempo runs—longer runs at higher rates of exertion—teach your body to use fat for fuel. If you rely just on carbohydrate to fuel a marathon, you'll become tired when you run low on it. (The energy supply of carbohydrate and fat is inversely related. The more carbohydrate you burn, the less fat you burn.) Burning more fat and delaying burning carbohydrate produces a more stable and longer energy supply. Even if you have just 6 percent body fat, you have plenty of fat to fuel running for many hours.

How do long and tempo runs help? These runs increase the number and size of mitochondria, the organelles that convert fat in the presence of oxygen into energy. The more mitochondria you have, the more fat you metabolize, the more you produce adenosine triphosphate (ATP), a molecule that exists in all cells. The body's major currency of energy, ATP temporarily stores energy and then releases in its high phosphate bonds. The more ATP you have, the more energy you have. Long runs of 90 minutes produce more mitochondria than 60-minute runs and more mitochondria than you'd build by splitting your 90-minute run into two 45-minute runs (Schulman 2000). Some research has shown that in highly trained endurance athletes, the activity of enzymes that break down fat is as much as 100 percent higher than in untrained subjects (Schulman 2000). Endurance athletes then have a much greater ability to regenerate the ATP that fuels muscle contraction than do untrained subjects who rely more on carbohydrate.

Third, both long runs and tempo runs build strength. Speed comes from strength. Joan Miller, 57, one of my masters athletes who ran her first marathon at age 56, was concerned that she would lose her 5K speed. Hardly. Running in the Freihofer's 5K race just six weeks after the Boston Marathon she ran her fastest 5K ever, thanks to her marathon training.

All of this is not to say that short intervals are unnecessary. They should be included in training to help increase raw speed, stride rate, and running economy.

Trusting perceived exertion on long and tempo runs can be especially challenging because you're running so many miles. In marathon training and racing, focusing on effort, or perceived exertion, for long or tempo runs can give you a feeling of control, confidence, and motivation that is essential for performance. By contrast, focusing on pace can be demoralizing because it is outside your control: it will vary depending on how you feel, the weather, your sneakers, or the course, for example.

Not only masters but also elite open runners have reported that focusing on effort rather than pace in marathon training and in the race itself resulted not just in increased confidence, control, and motivation but also in improved results. Boston College assistant men's track and field coach, Tim Ritchie, 26, described his experience of focusing on pace while training for his first marathon, the 2013 Boston Marathon, and his experience focusing on effort for his second marathon, the 2013 Twin Cities Marathon:

> On the buildup for Boston I did a series of long runs at a pace believed to be my potential marathon pace. Most of these runs were done on the Boston course and began at a steady-run pace and quickly progressed to a fast sustainable pace over 10 to 20 miles (16-32 km). Although this without a doubt increased my fitness, it also brought along expectations of what a certain minute per mile pace felt like and the incorrect assessment that a certain pace one day would feel the same the next. I sacrificed long runs over two hours for fast runs under two hours. The result was facing the unknown when I found myself running 2:10 into the marathon, and I still had 2 miles to go.
>
> Many things on race day influence your perceived effort: the crowd, the hype, the weather, the course, your emotions, and so on. When I was hitting mile splits slower than I had been in training, but feeling worse, it was detrimental to my confidence going forward in the race. The marathon is quite long and there are good miles and bad miles, but my expectations of a certain pace prevented me from racing based on effort.
>
> Going into the Twin Cities Marathon, I opted for long runs for time or mileage instead of pace. To balance this I added in more races and a few key quality workouts. This balance allowed me to get used to both running fast (pace) and running long. All of my long runs and workouts were based on effort to the point where I was aware of what a comfortable marathon pace felt like, but did not have a specific minute per mile pace tied to that.
>
> For the race itself, I began to run at a familiar effort (not time) and let the splits be what they were. I let that effort dictate how I ran up the hills and down the hills, how I ran the first 10 miles (16 km) compared to how I ran the last 10 miles. I was very much in control of my effort; whereas, splits are much harder to control. The marathon being what it is, means control is a key element of success. When you lose control, the battle to the finish line becomes a much more difficult one.
>
> The result in Boston was a 2:21:31, after coming through the half in 1:06:30 and bonking the whole way down Beacon Street. The result in Twin Cities was a 2:14:50, coming through the half in 1:07:40, feeling consistent and controlled from mile 1 to mile 26.

RECOVERY AND SLEEP

As you put in more miles of training, you may well need more sleep. Over the years, masters have reported that they need an hour more of sleep each night during peak marathon training, a time when they're often running 20 more miles

(32 km) a week than their usual mileage. Establish consistent sleep habits if you haven't already. Plan to leave social occasions before 10:30 p.m. the week before the marathon. On the night before the marathon, it's hard for many runners to get a full night's sleep, given race day anxiety and the logistics of waking up early to get to the start. Don't worry if you get just five hours of sleep that night. It's still possible to run a fast marathon the next day. While a completely sleepless night may adversely affect performance because it can limit the muscles' ability to use glucose, as little as four and a half hours of sleep have no negative effect on glucose metabolism (Schmid et al. 2008).

HABITS FOR INJURY PREVENTION

Get used to listening to your body and respecting its needs. If it's telling you to take a day off or back off, do that. If you miss a day or two of training, don't try to make up missed mileage. See a chiropractor or massage therapist—if possible, the same person, so he or she knows your body—at least once every two weeks. Make a practice of massaging your legs with a stick or roller after long runs. Don't forget to stretch. Buy new shoes at least once every 300 to 500 miles (482-805 km). Cross-train if your body is telling you not to run. All these habits will help you get to the marathon starting line healthy.

HYDRATING HABITS

Like everything related to the marathon, hydrating is something to practice. Staying hydrated is essential not just for running performance, but it also prevents heat-related illnesses: dehydration (which leads to fatigue), headaches, impaired coordination, and muscle cramping. While losing 2 percent of your starting body weight in a marathon is expected, losing more than that through dehydration often results in slower performance. If, for example, you weigh 140 pounds (63 kg) at the beginning of a marathon and finish weighing 137 pounds (62 kg), you have kept your weight nearly neutral for body water loss and hydrated adequately. If your weight drops significantly below 137 pounds, however, your performance may be impaired.

Marathon hydrating guidelines follow and reiterate and expand on the general hydrating guidelines outlined in chapter 3. First, limit consumption of alcohol during the two or three days before the marathon. Alcohol dehydrates the body, inhibiting its ability to store glycogen. Alcohol also impairs sleep. Second, don't always trust thirst as the perfect indication of a fluid deficit.

Sometimes you need fluids before you start to feel thirsty. If you don't know your sweat rate (discussed later), depending on the weather conditions and your size, sip four to eight ounces (118-237 ml) of fluid every 15 to 20 minutes, or every two to three miles (3.2-4.8 km). Third, foods or sport drinks containing 5 to 6 percent carbohydrate and containing electrolytes such as sodium and potassium help promote fluid retention. You're well hydrated if you void large volumes of pale urine (the color of light lemonade, not apple juice) at least six times a day.

You can practice learning specifically how much fluid you should ingest in a marathon by figuring out your sweat rate. It's simple.

Runner Profile: Linda Somers Smith

Date of birth: May 7, 1961

Personal Information

- Attorney in San Luis Obispo, California
- Married to Scott Smith
- One daughter, Monica
- Started focused training at age 27

Open Personal Bests

- 5K (road) 15:48 (35)
- 10K (road) 31:40 (35)
- Half marathon 1:11:01 (36)
- Marathon 2:30:06 (35)

Personal Bests at 40 to 49

- 5K (road) 16:14 (48)
- 10K (road) 33:39 (49)
- Half marathon 1:13:32 (49)
- Marathon 2:36:33 (48)

Personal Bests at 50 to 59

- 10K (road) 34:14 (51)
- Half marathon 1:15:18 (50)
- Marathon 2:37:36 (50)

Courtesy of Scott Smith

Cathy Utzschneider: Since you started running, what lessons have you learned about masters running that you would want other masters to know?

Linda Somers Smith: I started running at 21 and actually was much stronger in my 30s than in my 20s. After turning 30, I had almost seven years of running behind me (I didn't run from 23 to 26) and could handle a lot more work. In addition, life had progressed where it was more stable—stable job, not moving around—so I had the opportunity and ability to join a consistent training group, combined with a stable lifestyle. I did a great deal of heavy training and racing in my 30s, and the real change came when I hit about 38. Whether it was the miles, age, or genetics (or all three), I am not sure, but I started to have chronic problems that limited training and reduced my enjoyment of running considerably. I had assumed the chronic conditions were permanent and struggled through the next four to five years, not enjoying running much. When I assumed I would be OK with not running again, I decided to try the surgeries recommended. These actually addressed both my chronic problems, by which time I was 45. I feel like I missed years 39 to 45 in terms of exploring my real running potential at those times; but at 45, not having the pain felt so great, it was like starting over and I felt younger and better than before.

Cathy: Do you have a favorite race distance and if so, what is it?

Linda: My favorite distance has changed over time. It used to be 5 miles (8 km), then the marathon, and now it is the half marathon. The marathon is just so hard on my body, but I can get through a half pretty well.

Cathy: Injuries are part of our lives as runners. How do you view them when you encounter them?

Linda: I have had an injury-plagued career, which may be a reason I have run as long as I have; I've had a lot of time, years, off. My attitude toward injuries depends on the injury. I have been running so long, I am pretty good, not always right but close, at gauging pain and its significance. I can tell if an injury is serious right way or one that just requires training modifications.

That is not to say I don't cross the line. For example, when the 2012 marathon trials were coming up, I had an Achilles and ankle injury that required modification at a key time in training, but I pushed through it, knowing after the marathon it would be a true injury. I would not recommend a younger athlete with plenty of time do this, because significant injuries can risk a career. Basically, I treat injures in a hierarchy from treatment and complete time off to running through them. I am very good at cross-training, so if I can't run I don't find it difficult to cross-train. I don't like not being able to run, but if you can't, you can't and there is no sense being miserable about it.

In terms of cross-training, I used to be much better at it, and would hit the pool, bike, or gym immediately. Now, I am less intense, maybe because I don't have the energy or sense of urgency to maintain fitness. I figure the fitness will come back when I start running, and I don't feel as if it is going to give me a make-or-break performance if I stay in the best shape I can.

Cathy: Many masters today enter marathons. Can you give a sample week of peak training for a marathon?

Linda:

> Monday – easy 8-12 miles (13-19 km), off, or swim
>
> Tuesday – tempo 4-12 miles (6.4-19 km) at below marathon pace
>
> Wednesday – easy 8-12 miles
>
> Thursday – easy 12-13 miles (19-20.9 km) with pickups or, if feeling good, run last 4 miles (6.4 km) at tempo pace (marathon pace plus 20 seconds)
>
> Friday – intervals on track (400 to 1,600 meters or 3,200-meter reps), total of 6 miles (9.6 km)
>
> Saturday – easy 8-12 miles and swim
>
> Sunday – easy 16-22 miles (26-35 km) and swim

On alternate weeks:

> Monday – easy 8-12 miles (13-19 km)
>
> Tuesday – interval workouts (400 to 1,600 meters or 3,200-meter reps), total of 6 miles (9.6 km)
>
> Wednesday – easy 8-12 miles
>
> Thursday – 8-12 miles, last 6-8 miles (9.7-13 km) run at tempo pace (marathon pace plus 20 seconds)
>
> Friday – easy 5-8 mile (8-13 km) run or swim 1 hour and 10 minutes
>
> Saturday – bike 30-40 miles (48-64 km) at effort followed by 8-10 miles (13-16 km) at marathon pace
>
> Sunday – 16-22 miles (26-35 km) plus swim

Cathy: What advice would you give masters runners who want to set a marathon possible goal, train for it, and reflect on it afterward?

(continued)

Linda: Depending on your level of commitment and your goal, the marathon can be a hard event to train for as a master and can also be difficult to recover from. Keep in mind, I say this as a competitive runner, so I don't run a marathon unless I train for it. As a master, you can run a marathon off basic training if you do so in a relaxed fashion and set a realistic goal; however, if you want to set a time goal, then that requires discipline in training, type of training, rest, and managing all that with the rest of your life. You can do it—plenty of people do—but you have to stay organized. Most masters runners have jobs and families, so all training has to be integrated into one's life. I use my training both for training and also as a social outlet. If you truly want to train and set goals as a masters runner, I recommend training with a consistent training group. The training group helps you improve and also allows you to set realistic goals. For example, if you are running with 2:50 marathoners in training and races, you have a good idea of what you can do; however, if you are running with the 3:20 group, it probably isn't wise to set a goal of a 2:50 marathon until you can complete the workouts that would suggest that goal is achievable.

Cathy: If there's a day when you're unusually tired or stressed, do you adjust your training and, if so, can you give an example?

Linda: Inevitably during any one week, I have a day with too much going on, too much stress, or not enough time to run. I try to run in the early morning so my day doesn't get away from me. However, some days, if I have an early-morning meeting, I can't fit the run in without getting up at a ridiculously early hour. I don't ever set a day off, but allow myself a floating day off each week. I let the week dictate which day I will take off. It might be a day I had a workout planned, and if so, I just move it to the next day. If I don't do it this way and have a planned day off, I sometimes end up having to take two off.

Cathy: Do you have recommendations regarding sleep during preparation for the marathon?

Linda: Sleep is probably the most difficult issue for me because I love to sleep and hard training increases the need; however, there are sometimes just not enough hours in the day. I tend to sleep in on weekends, which makes it difficult to meet a training group, but if I didn't do that, I would not get enough sleep.

Cathy: Any thoughts on the marathon and fueling and hydrating?

Linda: I have never put much thought into this, because fueling and hydration seem like easy issues. However, having watched my husband in triathlons, I understand that the type of fuel and hydration, as well as timing, can be crucial. I have always had the luxury of having my own water bottles on my marathon courses, so I haven't had to worry too much. My bottles have my drink in the mixture I prefer and have tested in training runs. In a marathon I carry one or two power gels with me, so I can take those at 15 to 21 miles (24-34 km). I try to take the gels regardless of whether I want to, because your body's signals aren't always timed to need in a marathon. For example, by the time you are thirsty, you have probably gone too long without hydration.

In terms of prerace fueling, I eat sensibly the day before. I do not carbo-load. If I am going to stuff carbs, I'll do it two or three days before the race, not the day before. The day before, I eat lightly and avoid heavy foods. Some people can drink the night before a race, maybe a glass of wine; I can't. I avoid all alcohol for two to three weeks leading up to a race.

Cathy: Do you have a perspective on the marathon that can help with training and racing the distance?

Linda: In term of perspective, just run what makes you happy. If running the local 10K with friends leaves you refreshed and keeps you motivated, then enjoy that. If traveling to London, combined with a marathon, sounds like fun, plan that. If you want to set a time goal, pick a flat course and consider the weather. There is no one-size-fits-all advice except to keep putting one foot in front of the other and stay uninjured. I find a marathon takes care of itself, provided you prepare. The best way to prepare is to do the necessary training, in particular the longer tempo runs. I find longer tempo runs much more helpful than marathon long runs for performance. Ideally, you should do both, but if you can't do both, 8- to 16-mile (13-26 km) tempo runs in the weeks leading up to the race will get you ready more than just long slow runs.

Masters running is about perspective and balance. Once you are over 40, you have to accept that your best times are behind you. You don't see a lot of really great runners racing later in life because the return is so minimal. With some exceptions, you will not win races or make a living at it, and the investment compared to rate of return just isn't worth it. However, if you continue to incorporate running into your life, socially or for health, you can continue it despite knowing there are no PRs ahead and it might not always be easy or pain free.

I also think it is important to listen to experts and avoid fads. I have been running so long that when someone tells me I should try barefoot running, I can smile and politely decline the recommendation. If someone tells me yogurt is the secret to PRs, I don't need to hang out in the dairy section of the grocery store. Again, masters running is one foot in front of the other, maintaining proper nutrition, staying uninjured, hanging out with other runners who help you maintain your motivation, and working it into a busy lifestyle so that it augments you, not takes away. It can be easy, not always, but usually.

1. Weigh yourself nude before a run.
2. Run (at race pace) for one hour. Do not drink during that hour.
3. After the run, reweigh yourself nude, having toweled off sweat.
4. Subtract your weight after the run from your weight before the run and convert to ounces.
5. To determine how much you should drink about every 15 minutes, divide that number by four. If you have lost 32 ounces (946 ml), drink about 8 ounces (237 ml) of fluid every 15 minutes.
6. Because the test reflects sweat loss based on environmental conditions that day, repeat the test under different conditions to see how they affect your sweat rate. You'll likely get different results under different temperatures, altitudes, and paces.

As important as drinking enough is, make sure you are not overhydrating. Overhydrating can lead to hyponatremia, dangerously low blood salt levels caused by abnormal fluid retention. Such low levels make it difficult for your kidneys to clear extra body fluid. If your weight after a marathon is higher than it was when you started, you have drunk too much. If you are running longer than four hours for the marathon and you do not know your sweat rate, drink each time you feel thirsty to avoid both hyponatremia and dehydration. Also, ingesting snacks like pretzels or fluids with sodium will help promote fluid retention and prevent hyponatremia.

Warning Signs of Dehydration

- Feeling faint or light-headed while standing
- Rapid heart rate
- Sunken eyes
- Dry mouth
- Feeling very thirsty
- Dull headache

Warning Signs of Hyponatremia

- Feeling like water is sloshing in your stomach
- Severe and worsening headache and confusion
- Feeling puffy or bloated in the hands and feet
- Nausea and vomiting
- Upset stomach
- Wheezy breathing
- Fatigue
- Irritability
- Muscle spasms or cramps
- Seizures and even unconsciousness

BALANCED NUTRITION

Balanced nutrition throughout the year and particularly throughout the marathon training months is essential for promoting good health and preventing disease. Months of daily focus on a diet that includes a balance of whole grains, fresh fruits, vegetables, protein-rich foods, and specific polyunsaturated fat will contribute to your best marathon. Balanced nutrition is discussed in chapter 3.

FUELING ON LONG RUNS

Fueling on long runs is individual. During runs longer than 10 miles (16 km), you should consume enough carbohydrate to maintain normal blood sugar levels and to spare your muscle glycogen. Fueling depends to a certain extent on your weight and your preferences. A rule of thumb is to take in about 100 calories of carbohydrate after an hour of running, and then another 100 calories every 40 to 45 minutes after that either as a carbohydrate drink or as food. Find food that is easy to carry and digest, whether a gel, gummies, a sport bar, or sport beans. Many are offered in 100-calorie packets.

Carbohydrate Loading During Training

Your marathon training will help you run better on fat metabolism and store more carbohydrate (CHO) as glycogen. The purpose of carbohydrate loading is to store even more glycogen in your muscles after the normal stores are used up. Normal stores will last for one and a half to two hours of running. Carbohydrate loading is useful for anything longer, such as a marathon.

Loading complex carbohydrate for the three days before the marathon by increasing their percentage to 70 to 80 percent of your daily caloric intake while significantly reducing your training load works as well as any method. Complex carbohydrate produces greater muscle glycogen storage than simple carbohydrate, and the more carbohydrate eaten, the more will be stored. Complex carbohydrate includes whole wheat pasta, spaghetti squash, wild or brown rice, potatoes, sweet potatoes, and grains such as barley. As always with dietary changes, try carbohydrate-loading methods before you use them in your marathon. Table 13.1 outlines a carbohydrate-loading method.

Carbohydrate Loading During Marathon Week

The first day of loading—Thursday, on table 13.1—is the most important. Begin with a breakfast high in carbohydrate, such as pancakes or French toast. This is the day for the traditional pasta dinner of spaghetti and bread. Try to eat as much complex carbohydrate as possible in these two meals. Taper the bulk as the days progress. Do not load on large quantities of fruit or other foods that you don't normally eat. Because fiber in fruit takes longer to digest, eating too much fruit, particularly the night or day before a long run or race, can lead to an upset stomach. The last major meal should be 12 to 15 hours before the race and should not include too much bulk. It should be easily digestible so that it will pass through your system before the race. How will you know if you are effectively loading? If you are keeping a record of your daily weight, you may notice a weight gain of a few pounds over the three-day period. As carbohydrate is stored, water is also stored in your muscles. That leads to weight gain. This water storage may make your legs feel sluggish during your few miles of easy runs, but it may come in handy during the marathon as a source of sweat. You may also feel sleepy, cranky, or tired because of the blood sugar and insulin responses to the carbohydrate. During the race, however, you should feel charged and ready to go.

Table 13.1 Carbohydrate Loading During Marathon Week

Monday	Tuesday	Wednesday	Thursday	Friday	Saturday	Sunday
Regular exercise			Low exercise			
Regular diet			High-carbohydrate diet			Race
(55–60% CHO)			(70–80% CHO)			

Loading carbohydrate coincides with reduced exercise.

DAY BEFORE THE MARATHON

The day before the marathon do nothing but hang around with your feet mostly elevated. Read a book; watch a movie. A runner I know spent the day before the marathon shopping for several hours with her daughter. That was a mistake. She didn't consider shopping exercise, but the day before a marathon it is. Save all extra energy for your race. Also, 24 hours before the marathon, drink 64 to 88 ounces (2-2.6 L). Your body will appreciate the hydrating the next day.

Make a checklist of everything you'll need on race day. Of course you'll need your number and pins to attach to your singlet and the timing chip. Other items you might want to put in your bag include the following:

Clothing for rainy or cold conditions: gloves and a hat or compression tights if you wear them

Small towel

Water bottle

Toilet paper, tissues

Petroleum jelly or Bodyglide to prevent chafing and blisters

Pain reliever

Second pair of running shoes to walk around in before the start of the race

Extra pair of socks

Sunglasses

Sunscreen

Adhesive strips

Small plastic bags for snacks such as jelly beans, energy gel, peanut butter and jelly sandwiches, sport bars

Old clothing and something to sit on while waiting for the marathon to start (These items are usually discarded and donated to charity.)

Know before race day where you will plan to meet family and friends after the marathon.

LAST DINNER: THE NIGHT BEFORE THE MARATHON

Many runners feel nervous the night before a marathon. Because nervousness can upset and hinder the digestive process, it can be helpful to eat a very large snack rather than a full dinner the night before. Smaller meals digest faster than larger ones. Components of a good meal the night before the marathon include the following:

- More carbohydrate and small amounts of fat and protein. Fat and protein take much longer to digest than carbohydrate.
- Foods that are rather bland. Avoid foods that are spicy and that produce gas and may upset the digestive system, such as pepper, broccoli, carbonated beverages, chili powder, cabbage, broccoli, and onions.
- Low-fiber foods. Avoid foods like nuts, raw vegetables, bran, and beans.
- Foods with which you're familiar. Never try new foods during the few days before your marathon.

RACE DAY FUELING AND HYDRATING

Never try anything new on race day. If you usually have a cup of coffee or tea in the morning, have it on marathon day. However, caffeine decreases your ability to spare glycogen so limit it. Two to four hours before your race, eat a light, low-fiber carbohydrate meal that is easily digested, such as a bagel or cereal and a banana. No carbohydrate, especially simple sugars, should be ingested within two hours of the start; this could lead to a blood insulin reaction, causing weakness and fatigue. About two hours before the start, drink 12 to 20 ounces (355-591 ml) of water, giving your body time to process extra fluid. It takes one to one and a half hours to eliminate excess fluids through urination. Ideally, you don't want to have to use the portable toilet at the starting line or soon after you start. Ten to 20 minutes before the race start, drink 6 to 10 ounces (177-296 ml) of cool water. Because your kidneys slow when you start running, last-minute fluid intake will remain in your body, available for sweat and to improve the stomach's ability to digest fluids (Bergeron et al. 2007).

As mentioned earlier, in the marathon itself every 15 to 20 minutes try to drink four to eight ounces (118-237 ml) of water or a combination of water and a sport drink (or the amount you have calculated necessary based on your sweat rate test). Many of my marathoners drink fluids that are 50 percent water and 50 percent sport drink because their stomachs often don't tolerate sport drinks at full strength. Sport drinks are helpful because they enter the bloodstream rapidly and provide water, energy, and electrolytes. Additionally, sip, don't gulp, the fluid to avoid choking. Some runners carry straws for sipping while running.

In terms of fueling, consume about 100 calories of carbohydrate after an hour of running and then another 100 calories every 40 to 45 minutes after that either as a carbohydrate drink or as food. That will help you maintain normal blood sugar levels and avoid bonking. If you're carrying food such as sport bars or sport beans, you can put them in a plastic bag and pin that to your shorts or put it in your bra.

MARATHON TRAINING PLANS

The endurance phase in all plans (weeks 1 through 5) focuses on plus-pace running, strides, building mileage, and on introducing a first tempo run. These are all defined in table 8.1. Besides, plus-pace running builds psychological and physical variety into your runs, and strides wake up your fast-twitch muscle fibers and help you focus on form. The endurance phase includes a 10K race at the end of the third week to establish a time to find your current $\dot{V}O_2$max. The strengthening phase (weeks 6 through 11) continues to build mileage and includes speed work, including intervals and tempo runs longer than those for shorter-distance events, a 10-mile race at the end of week 6, and a half marathon at the end of week 10. The two-week sharpening phase (weeks 12 and 13) focuses on more tempo running and more intensive speed work. The three-week tapering phase (weeks 14 through 16) includes some speed work and lowers mileage. In this phase, weekly mileage is lowered from maximum mileage to about 80 percent in week 14, 60 percent in week 15, and about 30 percent in the last week leading to the marathon.

The plan for runners with a base of 20 miles (32 km) builds to a maximum of 44 miles (71 km) per week and includes one 18-mile (29 km) and two 20-mile (32 km) runs. The plan for runners with a base of 30 miles (48 km) builds to a maximum of 54 miles (87 km) per week and includes one 18-mile, two 20-mile, and one 22-mile (35 km) runs. The plan for runners with a base of 40 miles (64 km) builds to a maximum of 64 miles (103 km) per week and includes two 18-mile runs, one 20-mile run, and two 22-mile runs.

Marathon Training From a 20-Mile (32 km) Base*

Phase	Week	Monday	Tuesday	Wednesday	Thursday**
Endurance	1	Off	4 miles**, 5 × 30-sec strides (PE 8.5)	3 miles easy***	2-4 miles easy
Endurance	2	Off	4 miles, 5 × 30-sec strides (PE 8.5)	3 miles easy	3-5 miles easy
Endurance	3	3 miles easy	5 miles, 5 × 30-sec strides (PE 8.5)	3-5 miles easy	3 miles, 8 × 3 min (PE 6.5)
Endurance	4	Off	5 miles easy	4 miles easy	3-5 miles easy
Endurance	5	Off	4 miles easy	7 miles, 7 × 5-min cruise intervals (PE 7.5)	3-5 miles easy
Strengthening	6	4 miles easy	5 miles, 3 × 800 meter, 2-4 × 400 meter intervals (PE 8.5-9)	4 miles easy	5-7 miles easy
Strengthening	7	Off	7 miles easy	4 miles easy	4-6 miles easy
Strengthening	8	Off	7 miles, 3 × 1,000 meter cruise intervals (PE 7.5), 2 × 1,000 meter intervals (PE 8.5-9)	9 miles easy	6 miles easy
Strengthening	9	Off	7 miles easy	8 miles, 5 or 6 × 1 mile cruise intervals (PE 7.5), 10 min plus pace	5 miles easy
Strengthening	10	5 miles easy	6 miles, 4 × 45-sec, 4 × 30-sec hill repeats (PE of 8.5), 2 × 10-sec hill repeats (PE 9.5)	7 miles easy	6-8 miles, 5 × 30-sec strides (PE 8.5)
Strengthening	11	Off	5 miles easy	8 miles easy	4-6 miles easy
Sharpening	12	3 miles easy	8 miles, 6-mile tempo run (PE 7.5)	4 miles easy	3-5 miles easy
Sharpening	13	Off	7 miles, 5-6 × 1-mile cruise intervals (PE 7.5)	4 miles easy	5-7 miles, 3 × 800 meter intervals (PE 8.5- 9), 2 × 200-meter reps (PE 9.5)
Tapering	14	Off	5 miles easy	8 miles, 8 × 2 min intervals (PE 8.5- 9)	3-5 miles easy
Tapering	15	Off	5 miles, 8 × 1 min strides (PE 8.5)	5 miles easy	Off
Tapering	16	Off	5 miles, 4 × 45 sec (PE 7.5)	6 miles easy	Off

* Use a site such as www.worldwidemetric.com/measurements.html to calculate metric conversions.

** Daily mileage totals **include** recommended speed work.

*** All easy running should be done at a PE of 5.

Friday	Saturday	Sunday	Total weekly mileage
3 miles, 6 × 3 min plus pace (PE 6.5)	3 miles easy	6 miles, 5 × 30-sec strides (PE 8.5)	21-23 miles
4 miles, 7 × 3 min plus pace (PE 6.5)	3 miles easy	7 miles, 5 × 30-sec strides (PE 8.5)	24-26 miles
3 miles easy	Off	10K race, 9 miles total	26-28 miles
4 miles easy	4 miles, 5 × 30-sec strides (PE 8.5)	10 miles easy	30-32 miles
5 miles, 5 × 30-sec strides (PE 8.5)	Off	14 miles easy	33-35 miles
3 miles easy	Off	10-mile race, 12 miles total	35-37 miles
4 miles easy	3 miles, 5 × 30-sec strides (PE 8.5)	18 miles easy	38-40 miles
8 miles, 5 × 8-min cruise intervals (PE 7.5)	Off	14 miles easy	42-44 miles
4 miles easy, 5 × 30-sec strides (PE 8.5)	Off	20 miles easy	42-44 miles
4 miles easy	Off	Half marathon race, 14 miles total	42-44 miles
5 miles, 5 × 30-sec strides (PE 8.5)	4 miles easy	16 miles easy	42-44 miles
6 miles, 5 × 1-min, 4 × 45-sec hill repeats (PE 8.5), 4 × 10-sec hill repeats (PE 9.5)	Off	14 miles easy	38-40 miles
Off	Off	20 miles easy	36-38 miles
4 miles, 6 × 30-sec strides (PE 8.5)	Off	14 miles easy	34-36 miles
6 miles, 6 × 30-sec strides (PE 8.5)	Off	10 miles easy	24-26 miles
3 miles easy	Off	Marathon	14 miles before race

Length of easy jog or walk recovery:

Cruise intervals: one to two minutes

Intervals: one-third to equal the interval

Repetitions and sprints: up to five times the length of the repetition

Hill repeats: equal the effort (PE of 8.5 to 9) or up to four times the effort (PE of 9 to 9.8)

Fartlek, including hill fartlek: one to four minutes

Strides: equal the effort

Marathon Training From a 30-Mile (48 km) Base*

Phase	Week	Monday	Tuesday	Wednesday	Thursday	
Endurance	1	Off	6 miles**, 5 × 30-sec strides (PE 8.5)	5 miles easy***	3-5 miles easy	
Endurance	2	Off	7 miles. 5 × 30-sec strides (PE 8.5)	5 miles easy	3-5 miles easy	
Endurance	3	5 miles easy	7 miles, 5 × 30-sec strides (PE 8.5)	5-7 miles easy	5 miles, 10 × 3 min plus pace (PE 6.5)	
Endurance	4	Off	5 miles easy	5-7 miles easy	8 miles easy	
Endurance	5	Off	7 miles, 8 × 5-min cruise intervals (PE 7.5)	5-7 miles easy	8 miles easy	
Strengthening	6	7 miles easy	7 miles, 4 × 800 meter, 2-4 × 400 meter intervals (PE 8.5)	7-9 miles easy	6-8 miles easy	
Strengthening	7	Off	7 miles easy	6-8 miles easy	7 miles easy	
Strengthening	8	7 miles easy	8 miles, 4 × 1,200 meters, 4 × 400 meter intervals (PE 8.5-9)	9 miles easy	8 miles, 6 × 8-min cruise intervals (PE 7.5)	
Strengthening	9	5 miles easy	7 miles easy	9 miles: 6 or 7 × 1 mile cruise intervals (PE 7.5), 10 min plus pace	5-7 miles easy	
Strengthening	10	4 miles easy	8 miles, 4 × 1-min, 4 × 30-sec hill repeats (PE 8.5), 2 × 10-sec hill repeats (PE 9.5)	9 miles easy	5-7 miles, 5 × 30-sec strides (PE 8.5)	
Strengthening	11	Off	7 miles easy	4-6 miles easy	9 miles easy	
Sharpening	12	Off	7 miles easy	9 miles: 6-8 mile tempo run (PE 7.5)	5-7 miles easy	
Sharpening	13	5 miles easy	9 miles: 6-7 × 1-mile cruise intervals (PE 7.5)	6 miles easy	6-8 miles, 4-5 × 800 meter intervals (PE 8.5-9), 2 × 200-meter reps (PE 9.5)	
Tapering	14	Off	6 miles easy	10 miles, 8 × 2 min intervals (PE 8.5-9)	3-5 miles easy	
Tapering	15	Off	6 miles, 8 × 1 min strides (PE 8.5)	4 miles easy	3-5 miles easy	
Tapering	16	Off	7 miles, 5 × 45 sec strides (PE 8.5)	5 miles easy	Off	

* Use a site such as www.worldwidemetric.com/measurements.html to calculate metric conversions.

** Daily mileage totals **include** recommended speed work.

***All easy running should be done at a PE of 5.

Friday	Saturday	Sunday	Total weekly mileage
6 miles, 7 × 3 min plus pace (PE 6.5)	4 miles easy	8 miles, 5 × 30-sec strides (PE 8.5)	32-34 miles
6 miles, 9 × 3 min plus pace (PE 6.5)	4 miles easy	10 miles, 5 × 30-sec strides (PE 8.5)	35-37 miles
4 miles easy	Off	10K race, 12 miles total	38-40 miles
5 miles easy	5 miles, 5 × 30-sec strides (PE 8.5)	14 miles easy	42-44 miles
6 miles, 5 × 30-sec strides (PE 8.5)	4 miles easy	16 miles easy	46-48 miles
7 miles easy	Off	10-mile race, 14 miles total	50-52 miles
6 miles easy	6 miles, 5 × 30-sec strides (PE 8.5)	18 miles easy	52-54 miles
6 miles easy	Off	14 miles easy	52-54 miles
6 miles easy, 5 × 30-sec strides (PE 8.5)	Off	20 miles easy	52-54 miles
4 miles easy	Off	Half marathon race, 16 miles total	46-48 miles
6 miles easy	4 miles, 5 × 30-sec strides (PE 8.5)	22 miles easy	52-54 miles
8 miles, 6 × 30-sec strides (PE 8.5), 2 × 30-sec sprints (PE 9.5)	5 miles easy	16 miles easy	50-52 miles
Off	Off	20 miles easy	46-48 miles
4 miles easy	3 miles, 6 × 30-sec strides (PE 8.5)	14 miles easy	40-42 miles
7 miles, 6 × 30-sec strides (PE 8.5)	Off	10 miles easy	30-32 miles
4 miles easy	Off	Marathon	16 miles before race

Length of easy jog or walk recovery:
Cruise intervals: one to two minutes
Intervals: one-third to equal the interval
Repetitions and sprints: up to five times the length of the repetition

Hill repeats: equal the effort (PE of 8.5 to 9) or up to four times the effort (PE of 9 to 9.8)
Fartlek, including hill fartlek: one to four minutes
Strides: equal the effort

Marathon Training From a 40-Mile (64 km) Base*

Phase	Week	Monday	Tuesday	Wednesday	Thursday
Endurance	1	Off	8 miles**, 5 × 30-sec strides (PE 8.5)	5 miles easy***	6-8 miles easy
Endurance	2	Off	9 miles, 5 × 30-sec strides (PE 8.5)	5 miles easy	6-8 miles easy
Endurance	3	9 miles easy	9 miles, 5 × 30-sec strides (PE 8.5)	6-8 miles easy	7 miles, 10 × 3 min plus pace (PE 6.5)
Endurance	4	Off	6 miles easy	5-7 miles easy	9 miles easy
Endurance	5	Off	7 miles easy	10 miles, 9 × 5-min cruise intervals (PE 7.5)	5-7 miles easy
Strengthening	6	8 miles easy	8 miles, 5 or 6 × 800 meter intervals (PE 8.5- 9)	7-9 miles easy	8 miles easy
Strengthening	7	5 miles easy	7 miles easy	8-10 miles easy	8 miles easy
Strengthening	8	8 miles easy	8 miles easy	9 miles easy, 4 × 1,200 meter, 2 × 800 meter intervals (PE 8.5-9)	6-8 miles easy
Strengthening	9	7 miles easy	5-7 miles easy	10 miles: 7 or 8 × 1 mile cruise intervals (PE 7.5), 10 min plus pace	5 miles easy
Strengthening	10	8 miles easy	9 miles, 6 × 1-min, 4 × 30-sec hill repeats (PE 8.5). 2 × 10-sec hill repeats (PE 9.5)	8 miles easy	7-9 miles, 5 × 30-sec strides (PE 8.5)
Strengthening	11	6 miles easy	9 miles easy	7 miles easy	8-10 miles easy
Sharpening	12	5 miles easy	9 miles, 6 × 30-sec strides (PE 8.5), 2 × 30-sec sprints (PE 9.5)	6-8 miles easy	11 miles: 8- to 9-mile tempo run (PE 7.5)
Sharpening	13	5 miles easy	10 miles: 7-8 × 1-mile cruise intervals (PE 7.5)	4 miles easy	8 miles, 5-6 × 800 meter intervals (PE 8.5-9), 2 × 200 meter reps (PE 9.5)
Tapering	14	Off	5 miles easy	6 miles easy	8-10 miles, 10 × 2 min intervals (PE 8.5-9)
Tapering	15	Off	6 miles, 10 × 1 min strides (PE 8.5)	9 miles easy	4-6 miles easy
Tapering	16	6 miles easy	7 miles, 5 × 45 sec (PE 7.5)	5 miles easy	Off

* Use a site such as www.worldwidemetric.com/measurements.html to calculate metric conversions.
** Daily mileage totals **include** recommended speed work.
*** All easy running should be done at a PE of 5.

Friday	Saturday	Sunday	Total weekly mileage
8 miles, 7 × 3 min plus pace (PE 6.5)	5 miles easy	10 miles, 5 × 30-sec strides (PE 8.5)	42-44 miles
8 miles, 9 × 3 min plus pace (PE 6.5)	6 miles easy	12 miles, 5 × 30-sec strides (PE 8.5)	46-48 miles
7 miles easy	Off	10K race, 14 miles total	50-52 miles
5 miles easy	5 miles, 5 × 30-sec strides (PE 8.5)	16 miles easy	46-48 miles
6 miles, 5 × 30-sec strides (PE 8.5)	4 miles easy	18 miles easy	50-52 miles
7 miles easy	Off	10-mile race, 16 miles total	54-56 miles
7 miles easy	5 miles, 5 × 30-sec strides (PE 8.5)	18 miles easy	58-60 miles
8 miles easy	7 miles easy	16 miles: 7 or 8 × 8-min cruise intervals (PE 7.5)	62-64 miles
5 miles easy, 5 × 30-sec strides (PE 8.5)	Off	22 miles easy	54-56 miles
6 miles easy	4 miles easy	Half marathon race, 16 miles total	58-60 miles
8 miles easy	4 miles easy, 5 × 30-sec strides (PE 8.5)	20 miles easy	60-64 miles
7 miles easy	6 miles easy	16 miles easy	58-60 miles
5-7 miles easy	Off	22 miles easy	54-56 miles
6 miles easy	7 miles, 6 × 30-sec strides (PE 8.5)	16 miles easy	48-50 miles
7 miles, 6 × 30-sec strides (PE 8.5)	Off	12 miles easy	38-40 miles
4 miles easy	Off	Marathon	20 miles before race

Length of easy jog or walk recovery:
Cruise intervals: one to two minutes
Intervals: one-third to equal the interval
Repetitions and sprints: up to five times the length of the repetition

Hill repeats: equal the effort (PE of 8.5 to 9) or up to four times the effort (PE of 9 to 9.8)
Fartlek, including hill fartlek: one to four minutes
Strides: equal the effort

RECOVERY

Finishing a marathon might come as a shock once it's over. The buildup is so long that the finish takes days and weeks to process. Recovery in the immediate and near terms should be on your mind amid the excitement of the huge accomplishment. Main tasks of recovery are rehydrating, replenishing depleted glycogen stores, repairing and regenerating muscle tissue, replacing electrolytes, and rebuilding your immune system.

Immediate Refueling

Fueling within 30 minutes after finishing the marathon helps replenish glycogen stores and lost electrolytes. For about 30 minutes after exercise the body secretes a hormone called glycogen synthase that converts carbohydrate to muscle glycogen. Secretion of glycogen synthase begins to decline significantly after 30 minutes of exertion, so these minutes are an opportune time for ingesting carbohydrate to replenish glycogen stores along with protein to start the process of protein synthesis, or muscle rebuilding. Consuming protein along with carbohydrate stimulates even greater protein synthesis. According to the International Society of Sports Nutrition, consuming four grams of carbohydrate for each gram of protein (a carbohydrate to protein ratio of 3-4:1) may increase endurance performance and maximally promote protein synthesis (Kerksick et al. 2008). Studies have shown that as early as two hours after exertion, muscle glycogen resynthesis is already 50 percent less effective (Betts and Williams 2010). Lost electrolytes can be replaced by eating salty foods like pretzels or nuts.

Examples of healthy and replenishing postmarathon snacks include the following:

- Chocolate milk
- Bread with peanut butter and jam or honey
- Smoothie made with fruit, yogurt, and milk or juice
- Sport bar and sport drink or water
- Yogurt
- Cereal with milk
- Banana with peanut butter

Refueling with a liquid option allows you to achieve glycogen replenishment, electrolyte replacement, and rehydration quickly, although solids can be just as effective. Your choice may depend on convenience and texture preferences. Just make sure to focus on high-glycemic, glucose-rich carbohydrate sources, such as fruit and yogurt, a peanut butter sandwich, or cereal with milk or yogurt. Low-fat chocolate milk and Accelerade are two drinks that have the recommended 3-4:1 carbohydrate-to-protein ratio. In terms of rehydrating, drink at least 8 ounces (237 ml) of fluids every two hours for 24 hours after your marathon.

Refueling a Few Hours Postmarathon

Two to three hours after the marathon, eat a full meal that includes a balance of fruits, vegetables, whole grains, and protein. Stay away from alcohol and caffeine, which are dehydrating. It is normal to feel unusually hungry after the marathon.

Without a doubt, during the first two to seven hours after the marathon you can expect to feel delayed-onset muscle soreness (DOMS), caused by damage to muscle fiber from eccentric muscle contractions, particularly if you ran a lot of downhills. Muscle soreness peaks 24 to 48 hours after the marathon and may last 7 to 10 days.

Postmarathon Running Plan

The following rebuilding plan will help you recover after running a marathon. It's a reverse marathon taper over four weeks. Generally, the rule is to take one recovery day for each mile of the race. If you come back too soon after a marathon, you will pay for it later with chronic calf, hamstring, and quadriceps pain.

- Week 1 postmarathon: Immediately afterward, you should consider an ice bath as discussed in chapter 5. Fill the tub with ice and cold water; 55 degrees F (13 C) is optimal, but anything under 60 degrees F (16 C) works. Submerge your lower body for 10 minutes. After the ice bath, rest or take a short, easy walk to loosen the legs. At this point, you've done about all you can do for the day. Celebrate your accomplishment.

In the first three days after the marathon, do not run or cross-train. Continue to drink water, at least 64 ounces (2 L) per day. For the next few days, eat lots of fruit, carbohydrate, and protein to help repair muscle damage and restore muscle glycogen. Soak in a hot tub for 10 to 15 minutes or soak in a tub with Epsom salt and stretch afterward. Sitting in a whirlpool for 20 minutes can also help increase circulation and reduce inflammation. Massage your legs with a stick or roller. Get a light massage to help loosen your muscles. In the second half of the week, cross-train at an easy effort for 30 to 40 minutes to promote blood flow to your legs.

- Week 2 postmarathon: Return to easy running only. Limit your running to 40 percent of your maximum marathon mileage.

- Week 3 postmarathon: Run 60 percent of your maximum marathon mileage. All running should still be easy.

- Week 4 postmarathon: Run 80 percent of your maximum marathon mileage, which may be where you want to remain until you start your next marathon training plan. During this week, try running 15 minutes once or twice a week at a PE of 7.5, comfortably hard. Otherwise run easy. This week you can start thinking about racing again, as long as you don't feel any muscle soreness.

Once is not enough for most marathoners. Neither is twice. There's so much to learn. One of our Liberty Athletic Club members has run the Boston Marathon 38 times. Whirlaway Racing Team member, Reno Stirrat, 60, is one of many runners who continues to strive to perfect marathon performance.

I have run 28 marathons and try to make them all count. The marathon distance is not for everyone, but when someone decides to attempt it, it should be respected and the proper training done for it. I was born on April 19, the true Patriots Day when the Boston Marathon was always run. With a name like Reno, I was meant to run the marathon. The marathon is not so forgiving, but run the race you prepared to run and the returns are satisfaction beyond one's wildest dreams. I have run sub-three hours for five decades, and this accomplishment makes me a member of a very small club that includes Olympians and a Boston Marathon champion. I still enjoy each and every marathon, and when I do finish one, it's with a smile knowing that I have finished and completed the distance to the best of my abilities.

Part IV

Competing

Chapter 14

Race Strategy

A great race is never the result just of luck and good training. Strategy is important, too. It is also very individual—and best with doses of humor and perspective. Every runner and coach has his or her own best strategy. So what if one strategy doesn't work? You learn from what went wrong and move on, now more informed. As a masters runner, strategy includes race tactics, travel arrangements (your coach won't be arranging those), the right shoes, fueling, hydrating, and pacing. This chapter provides a timetable that spans the months before the race to recovery weeks afterward. These are suggestions; there are many other strategies.

FOUR OR MORE WEEKS PRERACE: YOU'VE ENTERED YOUR RACE

Once you've entered the race—maybe it's 4, 8, 10, or even 16 weeks before the race, if it's a marathon—read the race website carefully. Race websites provide information about travel and flights, hotels, the course, race history with past results, the race schedule, and information on packet pickup. If the race is a national or world championship, the website contains information on when and where to declare your entry, eligibility requirements (e.g., your age division based on your birth date, which you may have to verify with a passport or birth certificate), and yes, drug testing. If you've entered a race that requires travel, make flight and hotel reservations as soon as possible to ensure they are convenient and you get the best prices. Determine if you have to be a member of USA Track & Field or your national organization. If you're competing, you want to know whether there are age group awards, and if so, whether they are in 5- or 10-year age brackets.

Race websites may tell you a lot about the race course. If you've entered a road, cross country, mountain, ultra, or trail race, the race website may offer details about elevation increases or decreases. Say you're running a 10K road race. Is the course a loop that begins and ends in the same place? Is it an out-and-back course that starts and finishes in the same location, following a linear route to a halfway point before making a 180-degree turn and returning the same way? Is it a point-to-point course that ends quite a distance from the start, or is it a course with multiple out-and-back sections or multiple loops?

Write Down Your Goals

Once you've entered the race, it's a good time to set process goals and also preliminary performance goals (based on time) or outcome goals (based on place) in the goal pyramid discussed in chapter 7. (You may want to review the discussion of performance, outcome, and process goals in that chapter.) Although performance or outcome goals set now will be preliminary, they will help you with pacing and give you a sense of control. Even if you are an experienced runner, check with a coach or more experienced runner to see whether your thoughts are reasonable.

In the triangle at the top of the goal pyramid found in chapter 7, write an estimate of your performance or outcome goal. If this is your first race ever, set a performance goal of finishing the race and enjoying the experience. That will likely lure you back to another race.

Guidelines for Performance Goals

In general, performance goals are more useful for track and road races than for mountain or cross country races. Following are guidelines for setting performance goals.

- Set performance or time goals based on your recent training times or most recent road race result. For example, if you are about to race a 10K and you recently ran a 5K in 20:35. The Jack Daniels VDOT chart found in the appendix shows that your VDOT number is 48. That corresponds with a 42:50 10K at a 6:54 per mile pace.

- Setting performance goals in terms of ranges allows for variability and unpredictable circumstances. Runners who I coach sometimes set A (highest), B (higher), and C (high) goals, even though goal setting is hardly an exact science. The range for setting performance goals is individual, depending on your level of experience, the race course, and the distance. In general, the more experienced runner you are, the narrower the range. And the longer the race distance, the wider the range. For example, if you are racing the mile, you might set A, B, and C goals spanning 2 to 3 seconds. An A goal might be 6:00 to 6:03, a B goal might be 6:03 to 6:06, and a C goal might be 6:06 to 6:09. A, B, and C goals might span 6 to 8 seconds each for a 5K, 10 to 15 seconds each for a 10K, 1 to 3 minutes each for a half marathon, or 3 to 8 minutes or more for a marathon. Even though setting range goals is not an exact science, doing so encourages you to consider everything that contributes to your performance and increases the chances that you'll evaluate your performance objectively afterward.

- Many masters runners prefer to set performance goals based on age grading. Say you're a 45-year-old woman who has just run a 10K in 46:00 and you're about to run a 5K. Looking at the masters age-grading calculator (www.usatf. org/statistics/calculators/agegrading), you see that your 46:00 age grades to 70.76 percent. You might set an A goal of running the 5K in an age-graded time of about 72 percent (22:00), a B goal of running of 71 percent (22:20), and a C goal of 70 percent (22:58).

As mentioned, performance goals are worth setting even if you don't achieve them. Weather—snow, cold, ice, heat, rain, and humidity—on race day can thwart your plans. One of my runners recently ran a 5K road race and didn't meet her goals. The conditions were unusually hot and humid. Even though she was not able to achieve her goals, she ran a smart race. She ran each mile progressively faster. Her pace goals gave her a sense of control for her best possible result that day. Accept and expect the unexpected on race day.

Guidelines for Outcome Goals

Outcome goals—those based on your place relative to others (Do you want to win? Place in the top 10 percent of finishers?)—are useful if you are experienced and know your competition. While you can set preliminary outcome goals now, know that you will revise them a week before the race when and if the race website lists the entrants. You can usually find past performances of runners on the Internet.

Guidelines for Process Goals

Writing down process goals—the tasks you will complete each week—will help you identify what you are focusing on. If you are an experienced racer who has raced a distance many times before, consider adding new training tasks to energize your training plan. Focused on strengthening her hip flexors, one of my experienced racers added strength-training exercises, including hill runs every 10 days, lunges, and step-ups with weights to her weekly process goals. These additions improved her age-graded performance from 88 to 89 percent.

ONE MONTH BEFORE YOUR RACE: FIND THE RIGHT SHOES FOR YOUR RACE

Having reviewed the race website, you know something about the course. That will help you select race day sneakers, which you should wear several times before your race to make sure that they are comfortable and allow your feet to move naturally. The following generalities about choosing sneakers hold. The stronger and healthier your feet and ankles are (you have no bunions or Achilles tendon issues, for example), the less cushioning you need in your shoes, and the lighter they will be. There are many kinds of lightweight racing flats and spikes, and it's important to consult a coach and the race website before choosing a pair (longer spikes are not allowed on some tracks, for example). During longer races such as the half marathon and marathon, feet tend to swell and fatigue, so you may want to shy away from a snug-fitting minimalist shoe and opt for a more cushioned lightweight trainer with a modest-sized toe box and with supplemental support. Last but not least, all things being equal, as long as the shoe provides adequate support, the lighter it is, the faster you'll race. The rule of thumb is that you'll save one second per mile for every "saved" ounce (28 g) in your running shoes. If you, then, normally train in a 12-ounce (.34 kg) shoe, and you switch to a 5.5-ounce (.16 kg) shoe, you reduce the shoe weight by 6.5 ounces (.18 kg), roughly saving 6 seconds per mile. Over a 10K that adds up to 40 seconds.

Ultimately, the correct shoe depends on you, your level of experience, and your feet. More experienced runners often have stronger feet and require less cushioning, and therefore lighter sneakers. Everyone is different, though, needing different levels of cushioning in the heel, support in the forefoot, and general flexibility. Some of my masters run best in their lightweight training shoes because they have bunions, which need a wider toe box, or they have flat feet, which require more arch support. While many runners wear sneakers with support in longer races, some experienced runners wear very light shoes even for the marathon.

Options that are lighter than everyday training shoes, which weigh 11 or 12 ounces (.31 or .34 kg), follow:

- Lightweight trainers have the same look and benefits of a regular-weight shoe but generally weigh approximately 3 ounces (.08 kg) less. They range from 8 to 10 ounces (.23-.28 oz).

- Spikes, roughly 5 ounces (.14 kg) per shoe, have sharp metal or ceramic spikes that are screwed into the sole. Some cross country spikes have rubber spikes attached to the sole. Because they are designed for minimal weight and high traction, spikes can improve times in races on the track as well as in cross country races. Spikes encourage you to run on your toes, helping you achieve maximum traction on the track surface, and cross country spikes provide better traction on dirt, loose gravel, mushy snow, and sandy surfaces than any other type of running shoe. Because spikes are generally narrow and offer little or no support or stability, be sure you spend extra time stretching your hamstring, calves, and Achilles tendons beforehand. Spikes can lead to pulled calves or Achilles if you are not used to them.

Also, spikes come in various lengths and types. Most racing venues and organizations dictate which spikes are legal for their events, and some meets don't allow spikes. Know what's allowed and what's not. Three-eighths-inch spikes (9 mm) are fairly standard for cross country races, while quarter-inch (6 mm) spikes are standard for track races. Bring to the race not only spikes in a variety of lengths but also extras in case some are lost.

- Flats, about five to eight ounces (.14-.23 kg) per shoe, offer less cushioning and a lower heel than lightweight trainers. Many runners wear flats on all kinds of surfaces—track, roads, and cross country, particularly if the footing is hard and dry—and in distances from the mile to the marathon.

▪ Minimalist or "barely there" shoes—unlike flats, which provide a little cushioning—have no cushioning and no drop between the heel and forefoot. They offer no medial or lateral support and are very flexible. Few masters choose minimalist shoes. This is not surprising given that many of them need more support than younger runners do given increased vulnerability to injuries such as Achilles tendinitis, plantar fasciitis, and calf strains.

TWO WEEKS BEFORE YOUR RACE

Beginning now, and continuing through race day, you may want to practice a daily five-minute visualization that can help you steady your breathing during challenging moments of the race, whether that is the third quarter of the race, often the slowest section, or laps on a track when you are bunched up with others in a mile. Consult with your coach or more experienced runners about challenges to visualize.

Wear your racing shoes on portions of your runs at least three times during the two weeks before your race so you know they'll be comfortable on race day.

RACE WEEK

During this taper week, focus on gentle stretching, reducing mileage, and getting more sleep, if possible, than usual. Go to bed half an hour earlier than you normally do, even if that's to read or watch television.

Drink plenty of fluids (an average of 11.5 cups [2.7 L] for women and 15.5 cups [3.7 L] for men, as discussed in chapter 3), and as mentioned in chapter 13, if you are preparing for a marathon, begin fueling with more complex carbohydrate beginning four days before the race. Begin checking the weather prediction for your race so you can plan your race day clothing.

Refine Your Goals

During the week of your race, refine your goals based on your training over the last few weeks and months. Again, ask a coach or a more experienced runner for advice about attainable goals. Setting A, B, and C goals will give you guidelines for pace and also for evaluating your race and your training after the event. It will help you avoid reacting only emotionally to your race, by providing a built-in framework for judging your race objectively.

Choose a Segmenting Plan

Even though you have an idea of your goals, you'll be more prepared to race if you have a segmenting plan that divides the race into parts. Each plan has advantages and disadvantages and depends on your strengths, your weaknesses, experience, race distance, course conditions, and race logistics. Segmenting a race helps you focus on where you are in a race, whether it's a mile or a marathon. You can focus on even pacing, even effort, negative splits, or surges, for example.

Even Pacing

Many runners like even pacing, maintaining roughly the same pace per mile or kilometer throughout the race. Studies have shown that the top runners in most

Runner Profile: Kara Haas

Date of birth: Oct. 10, 1970

Personal Information

- Elementary school computer teacher and webmaster
- Middle school cross country coach
- Married, with a 2-year-old daughter, Ella
- Started focused training at 19

Open Personal Bests

- Mile (downhill) 4:41 (22)
- 1,500 meters 4:40 (22)
- 5K (road) 16:48 (23)
- 10K (road) 35:06 (23)
- Half marathon 1:18:54 (24)
- Marathon 2:54:17 (38)

Personal Bests at 40 to 49

- Mile (downhill) 4:38 (42)
- Mile (indoor track) 5:06 (40)
- 3,000 meters 9:49 (41)
- 5K (road) 16:28 (42)
- 10K (road) 37:41 (42)
- Half marathon 1:19:41 (40)

Age-Graded Personal Bests

- 5K (road) 94.36% (15:41 at age 42)
- 10K (road) 86.4% (35:06 at age 23)
- Half marathon 86.15% (1:16:25 at age 40)

Courtesy of Mike Haas

Cathy Utzschneider: You started to focus on running in college and have stayed with it since. As you've learned more about running over the years, what has surprised you most?

Kara Haas: The friendships, connections, and sense of belonging that is stronger than in any other community of people. Runners are just such special, unique people and I'm so proud to call myself a runner!

Cathy: What would you want collegiate runners and other runners to know about masters running?

Kara: It's a lifelong sport. When you are 19 years old and have a bad race, it feels like the end of the world. The older you get, you realize there will always be another race, and at the end of the day, it's just a race.

Cathy: What was your favorite win as a runner under 30?

Kara: I was running and working for Saucony, and I won the 3.5-mile World Corporate Challenge Championship in NYC. I ran out of my tree that day, and then got to have breakfast with Grete Waitz. That is one of my fondest memories as a runner. She was an amazing, classy lady.

Cathy: What was your favorite win as a runner under 40?

Kara: The Falmouth Road Race. The masters win at Falmouth, in the inaugural year of the separate women's elite start, was simply magical. It was one of those days you know will probably never happen again, so you just savor the moment.

Cathy: People often say that masters runners look forward to aging, to entering a new arena of competition. Given that you race a lot on the roads, where masters is usually defined as beginning at age 40, in your late 30s were you looking forward to turning 40?

Kara: Yes and no. I've tried all my life to live in the moment and not focus on what might be next. That being said, it's still so inspirational to see people in their 60s, 70s, and 80s running amazing times and simply loving to compete. My father is 73 and he has won the 70-plus division at Falmouth the last three years in a row, and I love how he continues to find such joy in running and competing. That is really what it is all about.

Cathy: You have one child and gave birth at 41. Did you take time off during your pregnancy?

Kara: I continued to run 40 to 50 miles (64-80 km) up until the last six weeks of my pregnancy and biked the last six weeks. I was running again three days after Ella was born. I really think being in such good shape helped me recover so quickly and was part of the reason I had such an easy, healthy pregnancy.

Cathy: You won the masters division of New Bedford Half Marathon at 41 just five months after having given birth to your first child. How did you do that?

Kara: I was so fortunate to recover really quickly after childbirth. I ran my 3,000-meter PR (9:49) and dipped under the American indoor record 11 weeks after Ella was born. I felt fantastic running after childbirth, but I also was able to stay home for five months. I had always worked at least one job, so to not have the stressors of multiple jobs was a huge factor. I think the happiness factor played a huge role, too. I was thrilled to have a child and to be able to spend some time at home with her.

Cathy: As a 43-year-old, do you think more in terms of personal bests or in terms of age grading?

Kara: Definitely personal bests. For me, every race is an internal competition against my 22-year-old self.

Cathy: As a fairly young masters runner, have you noticed differences yet between running as a college student and running in your early 40s, and if so, what are they?

Kara: In college, there is so much time to devote to training, nutrition, rest, and so on. Once you graduate and are working crazy hours, taking care of a household, then a family, running is just an outlet for sanity.

Cathy: What is a sample peak training week for a 10K these days?

Kara:

> Sunday: 10- to 15-mile (16-24 km) long run
>
> Monday: easy 8-9 miles (13-15 km)
>
> Tuesday: speed work: 2- to 3-mile (3.2-4.8 km) warm-up, four × 1 mile (1.6 km) at 5K race pace, 2-mile (3.2 km) cool-down, strides
>
> Wednesday: easy 8-9 miles (13-15 km)
>
> Thursday: easy 8-9 miles (13-15 km) plus strides
>
> Friday: 2-mile warm-up (3.2 km), 4- to 5-mile (6.4-8 km) tempo run at marathon pace, 2- to 3-mile (3.2-4.8 km) cool-down
>
> Saturday: easy 10-12 miles (16-19 km)

races tend to run the first half and the second half of the race in nearly equal times. This is a good plan for long races like the marathon where it is difficult to run negative splits.

Even-Effort Pacing

Even-effort pacing relies more on effort than it does on actual pace per mile or kilometer. Runners try to maintain the same perceived, not actual, effort throughout the race. Many beginning runners use this plan because it allows them to finish comfortably. If you plan on even-effort pacing, anticipate that your perceived effort level will increase with fatigue. Even-effort pacing is often a good strategy for more experienced runners in mountain races, some cross country races, or very hilly events.

Negative Splits

Aiming for negative splits means trying to run the second half of a race faster than the first. A negative-split plan is excellent for race distances from the mile to the half marathon, as long as the second half of the course is not more difficult than the first. This strategy often results in top performances. It also keeps you from going out too fast at the race start (one of the biggest mistakes in racing), causing you to burn through your stored energy too quickly.

You can run negative splits by dividing the race into two, three, or four segments, running each progressively faster. Divide the race distance into segments that are progressively shorter as you intensify the pace. For example, if the race is a mile, or eight laps on an indoor track, run the first five laps at a hard perceived exertion and the last three at a very hard perceived exertion. If the race is a 5K, run the first 1.5 miles (2.4 km) at a comfortably hard perceived exertion, the next mile (1.6 km) at a hard perceived exertion, and the last .6 mile (1 km) very hard. With a 10K you might run the first 3 miles (4.8 km) comfortably hard, the next 2 miles (3.2 km) hard, and the last 1.2 miles (2 km) very hard. In a half marathon, my runners might run the first 8 miles (13 km) comfortably hard, the next 3 (4.8 km) hard, and the last 2 (3.2 km) very hard. An easier start gives you strength for a faster finish.

Many masters think that segmenting their races with cue words—words that describe feelings or evoke images—instead of perceived exertion helps them run negative splits, maintain focus, and also feel in control. In a 5K, for example, instead of focusing on running the first 1.5 miles (2.4 km) comfortably hard, you might focus on the words *relaxed* and *steady*. You might focus on the word *strong* until about 2.5 miles (4 km), and on *quick* and *smooth* for the final .6 miles (1 km).

Surging

When you surge, you change your pace suddenly at different points in the race depending on course conditions and where your competitors are. If you are in a competitive masters race hoping for a top position, surging can surprise and demoralize other runners, particularly if you can hold or accelerate your pace.

Front Running

Front running means starting strong and trying to lead throughout the race. Unless you are in an age group competition or know you're one of the fastest in the field, this is not a good strategy for most masters runners. During front running, you open a large lead in an attempt to discourage other runners. However, be prepared to be in a great deal of pain in the last part of the race.

Sometime during the week before the race, create a race day checklist. Include your race day schedule, including what time you will wake up and what time you will eat. Then list everything you'll need for the day. Lay out everything so you are sure you have it. These are things you should have:

- Information about where to pick up your bib number and timing chip, if you haven't picked it up already
- Identification
- Cash
- A raincoat or plastic trash bag (if it might rain)
- Water or carbohydrate beverage
- Towel
- Shoes
- Socks
- Safety pins
- Gels and food
- Tissues
- Adhesive strips
- Petroleum jelly or anti-chafing cream such as Bodyglide
- Pain relievers
- Hat
- Gloves
- Sunglasses
- Sunscreen

DAY BEFORE

If you're running a mountain, cross country, or road race, familiarize yourself with the race course. If you can, go to the race venue to see the start and to walk or jog parts of the course. Course conditions change from day to day. The course terrain—whether packed dirt, uneven grass, gravel, mud, snow, loose rubble, or sand—will affect your choice of racing shoes. If you are running a trail or cross country race and it's been wet and there are places with snow and mud, you will want to wear spikes rather than flats. If you can't visit the race site, review the course on the website again and speak with others who have seen the course in the last day or so.

If you are racing on a track and not familiar with its banking or the surface, it's worth visiting the track the day before you race on it. If you're running a mile, 5K, or 10K on the track, make sure you know how many laps you'll be running. A mile is approximately eight laps around a standard indoor track (200 meters) and four laps around a standard outdoor track (400 meters). (Because a mile is 1,609 meters, it is actually nine meters more than eight indoor and four outdoor laps.) The 5,000 meter race is 25 laps around a standard indoor track (200 meters) and 12.5 laps around a standard outdoor track (400 meters). The 10,000 meter race, the longest outdoor track event, is 25 times around a 400 meter outdoor track.

Always check the race website the day before a race for any changes. Sometimes start times, course routes, and parking areas are altered at the last minute to accommodate weather or unforeseen circumstances.

Double-check all the steps for getting to the start of the race. You'll be excited and nervous on race day, so the more familiar you are with what you should do and when you should do it, the more you can focus on your race.

Progressive Muscle Relaxation

So you've settled on a segmenting plan. And you're still nervous. Progressive muscle relaxation—tensing specific muscle groups and then relaxing them to create awareness of tension and relaxation—can help. Relaxing one muscle group at a time eventually leads to total muscle relaxation. Here are the steps.

1. Lie in a comfortable position, loosen any tight clothing, close your eyes, and be quiet. Tune out all other thoughts.

2. Tense each muscle group for five seconds and then relax it as follows:

   - Forehead: Wrinkle your forehead, trying to make your eyebrows touch your hairline. Relax.
   - Eyes and nose: Close your eyes as tightly as you can. Relax.
   - Lips, cheeks, and jaw: Draw the corners of your mouth back and grimace. Feel the warmth and calmness in your face. Relax.
   - Hands: Extend your arms in front of you. Clench your fists tightly for five seconds. Feel the warmth and calmness in your hands. Relax.
   - Forearms: Extend your arms out against an invisible wall and push forward with your hands for five seconds. Relax.
   - Upper arms: Bend your elbows. Tense your biceps for five seconds. Feel the tension leave your arms as you relax them. Relax.
   - Shoulders: Shrug your shoulders up to your ears for five seconds. Relax.
   - Back: Arch your back off the floor for five seconds. Relax. Feel the anxiety and tension disappear.
   - Abdomen: Tighten your abdominal muscles for five seconds. Relax.
   - Hips and buttocks: Tighten your hip and buttock muscles for five seconds. Relax.
   - Thighs: Tighten your thigh muscles by pressing your legs together as tightly as you can for five seconds. Relax.
   - Feet: Bend your ankles toward your body as far as you can for five seconds. Relax.
   - Toes: Curl your toes as tightly as you can for five seconds. Relax.

3. Focus on any muscles that may still be tense. Tighten and relax that muscle three or four times.

4. Fix the feeling of relaxation in your mind.

The day before your race is the time to eat your last large meal. It should be eaten at least 12 hours before your race. The following are guidelines for your last meal before your race:

- High in carbohydrate, which digests more quickly than fat and protein
- Rather bland
- Low in fiber
- Taken without alcohol or caffeine

RACE DAY

All day long, from the time you wake up to the end of the race, repeat a positive mantra to counteract negative thoughts and race day jitters. "Only positive thoughts" is a theme that works for many. Others are "I'm so lucky to be here," "I am so well prepared," "I have lots of energy," and "I know I can do this."

Be sure that your wake-up plan is foolproof. Don't just rely on an alarm clock. Perhaps ask a friend to call you also.

Tips for Starting the Race

Being smart and prepared at the start is an important part of a successful race, even though you're probably thinking more about the finish than the start. Here are tips to consider. Some of them have been discussed in earlier chapters:

- If you are already registered and the race is not too large, get to the start at least an hour early, especially if you need to pick up your race packet. If you haven't registered, arrive an hour and a half early. For large marathons, plan to arrive two to three hours early.

- Eat your last light meal two to four hours before your race. It should be low-fiber food that is easily digested, such as cereals, toast, and a banana.

- About two hours before the start, as mentioned in chapter 13, drink 12 to 20 ounces (355-591 ml) of water, giving your body time to process extra fluid. Then drink 6 to 10 ounces (177-295 ml) of cold water 10 to 20 minutes before the race start.

- Allow plenty of time for portapotty lines. They can be long, particularly at big races.

- Warm up 40 to 45 minutes before the race starts. A prerace warm-up is especially important in cold weather. Begin with easy running for one and a half to two miles (2.4-3.2 km). If you're running a marathon, a one-mile (1.6 km) warm-up is enough. After you've run a mile, stop and do dynamic stretches and leg swings for 5 to 10 minutes. Then complete your run, incorporating four times 20-second strides, focusing on your form. The strides help elevate your heart rate and get your body ready for racing.

- When you're done with your warm-up, relax—whether that means listening to music, doing light stretching, reading, meditating, or talking with others.

- For marathons and other big races, get to your corral early (that means you've already checked your race bag with your extra layers). If you're going to be waiting at the starting line for a while, wear an old long-sleeve shirt (that you can throw away at a water stop) over your race clothes for warmth. If it's rainy or windy, a garbage bag with holes cut for your arms and neck is handy also and easy to discard once the race begins.

- Line up in the right spot. Faster runners line up closest to the starting line, and slower runners are farther back. Some races, especially big half marathons and marathons, have corrals based on estimated pace. Your race bib should indicate the corral to which you've been assigned. If the race doesn't have corrals, look for pace-per-mile signs. If there aren't any, seed yourself near runners whose anticipated pace is close to yours. If theirs is faster than yours, move farther back. (You don't have to worry about the minutes it takes to cross the starting line because most races use timing chips.)

- Be cautious once you start running. Starts are often crowded and chaotic, and runners jostle each other. Pay attention to other runners, and watch out for discarded items so you don't stumble. If you have to throw something away, make sure you toss it off to the side, away from other runners.

- Take advantage of drafting or trailing directly behind or just off to the side of a runner. This lowers wind resistance, allowing you to run at least four seconds per mile faster at the same effort (Davies 1980).

- Run the tangents, meaning cover the shortest distance possible by running straight from one curve to the next. Even though race courses are measured accurately, many racers run a longer distance (and therefore a slower finish time) by following every curve in the road. A tangent is a straight line that just touches a curve.

Hydrating and Fueling During the Race

If you don't know your sweat rate, as discussed in chapter 13, then during the race, depending on the weather conditions and your size, you should sip four to eight ounces (118-237 ml) of fluid every 15 to 20 minutes. You can save time on the water stops if you pass the first table, which is usually the most crowded, and head for a table toward the end of the row and on the left-hand side if there are tables on both sides of the street. (Most people are right handed and naturally go to the tables on the right side.)

As mentioned in chapter 13, in races of 10 miles (16 km) or longer consume about 100 calories of carbohydrate after an hour of running and then another 100 calories every 40 to 45 minutes after that either as a carbohydrate drink or as food.

If you are racing for 90 minutes or more, or a race longer than 10 miles (16 km), some of your fluid intake should include a sport drink consisting of 5 to 6 percent carbohydrate and electrolytes that will replace lost sodium and other minerals as well as help the fluids absorb faster.

POSTRACE FUELING AND HYDRATING

Replacing fluid after a race, be it the mile or the marathon, is important, particularly if you'll begin training again soon. As mentioned in chapter 13, replace fluids and carbohydrate within 30 minutes of exercise. That applies not just to the marathon but the shorter distances as well. The American College of Sports Medicine (2007) recommends drinking 2 cups (.5 L) of fluid for every pound (.4 kg) of body weight lost while running (ACSM 2007). Check your urine for a day or two after the event to help you determine whether you are hydrated. It should be pale yellow.

As also mentioned in chapter 13, replace muscle and liver glycogen stores within 30 to 60 minutes of finishing exercising because, within that period, the body secretes a hormone called glycogen synthase that converts carbohydrate to glycogen. Ingesting carbohydrate and protein in a ratio of 4:1 (4 grams of carbohydrates for every gram of protein) helps increase muscle glycogen recovery (Ivy et al. 2002). Low-fat chocolate milk provides this 4-to-1 carbohydrate-to-protein ratio, as does a piece of whole grain bread with peanut butter and jelly or yogurt and granola. (Consuming protein along with carbohydrate stimulates even greater protein synthesis for muscle rebuilding.) You can easily replenish lost electrolytes through a balanced diet. Sodium almost never needs to be supplemented because a balanced diet containing salty foods such as pretzels or nuts provides enough sodium. Potassium is found in many foods, including orange juice, bananas, potatoes, cantaloupe, yogurt, and apricots.

Within a half an hour of finishing your race, stretch gently, focusing on your major muscle groups. You can use a foam roller or a stick roller to break up tightness.

Within about two hours after your race, eat a well-balanced meal, and then rest. While ice baths, discussed in chapter 13, are worth taking after a marathon, a bath in Epsom salt, also known as magnesium sulfate, can ease pain and relieve inflammation. Epsom salt is absorbed through the skin (avoid using soap with it because it blocks its effectiveness). Put two cups of Epsom salt in warm water and soak for 10 minutes. If you also want to moisturize your skin, add half a cup (118 ml) of olive or baby oil.

POSTGOAL ANALYSIS

Your race is over. You're exhausted, relieved, thrilled, or, perhaps, disappointed. How do you think about your race objectively? The postgoal analysis described in chapter 7 can help you evaluate your training and the race objectively for future improvement. The form asks you to summarize your training over the past months, comment on particular circumstances related to race day, and recall recent life events that occurred over the course of your training. It also asks you to identify how you would improve your training for a similar race in the future.

RECOVERY AND REBUILDING

How much should you run after a race? Your return depends largely on your age and experience. For suggestions on recovery from the marathon refer to chapter 13. For all other distances, take a day or even two days off after the race and run easy the following week, lowering your mileage by 50 to 75 percent. The following list suggests when you might consider running 10 single minutes at a comfortably hard pace again.

Race Distance	Time Until 10 × 1 Minute of Comfortably Hard Running
Mile	1 week
5K	10 days
10K	2 weeks
Half marathon	3 weeks
Marathon	4 weeks

Perseverance, patience, and passion—not perfection—are components of the best strategy. You always learn from experience and mistakes. So, as Nike says, Just do it! Every race is an excellent teacher as long as you remember and analyze past details for your next strategy and improved race.

Chapter 15

Beyond the Standard Events

You've achieved your goals: run the races, distances, times, the age-graded percentages you aimed for. You've run the mile, 5K, 10K, half marathon, and marathon. You're ready for a change. You love running—the joy of moving, its efficiency, the feeling of freedom, the satisfaction of having covered a distance—and you know you don't want to stop. And you enjoy the challenge, the excitement and challenges of racing. What about trying a triathlon or duathlon or a mountain, trail, or ultra run? Clearly some of these events require learning more new skills than others. This chapter presents an overview of these events, beginning with a few thoughts about making the transition to these events.

SHIFTING TO OTHER EVENTS

Maybe you've run for decades. You want to keep running but would also like to try something new, and yet you may hesitate. *I like my training routine. I'd like to try a new event but I'm not sure which one, not sure how to make adjustments to my routine,* you might think. True, transitions take time and also involve uncertainty. But they are invigorating. As William Bridges (2004) writes about all kinds of changes in *Transitions: Making Sense of Life's Changes,* transitions are "the difficult process of letting go of an old situation." They involve a "natural process of disorientation and reorientation marking the turning points in the path of growth" (p. 4). If you allow time to experiment and have patience and perspective (and trust the 10-year or 10,000-hours-to-excellence rule), you can relax as you try a new event.

Running is the best preparation for a mountain, trail, or ultrarun and an excellent base for a triathlon or duathlon. Many runners are amazed at how well they've done after taking on these events. Jody Dushay, 46, experienced success in her first major triathlon, having competed in cross country and track throughout high school and college and then in marathons with a personal best of 2:53. She enjoyed biking and swimming recreationally and decided to devote more time to these and try the triathlon experience. She entered the Miami Half Ironman, finished second in her age category (45 to 49), and qualified for the World Age Group Championship in September 2014. While Jody's initial success is unusual, many report that taking on a new event is inspiring. "Competing in marathons was starting to take a toll on my body, especially the very long runs. I was also finding marathon training more of a chore than a positive experience day after day. The addition of swimming and biking, in combination with reduced running, has been absolutely invigorating," Jody told me recently.

If you undertake a duathlon or triathlon or mountain, ultra, or trail run, consult a coach or at least an athlete experienced in the discipline. He or she can help you navigate the transitions in your training based on your current level of fitness and experience. Next, consider your strengths and weaknesses as an athlete as well as resources available, equipment required, clubs available, and your current life commitments. If a triathlon interests you, basic first questions include: Can you swim? Do you have access to a pool? Where can you get coaching if you want to improve your swimming? Do you have a bike and if not where can you buy one and where can you ride it? If mountain or trail running interest you, are trails nearby? Where can you run regularly on inclines? Events and training courses are listed on national websites (www.usatf.org/groups/MountainUltraTrail and www.usatriathlon.org for duathlons and triathlons) and regional websites usually include listings of experts from whom you can gain information about coaches and clubs. Local running and bike stores, other books, and running and swim coaches at high schools and colleges can also be sources of information. Specific considerations for first-timers in each event are covered in the following sections.

TRIATHLONS

What about trying a tri? The triathlon—the most common form includes swimming, cycling, and running—is surging in popularity, and many new entrants to the sport are masters runners. Overall, triathlon participation in the United States is at an all-time high, following unprecedented growth over the past 10 to 15 years. USA Triathlon membership in 2012 was 550,446 compared to 100,000 to 130,000 from 1998 to 2000. Masters runners have contributed to the growth in number of triathletes: 55 percent are between 30 and 49 years old. In 2012, 11 percent of USA Triathlon members were 30 to 34, 14 percent were 35 to 39, 17 percent were 40 to 44, and 13 percent were 45 to 49 (USA Triathlon 2013).

Triathlon races vary in distance. Consider starting with a shorter event:

- The sprint triathlon consists of a .5K to .75K (.3 to .5 mile) swim, 20K to 22K (12.4-13 miles) bike, and 5K run. Of all triathlon race distances, the sprint triathlon has seen the largest growth in the United States: 818 races held in 2004 compared to 1,507 in 2010 (USA Triathlon 2013). Because they are short, sprint triathlons are a good first-time triathlon choice for runners. (Supersprints are slightly shorter races, consisting of a .4K (.25-mile) swim, 10K bike, and 2.5K (1.5 miles) run.

- The Olympic distance triathlon consists of a 1.5K (.9 mile) swim, 40K (24.9 miles) bike, and 10K run.

- The Half Ironman, also known as an Ironman 70.3 because it refers to the total distance in miles (113K) covered in the race, consists of a 1.9K (1.2-mile) swim, a 90K (56-mile) bike ride, and a 21.1K (13.1-mile) run. Each distance of the swim, bike, and run segments are half the distances of those segments in an Ironman triathlon. Half Ironman events are used as qualifiers for Ironman triathlons.

- The Ironman consists of a 3.8K (2.4 miles) swim, 180K (111.8 miles) bike, and 42K (26.2 miles) run (a marathon). Each leg alone in this event challenges even an experienced endurance athlete. Train for an Ironman distance only after you've had experience in shorter races and have completed at least one Half Ironman.

General recommendations for first-time triathletes—and also for duathletes—begin with anticipating the gear you'll need. For your first triathlon, even your own Schwinn Varsity bike will work. If you happen to have a road bike, use it. Otherwise a mountain bike will serve, although it will not go as fast. You can improve its speed by replacing the fat, knobby tires with smooth, thinner tires meant for street riding. If you need to buy equipment, contact the closest triathlon club or the best local bike shop that specializes in serving triathletes. Most important is that the bike fits. To get properly fitted for your bike, a knowledgeable mechanic or cyclist can help you set your seat height, handlebar height, and other adjustable parts of the bike to give you the most comfortable and efficient riding position. You'll also want to get your bike tuned. Clean and lubricate the drive train, replace worn parts, and check the brakes and tires, for example. In addition, ask an expert about basic maintenance tasks such as how to fix a flat and oil the chain.

You can adjust your bike further for a race in several ways. If your bike has a kickstand, for instance, take it off. It just adds weight. Also, consider adding a clip-on aerobar. This will enable you to ride in an aerodynamic "time trial" position that saves a lot of energy by reducing wind drag. Also, consider replacing your flat pedals with a pair of clipless pedals and wearing bike shoes.

Other items you may need to purchase include padded bike shorts, bike shoes to increase pedal efficiency, a helmet, cycling glasses, a tire pump, a spare tube, and a hex wrench set for tightening and loosening bolts. If you are beginning triathlon training when you can't bike outside, start on a stationary bike in the gym or purchase a wind trainer, a stand that holds your bike and provides resistance so that you can ride indoors.

Essential gear for swimming includes a swimsuit, goggles, and a swim cap (if you have long hair). Consider buying a racing suit. Choose goggles that fit the shape of your face so they don't leak. (To prevent lens fogging, spread a tiny drop of baby shampoo on the inside of the lenses the night before your event and then rinse them out the morning of your race.)

For running, you can keep using the gear you have been using. You may want to purchase a triathlon suit, which combines a swimsuit with cycling shorts. Nothing beats it for this purpose.

In terms of training for your first triathlon, you should do equal numbers of swim, bike, and run workouts. Because the time during a triathlon is generally divided so that half is spent cycling, about 30 percent running, and 20 percent swimming, adjust your training time to reflect those percentages. That simply means that biking should take more time than running, which should take more time than swimming. The amount of actual time you spend training depends, of course, on your current level of fitness as well as your skill level. Once you have adjusted to the three disciplines, begin incorporating one and then two bricks (training two of the disciplines) a week: a swim and then bike, and a bike and then run because the order of triathlon events is swim, bike, run. If you are a beginning swimmer who needs lessons, figure on more time swimming. If you are afraid of open water, try a triathlon in a pool. In cold, snowy weather install an indoor trainer, which is more specific to biking than a stationary or spin bike. If you don't want to install a trainer, a spin class will keep you in shape until you can ride outside. When you get closer to your race, practice the transitions from swimming to biking and then from biking to running. As mentioned, consult a coach on all aspects of your first-time training.

DUATHLONS

If you hate to swim, you may want to try a duathlon: a race with a run, bike, run sequence. Duathlons may be found through USA Triathlon, the national governing body for duathlon (as well as for aquathlon [swim and run] and aquabike [swim and bike]). Duathlons vary a great deal. The following are typical distances:

- The supersprint duathlon consists of a 2.5K (1.6-mile) run, 10K (6.2-mile) cycle, and 2.5K (1.6-mile) run.

- The sprint duathlon consists of a 5K (3.1-mile) run, 20K (12.4-mile) cycle, and a 5K run.

- The standard-distance duathlon consists of a 10K run, 40K (24.9-mile) cycle, 10K run.

- The long-distance duathlon, an example of which is the world's premier duathlon, the Powerman Zofingen in Switzerland, is a 10K run, 150K (93.2-mile) cycle, and a 30K (18.6-mile) run.

The world's largest duathlon to date is the London Duathlon in Richmond Park in southwest London. It offers four individual competitions and one team challenge: a supersprint (5K run, 11K [6.8-mile] bike, 5K run), sprint (10K run, 22K [13.7-mile] bike, 5K run), classic (10K run, 44K [27.3-mile] bike, 5K run), ultra (20K run, 77K [47.9-mile] bike, 10K run), and classic relay (10K run, 44K bike, 5K run).

General recommendations for a first-time duathlon are to begin by dividing weekly workouts to include three cycling workouts and three runs. Consult with a duathlon coach to learn how to incorporate intervals and endurance training. Follow the suggestions about biking from the triathlon discussion.

MOUNTAIN, ULTRA, AND TRAIL RACES

More and more runners, masters among them, are turning to mountain, ultra, and trail races for variety and challenge. In the United States, these events are represented by the Mountain, Ultra and Trail (MUT) Sport Council, which assists USA Track & Field. MUT recognizes not just open but also masters runners of the year.

Mountain Races

Internationally, the World Mountain Running Association, the sport's global governing body, is responsible for world mountain running competitions, which include events for all ages. Mountain races, some of which may also be considered ultra and trail races, take place over a variety of distances, ascents, descents, and terrain, with courses for all abilities and age groups. While some mountain runs are staged on roads or semipaved surfaces, all must include significant elevation gains to be considered mountain runs. Significant elevation gains are the distinguishing difference between mountain and trail runs.

If you check your regional USATF division, you might find schedules for mountain races, including race series, in your area. Many of my New England runners participate in the shortest mountain races in the series, such as the Wachusett Mountain Race to prepare for larger races such as the Mount Washington Road Race. Awards are given in five-year age divisions. One of our Liberty Athletic Club runners, Carrie Parsi, has run Mount Washington 17 times, winning her age division numerous times. In 2013 she won the female 70 to 74 age group. The oldest age group winner that year was George Etzweiler, age 93.

Mountain races may also be ultradistances. The Ultra-Trail du Mont-Blanc, for example, is a mountain ultramarathon that covers 166 kilometers (103 miles). The total elevation gain is about 9,400 meters (30,840 feet), held in the Alps across France, Italy, and Switzerland. It's known as the most difficult footrace in Europe. The best runners complete the loop in a little over 20 hours, while most take 30 to 45 hours to finish.

General recommendations for training for your first mountain race include incorporating runs on hills or roads up small mountains, at first once and then at least twice a week. Add cycling to your training to strengthen your quadriceps, which are critical for mountain running. Strengthen your arms and abdominals, both of which work harder as you run uphill. Consider buying mountain running shoes with a reinforced toe bumper.

Ultradistances

Ultradistances are anything longer than a marathon, and even more than the marathon, they reflect a lifestyle, requiring many miles and hours of running to prepare for them. Ultradistances may also be trail or mountain runs. In general, there are two types of ultradistance events: events that cover a specified distance and events that take place during a specified time (with the winner covering the most distance in that time). The most common ultradistances are 50K (31 miles), 100K (62 miles), 50 miles (80K), and 100 miles (161K), although many races are run other distances. The 100K is an official International Association of Athletics Federation (IAAF) world record event. Other races include double marathons and timed events that range from 6, 12, and 24 hours to 3 to 10 days or even more.

The format of these events and the courses vary, including single or multiple loops, point-to-point road or trail races, and cross country orienteering, which involves both route planning and navigation between checkpoints using a variety of map types. Many ultramarathons, especially trail challenges, incorporate major course obstacles, including elevation changes over mountain paths and rugged terrain covering dirt and rocky roads. Aid stations are usually set up at regular intervals, where runners can replenish food and drink, supplies, or take a short break. This is also where race organizers track runners' progress, record their numbers, and make sure the runners are healthy and able to continue running.

General recommendations for your first ultramarathon are to consider an ultra only after you have run a few marathons and to choose an ultra that allows you to train on the terrain on which you expect to race. Perfect the art of fueling and hydrating, given the fact that even an easy 50-mile (80 km) run takes the average runner 8 to 11 hours to complete. Practice skills that develop the mental toughness required to withstand the hours of challenge. Focus your workouts not on the distance covered but rather on the hours on your feet. If you are working from a base of being able to run 15 miles (24 km), allow six months to train for your first ultra.

Trail Races

Trail races cover distances from 5K and up and are becoming increasingly popular. The sport is still fairly young. The American Trail Running Association, a member of USATF, was founded as recently as 1996 to represent trail races in the United States. Trail races include mountain single-track trails and may also include paved pathways in rural and even urban areas. Many trail races are held in national parks, and many overlap with mountain and ultrarunning if they traverse and climb mountains.

Short-course trail racing gives you a chance to try trail running without committing to long distances. The Cascadia Trail Series in Orem, Utah, offers race distances from 5K to 15K. The Georgia State Parks Trail Series just north of Atlanta, Georgia, includes race distances from 5K to 9.9 miles (16 km). The Endless Summer Trail Run Series in Minneapolis, Minnesota, features race distances from the 5K to 7 miles (11 km), and the Cougar Mountain Trail Run Series in Seattle, Washington, includes races from 5 to 26 miles (8-42 km).

Many of the most high-profile trail races are longer than marathons. Two famous trail runs in the United States, for example, are the Western States Endurance Run (commonly known as the Western States 100), a 100-mile (161 km) ultramarathon on trails in California's Sierra Nevada Mountains, and the Badwater Ultramarathon, which describes itself as the world's toughest footrace. It is a 135-mile (217 km) course from California's Death Valley to the trailhead at Mount Whitney.

While many trail races take place in a single day, some are divided into multiple stages and take place over several days because of their length. In both single-

Runner Profile: Meghan Arbogast

Date of birth: April 16, 1961

Personal Information

- Licensed massage therapist
- Widowed
- One daughter, born October 4, 1986
- Started focused training in mid-20s (I started competitive running with just the occasional and local 5K or 10K. I gradually worked up to running my first marathon at age 33. I was a high school "jock" and played volleyball and basketball and ran track.)
- Running is focused on ultra-endurance events: 50K to 100 miles (31 miles - 161 km)

Personal Bests at 40 to 49

- 5K (road) 17:56
- 10K (road) 36:57
- Half marathon 1:20
- Marathon 2:45

Personal Bests at 50 to 59

- 5K (road) 18:35
- Marathon 2:52

Cathy Utzschneider: When did you begin ultra-endurance running?

Meghan Arbogast: I ran my first ultra in the late 90s (I think I was 36 years old) but didn't like it. It was too much steep terrain for fast running, and I was still pursuing a fast marathon time. When I finally reached the Olympic Marathon Trials level in 2000, I was beginning to feel the call to get on the trails more. So, I came back to what I consider my real beginning to ultrarunning in 2003 at a 50K (31 miles) in Ashland, Oregon.

Cathy: What motivated you to start ultra-endurance running?

Meghan: The lure of the trail, the stories I would hear from my ultrarunning friends.

Cathy: How many ultra-endurance events do you do in a year?

Meghan: I probably run about 10 ultras a year: a couple of 50Ks (31 miles), a handful of 50 milers (80 km), a couple of 100Ks (62 miles), and one or two 100 milers (161 km).

Cathy: Do you run shorter races as well?

Meghan: Yes, I still like to run a fast marathon once or twice per year, and I love cross country, so I'll sometimes hop into a 5K cross country race, the occasional 5K and 10K road race, and a rare half marathon.

Cathy: What's the longest, most difficult ultra event you've done?

Meghan: The longest is the Western States 100-Mile Endurance Run. I have run it seven times. It isn't the most difficult, but it is the one I love the most.

Cathy: And how did you manage fueling and hydrating during it?

Meghan: I'm always learning. Now I try to consume a gel every 30 minutes, keep drinking whatever I'm carrying, and at every aid station I eat another gel or some fruit and drink from the cups while they refill my hydration pack. I'll usually drink Coke from the aid station for the

(continued)

extra sugar and caffeine boost. Soup starts to be really good at later stages as well, which I get from aid stations.

Cathy: Have you found that it's a certain kind of runner who is attracted to ultra-endurance events?

Meghan: People who are really happy in the outdoors, not worried about getting dirty or pooping in the woods.

Cathy: Are you ever scared when competitors are spread out and you're alone with wild animals?

Meghan: Ha! Nope. I'm more concerned about that on a training run when there may not be very many people out on a trail and I might be miles away from civilization. During a race I figure there are so many people out there before or behind me and lots of commotion with aid stations that the animals are hiding far away.

Cathy: What in your ultra-endurance competitions have been highlights for you and why?

Meghan: Crossing the finish line is usually the best. The entire event is then a story that I can share with everyone else who just did it, or anyone who wants to listen.

Cathy: Is there anything about ultra-endurance events that has surprised you?

Meghan: Maybe at how much I love them?

Cathy: How do you train for the longest events?

Meghan: I generally pick two or three races that I want to focus on every year: Western States 100-Mile, 100K World Championships (I'm a member of Team USA, who races every year, usually in Europe), and maybe another one. Other races leading up to the goal races are used as my long training runs. So by the time Western States 100 gets here, I'll have run a couple of 50Ks, a 50 miler, and a 100K in the four months leading up but each spread out by about one month. I also go to the Western States course for a long weekend either in April or May to get practice on the trail with my great training partners.

Cathy: How many miles do you run and where do you train?

Meghan: Anywhere from 50 to 100 miles (80-161 km) or more a week. I train wherever I am at the time. I travel a lot.

Cathy: As a massage therapist, you have to manage patients and a demanding training schedule. How do you do that?

Meghan: I work about half time at the most, so it isn't that hard to juggle.

Cathy: Have you had injuries during training or competition?

Meghan: No injuries during a competition, but I have had lots of injuries in the past. I've learned from each one, and now I work with a physical therapist once a month to keep my joints working smoothly and to keep working on my mechanics.

Cathy: I understand that you lost your husband in 2010 to brain cancer. I also gather he was a great supporter of yours. Do you have any perspective on endurance running and dealing with hardship that might be unique?

Meghan: I believe that in hard times, one must hold tight to their passions because they offer solace and remind us that time doesn't stop just because A, B, or C is happening in our world. My husband and I both believed that everyone else around him needed to keep living their lives. It gave him something to live through vicariously.

Cathy: For those who are not ultrarunners, is there an event that you'd recommend as a great one for first-timers?

Meghan: I would suggest finding a local and low-key 50K that you can get out on and run some of before the race.

Cathy: Do you have a final thought or story to share?

Meghan: I hope that folks recognize that the human species is incredibly able to adapt to a given situation, and that the only way to adapt is to stress ourselves. Through baby steps, most people can patiently train and build up to running ultramarathons. I don't feel like I'm more able than anyone else. My speed is something I was lucky to get from my parents, but determination and belief in human capacity keep me wanting to improve and uncover what I am ultimately capable of.

stage and multiday stage races, competitors are timed over the duration of their run, including stops at aid stations that supply food and beverages at intervals, often every 5K to 10K, along the course. Some multiday races like the TransRockies Run in Colorado offer support and runner amenities as complete as luggage service, medical stations, hot showers, tents, toilets, waste management, recycling services, and a catered dinner at the end of the day. The TransRockies Run offers two point-to-point courses. The three-day trail race covers 59 miles (95 km) and gains 8,400 feet (2,560 meters) of elevation. The six-day trail race covers 120 miles (193 km) and gains 20,000 feet (6,096 meters) of elevation. Runners can compete as individuals or as a team. A team consists of two runners whose ages combine to 80 years or more.

General recommendations for first-time trail runners are to recognize that trail running is slower and more difficult than running on a smooth surface because you are covering uneven surfaces through mud, rocks, tree roots, and sand and sometimes jumping over obstacles such as streams. Buy trail shoes that offer lateral support. Measure your workouts in terms of minutes rather than miles. Also begin incorporating trail running gradually by running the last mile or so of your workout on trails a few times a week. Strengthen your ankles, hips, quadriceps, and gluteal muscles. Perform exercises on a balance board or BOSU ball to improve balance. Standing on one leg for 30 to 60 seconds holding your body tall and your hips under your shoulders strengthens your ankles.

YOU HAVE OPTIONS

All these nonstandard events remind us that running is a foundation not just for track, cross country, and road events but also for those events which incorporate new challenges—different terrain or additional sports. As a runner you have choices to vary your goals, to expand your skills and experience. If you've been used to entering the same events for years, you may be energized by novelty. Why not step outside your comfort zone of the familiar and try something new? You may discover a new passion—or at least a new twist to your passion for running!

Appendix

Table A.1 VDOT Values Associated With Running Times of Some Popular Distances

VDOT	1,500	Mile	3,000	2 mile	5,000	10K	15K	Half marathon	Marathon	VDOT
30	8:30	9:11	17:56	19:19	30:40	63:46	98:14	2:21:04	4:49:17	30
31	8:15	8:55	17:27	18:48	29:51	62:03	95:36	2:17:21	4:41:57	31
32	8:02	8:41	16:59	18:18	29:05	60:26	93:07	2:13:49	4:34:59	32
33	7:49	8:27	16:33	17:50	28:21	58:54	90:45	2:10:27	4:28:22	33
34	7:37	8:14	16:09	17:24	27:39	57:26	88:30	2:07:16	4:22:03	34
35	7:25	8:01	15:45	16:58	27:00	56:03	86:22	2:04:13	4:16:03	35
36	7:14	7:49	15:23	16:34	26:22	54:44	84:20	2:01:19	4:10:19	36
37	7:04	7:38	15:01	16:11	25:46	53:29	82:24	1:58:34	4:04:50	37
38	6:54	7:27	14:41	15:49	25:12	52:17	80:33	1:55:55	3:59:35	38
39	6:44	7:17	14:21	15:29	24:39	51:09	78:47	1:53:24	3:54:34	39
40	6:35	7:07	14:03	15:08	24:08	50:03	77:06	1:50:59	3:49:45	40
41	6:27	6:58	13:45	14:49	23:38	49:01	75:29	1:48:40	3:45:09	41
42	6:19	6:49	13:28	14:31	23:09	48:01	73:56	1:46:27	3:40:43	42
43	6:11	6:41	13:11	14:13	22:41	47:04	72:27	1:44:20	3:36:28	43
44	6:03	6:32	12:55	13:56	22:15	46:09	71:02	1:42:17	3:32:23	44
45	5:56	6:25	12:40	13:40	21:50	45:16	69:40	1:40:20	3:28:26	45
46	5:49	6:17	12:26	13:25	21:25	44:25	68:22	1:38:27	3:24:39	46
47	5:42	6:10	12:12	13:10	21:02	43:36	67:06	1:36:38	3:21:00	47
48	5:36	6:03	11:58	12:55	20:39	42:50	65:53	1:34:53	3:17:29	48
49	5:30	5:56	11:45	12:41	20:18	42:04	64:44	1:33:12	3:14:06	49
50	5:24	5:50	11:33	12:28	19:57	41:21	63:36	1:31:35	3:10:49	50
51	5:18	5:44	11:21	12:15	19:36	40:39	62:31	1:30:02	3:07:39	51
52	5:13	5:38	11:09	12:02	19:17	39:59	61:29	1:28:31	3:04:36	52
53	5:07	5:32	10:58	11:50	18:58	39:20	60:28	1:27:04	3:01:39	53
54	5:02	5:27	10:47	11:39	18:40	38:42	59:30	1:25:40	2:58:47	54
55	4:57	5:21	10:37	11:28	18:22	38:06	58:33	1:24:18	2:56:01	55
56	4:53	5:16	10:27	11:17	18:05	37:31	57:39	1:23:00	2:53:20	56
57	4:48	5:11	10:17	11:06	17:49	36:57	56:46	1:21:43	2:50:45	57
58	4:44	5:06	10:08	10:56	17:33	36:24	55:55	1:20:30	2:48:14	58
59	4:39	5:02	9:58	10:46	17:17	35:52	55:06	1:19:18	2:45:47	59
60	4:35	4:57	9:50	10:37	17:03	35:22	54:18	1:18:09	2:43:25	60
61	4:31	4:53	9:41	10:27	16:48	34:52	53:32	1:17:02	2:41:08	61
62	4:27	4:49	9:33	10:18	16:34	34:23	52:47	1:15:57	2:38:54	62
63	4:24	4:45	9:25	10:10	16:20	33:55	52:03	1:14:54	2:36:44	63
64	4:20	4:41	9:17	10:01	16:07	33:28	51:21	1:13:53	2:34:38	64
65	4:16	4:37	9:09	9:53	15:54	33:01	50:40	1:12:53	2:32:35	65

(continued)

Table A.1 (Continued)

VDOT	1,500	Mile	3,000	2 mile	5,000	10K	15K	Half marathon	Marathon	VDOT
66	4:13	4:33	9:02	9:45	15:42	32:35	50:00	1:11:56	2:30:36	66
67	4:10	4:30	8:55	9:37	15:29	32:11	49:22	1:11:00	2:28:40	67
68	4:06	4:26	8:48	9:30	15:18	31:46	48:44	1:10:05	2:26:47	68
69	4:03	4:23	8:41	9:23	15:06	31:23	48:08	1:09:12	2:24:57	69
70	4:00	4:19	8:34	9:16	14:55	31:00	47:32	1:08:21	2:23:10	70
71	3:57	4:16	8:28	9:09	14:44	30:38	46:58	1:07:31	2:21:26	71
72	3:54	4:13	8:22	9:02	14:33	30:16	46:24	1:06:42	2:19:44	72
73	3:52	4:10	8:16	8:55	14:23	29:55	45:51	1:05:54	2:18:05	73
74	3:49	4:07	8:10	8:49	14:13	29:34	45:19	1:05:08	2:16:29	74
75	3:46	4:04	8:04	8:43	14:03	29:14	44:48	1:04:23	2:14:55	75
76	3:44	4:02	7:58	8:37	13:54	28:55	44:18	1:03:39	2:13:23	76
77	3:41+	3:58+	7:53	8:31	13:44	28:36	43:49	1:02:56	2:11:54	77
78	3:38.8	3:56.2	7:48	8:25	13:35	28:17	43:20	1:02:15	2:10:27	78
79	3:36.5	3:53.7	7:43	8:20	13:26	27:59	42:52	1:01:34	2:09:02	79
80	3:34.2	3:51.2	7:37.5	8:14.2	13:17.8	27:41	42:25	1:00:54	2:07:38	80
81	3:31.9	3:48.7	7:32.5	8:08.9	13:09.3	27:24	41:58	1:00:15	2:06:17	81
82	3:29.7	3:46.4	7:27.7	8:03.7	13:01.1	27:07	41:32	:59:38	2:04:57	82
83	3:27.6	3:44.0	7:23.0	7:58.6	12:53.0	26:51	41:06	:59:01	2:03:50	83
84	3:25.5	3:41.8	7:18.5	7:53.6	12:45.2	26:34	40:42	:58:25	2:02:24	84
85	3:23.5	3:39.6	7:14.0	7:48.8	12:37.4	26:19	40:17	:57:50	2:01:10	85

Reprinted, by permission, from J. Daniels, 2014, *Daniels' running formula,* 3rd ed. (Champaign, IL: Human Kinetics), 81-82. Table created by Jack Daniels' Running Calculator designed by the Run SMART Project.

Table A.2 Training Intensities Based on Current VDOT

VDOT	E (EASY) / L (LONG) Km	E (EASY) / L (LONG) Mile	M (MARATHON PACE) Km	M (MARATHON PACE) Mile	T (THRESHOLD PACE) 400	T (THRESHOLD PACE) Km	T (THRESHOLD PACE) Mile	I (INTERVAL PACE) 400	I (INTERVAL PACE) Km	I (INTERVAL PACE) 1.200	I (INTERVAL PACE) Mile	R (REPETITION PACE) 200	R (REPETITION PACE) 300	R (REPETITION PACE) 400	R (REPETITION PACE) 600	R (REPETITION PACE) 800
30	7:27-8:14	12:00-13:16	7:03	11:21	2:33	6:24	10:18	2:22	—	—	—	67	1:41	—	—	—
31	7:16-8:02	11:41-12:57	6:52	11:02	2:30	6:14	10:02	2:18	—	—	—	65	98	—	—	—
32	7:05-7:52	11:24-12:39	6:40	10:44	2:26	6:05	9:47	2:14	—	—	—	63	95	—	—	—
33	6:55-7:41	11:07-12:21	6:30	10:27	2:23	5:56	9:33	2:11	—	—	—	61	92	—	—	—
34	6:45-7:31	10:52-12:05	6:20	10:11	2:19	5:48	9:20	2:08	—	—	—	60	90	2:00	—	—
35	6:36-7:21	10:37-11:49	6:10	9:56	2:16	5:40	9:07	2:05	—	—	—	58	87	1:57	—	—
36	6:27-7:11	10:23-11:34	6:01	9:41	2:13	5:33	8:55	2:02	—	—	—	57	85	1:54	—	—
37	6:19-7:02	10:09-11:20	5:53	9:28	2:10	5:26	8:44	1:59	5:00	—	—	55	83	1:51	—	—
38	6:11-6:54	9:56-11:06	5:45	9:15	2:07	5:19	8:33	1:56	4:54	—	—	54	81	1:48	—	—
39	6:03-6:46	9:44-10:53	5:37	9:02	2:05	5:12	8:22	1:54	4:48	—	—	53	80	1:46	—	—
40	5:56-6:38	9:32-10:41	5:29	8:50	2:02	5:06	8:12	1:52	4:42	—	—	52	78	1:44	—	—
41	5:49-6:31	9:21-10:28	5:22	8:39	2:00	5:00	8:02	1:50	4:36	—	—	51	77	1:42	—	—
42	5:42-6:23	9:10-10:17	5:16	8:28	1:57	4:54	7:52	1:48	4:31	—	—	50	75	1:40	—	—
43	5:35-6:16	9:00-10:05	5:09	8:17	1:55	4:49	7:42	1:46	4:26	—	—	49	74	98	—	—
44	5:29-6:10	8:50-9:55	5:03	8:07	1:53	4:43	7:33	1:44	4:21	—	—	48	72	96	—	—
45	5:23-6:03	8:40-9:44	4:57	7:58	1:51	4:38	7:25	1:42	4:16	—	—	47	71	94	—	—
46	5:17-5:57	8:31-9:34	4:51	7:49	1:49	4:33	7:17	1:40	4:12	5:00	—	46	69	92	—	—
47	5:12-5:51	8:22-9:25	4:46	7:40	1:47	4:29	7:09	98	4:07	4:54	—	45	68	90	—	—
48	5:07-5:45	8:13-9:15	4:41	7:32	1:45	4:24	7:02	96	4:03	4:49	—	44	67	89	—	—
49	5:01-5:40	8:05-9:06	4:36	7:24	1:43	4:20	6:56	95	3:59	4:45	—	44	66	88	—	—
50	4:56-5:34	7:57-8:58	4:31	7:17	1:41	4:15	6:50	93	3:55	4:40	—	43	65	87	—	—
51	4:52-5:29	7:49-8:49	4:27	7:09	1:40	4:11	6:44	92	3:51	4:36	—	43	64	86	—	—
52	4:47-5:24	7:42-8:41	4:22	7:02	98	4:07	6:38	91	3:48	4:32	—	42	64	85	—	—

(continued)

221

Table A.2 *(continued)*

VDOT	E (EASY) / L (LONG) Km	E (EASY) / L (LONG) Mile	M (MARATHON PACE) Km	M (MARATHON PACE) Mile	T (THRESHOLD PACE) 400	T (THRESHOLD PACE) Km	T (THRESHOLD PACE) Mile	I (INTERVAL PACE) 400	I (INTERVAL PACE) Km	I (INTERVAL PACE) 1.200	I (INTERVAL PACE) Mile	R (REPETITION PACE) 200	R (REPETITION PACE) 300	R (REPETITION PACE) 400	R (REPETITION PACE) 600	R (REPETITION PACE) 800
53	4:43-5:19	7:35-8:33	4:18	6:56	97	4:04	6:32	90	3:44	4:29	—	42	63	84	—	—
54	4:38-5:14	7:28-8:26	4:14	6:49	95	4:00	6:26	88	3:41	4:25	—	41	62	82	—	—
55	4:34-5:10	7:21-8:18	4:10	6:43	94	3:56	6:20	87	3:37	4:21	—	40	61	81	—	—
56	4:30-5:05	7:15-8:11	4:06	6:37	93	3:53	6:15	86	3:34	4:18	—	40	60	80	2:00	—
57	4:26-5:01	7:08-8:04	4:03	6:31	91	3:50	6:09	85	3:31	4:14	—	39	59	79	1:57	—
58	4:22-4:57	7:02-7:58	3:59	6:25	90	3:46	6:04	83	3:28	4:10	—	38	58	77	1:55	—
59	4:19-4:53	6:56-7:51	3:56	6:19	89	3:43	5:59	82	3:25	4:07	—	38	57	76	1:54	—
60	4:15-4:49	6:50-7:45	3:52	6:14	88	3:40	5:54	81	3:23	4:03	—	37	56	75	1:52	—
61	4:11-4:45	6:45-7:39	3:49	6:09	86	3:37	5:50	80	3:20	4:00	—	37	55	74	1:51	—
62	4:08-4:41	6:39-7:33	3:46	6:04	85	3:34	5:45	79	3:17	3:57	—	36	54	73	1:49	—
63	4:05-4:38	6:34-7:27	3:43	5:59	84	3:32	5:41	78	3:15	3:54	—	36	53	72	1:48	—
64	4:02-4:34	6:29-7:21	3:40	5:54	83	3:29	5:36	77	3:12	3:51	—	35	52	71	1:46	—
65	3:59-4:31	6:24-7:16	3:37	5:49	82	3:26	5:32	76	3:10	3:48	—	35	52	70	1:45	—
66	3:56-4:28	6:19-7:10	3:34	5:45	81	3:24	5:28	75	3:08	3:45	5:00	34	51	69	1:43	—
67	3:53-4:24	6:15-7:05	3:31	5:40	80	3:21	5:24	74	3:05	3:42	4:57	34	51	68	1:42	—
68	3:50-4:21	6:10-7:00	3:29	5:36	79	3:19	5:20	73	3:03	3:39	4:53	33	50	67	1:40	—
69	3:47-4:18	6:06-6:55	3:26	5:32	78	3:16	5:16	72	3:01	3:36	4:50	33	49	66	99	—
70	3:44-4:15	6:01-6:50	3:24	5:28	77	3:14	5:13	71	2:59	3:34	4:46	32	48	65	97	—
71	3:42-4:12	5:57-6:46	3:21	5:24	76	3:12	5:09	70	2:57	3:31	4:43	32	48	64	96	—
72	3:40-4:00	5:53-6:41	3:19	5:20	76	3:10	5:05	69	2:55	3:29	4:40	31	47	63	94	—
73	3:37-4:07	5:49-6:37	3:16	5:16	75	3:08	5:02	69	2:53	3:27	4:37	31	47	63	93	—
74	3:34-4:04	5:45-6:32	3:14	5:12	74	3:06	4:59	68	2:51	3:25	4:34	31	46	62	92	—
75	3:32-4:01	5:41-6:28	3:12	5:09	74	3:04	4:56	67	2:49	3:22	4:31	30	46	61	91	—

VDOT	E (EASY) / L (LONG) Km	Mile	M (MARATHON PACE) Km	Mile	T (THRESHOLD PACE) 400	Km	Mile	I (INTERVAL PACE) 400	Km	1.200	Mile	R (REPETITION PACE) 200	300	400	600	800
76	3:30-3:58	5:38-6:24	3:10	5:05	73	3:02	4:52	66	2:48	3:20	4:28	30	45	60	90	—
77	3:28-3:56	5:34-6:20	3:08	5:02	72	3:00	4:49	65	2:46	3:18	4:25	29	45	59	89	2:00
78	3:25-3:53	5:30-6:16	3:06	4:58	71	2:58	4:46	65	2:44	3:16	4:23	29	44	59	88	1:59
79	3:23-3:51	5:27-6:12	3:03	4:55	70	2:56	4:43	64	2:42	3:14	4:20	29	44	58	87	1:58
80	3:21-3:49	5:24-6:08	3:01	4:52	70	2:54	4:41	64	2:41	3:12	4:17	29	43	58	87	1:56
81	3:19-3:46	5:20-6:04	3:00	4:49	69	2:53	4:38	63	2:39	3:10	4:15	28	43	57	86	1:55
82	3:17-3:44	5:17-6:01	2:58	4:46	68	2:51	4:35	62	2:38	3:08	4:12	28	42	56	85	1:54
83	3:15-3:42	5:14-5:57	2:56	4:43	68	2:49	4:32	62	2:36	3:07	4:10	28	42	56	84	1:53
84	3:13-3:40	5:11-5:54	2:54	4:40	67	2:48	4:30	61	2:35	3:05	4:08	27	41	55	83	1:52
85	3:11-3:38	5:08-5:50	2:52	4:37	66	2:46	4:27	61	2:33	3:03	4:05	27	41	55	82	1:51

Reprinted, by permission, from J. Daniels, 2014, *Daniels' running formula*, 3rd ed. (Champaign, IL: Human Kinetics), 84-87. Table created by Jack Daniels' Running Calculator designed by the Run SMART Project.

Table A.3   VDOT Values and Training Intensities for Beginning and Rehabilitating Runners

RACE TIMES Mile	5K	VDOT	R (REPETITION PACE) 200 m	300 m	I (INTERVAL PACE) 200 m	400 m	T (THRESHOLD PACE) 400 m	Km	Mile	M (MARATHON PACE) Time (hr:min)	min/km	min/mile
9:10	30:40	30	1:08	1:42	1:11	2:24	2:33	6:24	10:18	4:57	7:03	11:21
9:27	31:32	29	1:10	1:45	1:14	2:28	2:37	6:34	10:34	5:06	7:15	11:41
9:44	37:27	28	1:13	1:49	1:17	2:34	2:42	6:45	10:52	5:15	7:27	12:02
10:02	33:25	27	1:15	1:53	1:19	2:38	2:46	6:56	11:10	5:25	7:41	12:24
10:22	34:27	26	1:18	1:57	1:22	2:44	2:51	7:09	11:30	5:35	7:56	12:47
10:43	35:33	25	1:21	2:02	1:24	2:48	2:56	7:21	11:51	5:45	8:10	13:11
11:06	36:44	24	1:24	—	1:27	2:55	3:02	7:35	12:13	5:56	8:26	13:36
11:30	38:01	23	1:27	—	1:30	3:01	3:08	7:50	12:36	6:08	8:43	14:02
11:56	39:22	22	1:30	—	1:33	3:07	3:14	8:06	13:02	6:19	8:59	14:29
12:24	40:49	21	1:33	—	1:36	3:13	3:21	8:23	13:29	6:31	9:16	14:57
12:55	42:24	20	1:37	—	1:40	3:21	3:28	8:41	13:58	6:44	9:34	15:26

Reprinted, by permission, from J. Daniels, 2014, *Daniels' running formula*, 3rd ed. (Champaign, IL: Human Kinetics), 88. Table created by Jack Daniels' Running Calculator designed by the Run SMART Project.

Table A.4 Treadmill Pace Conversions

Treadmill MPH setting	Pace per mile	EQUIVALENT PACES BY INCLINE										
		0%	1%	2%	3%	4%	5%	6%	7%	8%	9%	10%
5.0	12:00	12:31	11:44	11:05	10:32	10:03	9:38	9:16	8:56	8:38	8:22	8:07
5.2	11:32	12:02	11:18	10:42	10:11	9:44	9:20	8:59	8:40	8:23	8:08	7:54
5.4	11:07	11:35	10:55	10:20	9:51	9:26	9:03	8:43	8:25	8:09	7:55	7:41
5.6	10:43	11:10	10:32	10:00	9:33	9:09	8:48	8:29	8:12	7:56	7:42	7:29
5.8	10:21	10:47	10:12	9:42	9:16	8:53	8:33	8:15	7:58	7:44	7:30	7:18
6.0	10:00	10:26	9:52	9:24	9:00	8:38	8:19	8:02	7:46	7:32	7:19	7:07
6.1	9:50	10:15	9:43	9:16	8:52	8:31	8:12	7:55	7:40	7:26	7:14	7:02
6.2	9:41	10:05	9:34	9:08	8:44	8:24	8:06	7:49	7:34	7:21	7:08	6:57
6.3	9:31	9:56	9:26	9:00	8:37	8:17	7:59	7:43	7:29	7:15	7:03	6:52
6.4	9:23	9:46	9:17	8:52	8:30	8:10	7:53	7:37	7:23	7:10	6:58	6:47
6.5	9:14	9:37	9:09	8:45	8:23	8:04	7:47	7:32	7:18	7:05	6:53	6:43
6.6	9:05	9:29	9:01	8:37	8:16	7:58	7:41	7:26	7:13	7:00	6:49	6:38
6.7	8:57	9:20	8:53	8:30	8:10	7:52	7:35	7:21	7:07	6:55	6:44	6:34
6.8	8:49	9:12	8:45	8:23	8:03	7:46	7:30	7:15	7:02	6:50	6:40	6:29
6.9	8:42	9:04	8:39	8:17	7:57	7:40	7:24	7:10	6:58	6:46	6:35	6:25
7.0	8:34	8:56	8:32	8:10	7:51	7:34	7:19	7:05	6:53	6:41	6:31	6:21
7.1	8:27	8:49	8:25	8:04	7:45	7:29	7:14	7:00	6:48	6:37	6:27	6:17
7.2	8:20	8:41	8:18	7:58	7:40	7:23	7:09	6:56	6:44	6:33	6:22	6:13
7.3	8:13	8:34	8:12	7:52	7:34	7:18	7:04	6:51	6:39	6:28	6:18	6:09
7.4	8:06	8:27	8:05	7:46	7:28	7:13	6:59	6:46	6:35	6:24	6:14	6:05
7.5	8:00	8:20	7:59	7:40	7:23	7:08	6:54	6:42	6:31	6:20	6:11	6:02
7.6	7:54	8:14	7:53	7:34	7:18	7:03	6:50	6:38	6:26	6:16	6:07	5:58
7.7	7:48	8:07	7:47	7:29	7:13	6:58	6:45	6:33	6:22	6:12	6:03	5:55
7.8	7:42	8:01	7:41	7:24	7:08	6:54	6:41	6:29	6:18	6:09	5:59	5:51
7.9	7:36	7:55	7:36	7:18	7:03	6:49	6:37	6:25	6:15	6:05	5:56	5:48
8.0	7:30	7:49	7:30	7:13	6:58	6:45	6:32	6:21	6:11	6:01	5:52	5:44
8.1	7:24	7:43	7:25	7:08	6:54	6:40	6:28	6:17	6:07	5:58	5:49	5:41
8.2	7:19	7:38	7:20	7:04	6:49	6:36	6:24	6:13	6:03	5:54	5:46	5:38
8.3	7:14	7:32	7:15	6:59	6:45	6:32	6:20	6:10	6:00	5:51	5:42	5:35
8.4	7:09	7:27	7:10	6:54	6:40	6:28	6:16	6:06	5:56	5:47	5:39	5:32
8.5	7:04	7:22	7:05	6:50	6:36	6:24	6:13	6:02	5:53	5:44	5:36	5:29
8.6	6:59	7:16	7:00	6:45	6:32	6:20	6:09	5:59	5:49	5:41	5:33	5:26
8.7	6:54	7:11	6:55	6:41	6:28	6:16	6:05	5:55	5:46	5:38	5:30	5:23
8.8	6:49	7:07	6:51	6:37	6:24	6:12	6:02	5:52	5:43	5:35	5:27	5:20
8.9	6:44	7:02	6:46	6:32	6:20	6:09	5:58	5:49	5:40	5:32	5:24	5:17
9.0	6:40	6:57	6:42	6:28	6:16	6:05	5:55	5:45	5:37	5:29	5:21	5:14
9.1	6:36	6:52	6:38	6:24	6:12	6:01	5:51	5:42	5:34	5:26	5:18	5:11
9.2	6:31	6:48	6:34	6:20	6:09	5:58	5:48	5:39	5:31	5:23	5:16	5:09

Treadmill MPH setting	Pace per mile	EQUIVALENT PACES BY INCLINE										
		0%	1%	2%	3%	4%	5%	6%	7%	8%	9%	10%
9.3	6:27	6:44	6:29	6:17	6:05	5:55	5:45	5:36	5:28	5:20	5:13	5:06
9.4	6:23	6:39	6:25	6:13	6:02	5:51	5:42	5:33	5:25	5:17	5:10	5:04
9.5	6:19	6:35	6:22	6:09	5:58	5:48	5:39	5:30	5:22	5:14	5:08	5:01
9.6	6:15	6:31	6:18	6:06	5:55	5:45	5:35	5:27	5:19	5:12	5:05	4:59
9.7	6:11	6:27	6:14	6:02	5:51	5:42	5:32	5:24	5:16	5:09	5:02	4:56
9.8	6:07	6:23	6:10	5:59	5:48	5:38	5:30	5:21	5:14	5:07	5:00	4:54
9.9	6:04	6:19	6:07	5:55	5:45	5:35	5:27	5:19	5:11	5:04	4:58	4:51
10.0	6:00	6:15	6:03	5:52	5:42	5:32	5:24	5:16	5:08	5:02	4:55	4:49
10.1	5:56	6:12	6:00	5:49	5:39	5:29	5:21	5:13	5:06	4:59	4:53	4:47
10.2	5:53	6:08	5:56	5:45	5:36	5:27	5:18	5:11	5:03	4:57	4:50	4:45
10.3	5:50	6:04	5:53	5:42	5:33	5:24	5:16	5:08	5:01	4:54	4:48	4:42
10.4	5:46	6:01	5:50	5:39	5:30	5:21	5:13	5:05	4:58	4:52	4:46	4:40
10.5	5:43	5:57	5:46	5:36	5:27	5:18	5:10	5:03	4:56	4:50	4:44	4:38
10.6	5:40	5:54	5:43	5:33	5:24	5:15	5:08	5:00	4:54	4:47	4:41	4:36
10.7	5:36	5:51	5:40	5:30	5:21	5:13	5:05	4:58	4:51	4:45	4:39	4:34
10.8	5:33	5:48	5:37	5:27	5:18	5:10	5:03	4:56	4:49	4:43	4:37	4:32
10.9	5:30	5:44	5:34	5:24	5:16	5:08	5:00	4:53	4:47	4:41	4:35	4:30
11.0	5:27	5:41	5:31	5:22	5:13	5:05	4:58	4:51	4:45	4:39	4:33	4:28
11.2	5:21	5:35	5:25	5:16	5:08	5:00	4:53	4:46	4:40	4:34	4:29	4:24
11.4	5:16	5:29	5:20	5:11	5:03	4:55	4:49	4:42	4:36	4:30	4:25	4:20
11.6	5:10	5:24	5:14	5:06	4:58	4:51	4:44	4:38	4:32	4:27	4:21	4:17
11.8	5:05	5:18	5:09	5:01	4:53	4:46	4:40	4:34	4:28	4:23	4:18	4:13
12.0	5:00	5:13	5:04	4:56	4:49	4:42	4:36	4:30	4:24	4:19	4:14	4:10

Reprinted from www.hillrunner.com. Available: http://www.hillrunner.com/training/tmillchart.php [March 10, 2014].

References

American College of Sports Medicine. 2007. The American College of Sports Medicine position stand on exercise and fluid replacement. *Medicine and Science in Sports*, 39, 377-390.

Baker, A.B., and Y.Q. Tang. 2010. Aging performance for masters records in athletics, swimming, rowing, cycling, triathlon, and weightlifting. *Experimental Aging Research*, 36 (4), 453-477.

Bandy W.D., J.M. Irion, and M. Briggler. 1997. The effect of time and frequency of static stretching on flexibility of the hamstring muscles. *Physical Therapy*. 77 (10), 1090-1096.

Bergeron, M.F., M. Hargreaves, E.M. Haymes, G.W. Mack, W.O. Roberts. 2007. ACSM position stand: exercise and fluid replacement. *Medicine & Science in Sports & Exercise* 39 (1) 2, 377-390.

Betts, J. A., & Williams, C. (2010). Short-term recovery from prolonged exercise: Exploring the potential for protein ingestion to accentuate the benefits of carbohydrate supplements. *Sports Medicine*, 40, 941–959.

Booth, F.W., S.H. Weeden, and B.S. Tseng. 1994. Effect of aging on human skeletal muscle and motor function. *Medicine & Science in Sports & Exercise*, 26 (5), 556-560.

Borg, Gunnar A. 1982. Psychophysical bases of perceived exertion. *Medicine & Science in Sports & Exercise* 14 (5), 377-381.

Bridges, W. 2004. *Transitions: Making Sense of Life's Changes*. Cambridge, MA: Perseus Books Group.

Burfoot, A., 2007. What's Your Ideal Weight? *Runner's World*. May 18.

Collins, K.J., A.N. Exton-Smith, M.H. James, D.J. Oliver. 1980. Functional changes in autonomic nervous responses with ageing. *Age and Ageing*, 9 (1), 17-24.

Conoboy, P., and R. Dyson. 2006. Effect of aging on the stride pattern of veteran marathon runners. *British Journal of Sports Medicine*, 40 (7), 601-604.

Daniels, J. 2014. *Daniels' Running Formula*. 3rd edition. Champaign, IL: Human Kinetics.

Daoud, A.I., G.J. Geissler, F. Wang, J. Saretsky, Y.A. Daoud, and D.E. Lieberman. 2012. Foot strike and injury rates in endurance runners: a retrospective study. *Medicine & Science in Sports & Exercise*, 44 (7), 1325-1334.

Davies, C. T. M., 1980. Effects of wind assistance and resistance on the forward motion of a runner. *Journal of Applied Physiology* 48 (4): 702-709.

Dion T., F.A. Savoie, A. Asselin, C. Gariepy, and E.D. Goulet. 2013. Half-marathon running performance is not improved by a rate of fluid intake above that dictated by thirst sensation in trained distance runners. *European Journal of Applied Physiology*, 113 (12), 3011-3020.

Duhigg, C. 2012. *The Power of Habit: Why We Do What We Do in Life and Business*. New York: Random House.

Ericsson, K.A., R.T. Krampe, and C. Tesch-Romer. 1993. The role of deliberate practice in the acquisition of expert performance. *Psychological Review*, 100 (3), 363-406.

Gagne, D.A., A. Von Holle, K.A. Brownley, C.D. Runfola, K.E. Branch, and C.M. Bulik. 2012. Eating disorder symptoms and weight and shape concerns in a large web-based convenience sample of women ages 50 and above: results of the Gender and Body Image study. *International Journal of Eating Disorders*, 45 (7), 832-844.

Grimby, G., and B. Saltin. 1983. The aging muscle. *Clinical Physiology and Functional Imaging*, 3 (3), 209-218.

Hay, P.J., J. Mond, P. Buttner, and A. Darby. 2008. Eating disorder behaviors are increasing: findings from sequential community surveys in South Australia. *PLOS ONE*. [Online]. 3 (2). Available: www.plosone.org/article/info:doi/10.1371/journal.pone.0001541.

Holloszy, J.O., and Kohrt, W.M. 1995. Exercise. In: E. Masoro (Ed.), *Handbook of Physiology*, Section 11: Aging, 633-666. New York: Oxford University Press.

Institute of Medicine of the National Academies. 2004. Newsletter. http://www8.nationalacademies.org/onpinews/newsitem.aspx?RecordID=10925

Ivy, J.L., H.W. Goforth Jr, B.M. Damon, T.R. McCauley, E.C. Parsons, and T.B. Price. 2002. Early post exercise muscle glycogen recovery is enhanced with a carbohydrate-protein supplement. *Journal of Applied Physiology* 93(4):1337- 1344.

Jacobs, S.J., and B.L. Berson. 1986. Injuries to runners: a study of entrants to a 10,000 meter race. *American Journal of Sports Medicine*, 14 (2), 151-155.

Joyner, M. 1993. Physiological limiting factors and distance running: influence of gender and age on record performances. *Exercise and Sport Sciences Reviews*, 21, 103-133.

Kay, A.D., and A.J. Blazevich. 2012. Effect of acute static stretch on maximal muscle performance: a systematic review. *Medicine & Science in Sports & Exercise*. 44 (1), 154-164.

Kerksick, C., T. Harvey, J. Stout, B. Campbell, C. Wilborn, R. Kreider, D. Kalman, T. Ziegenfuss, H. Lopez, J. Landis, J.L. Ivy, J. Antonio. 2008. International Society of Sports Nutrition position stand: nutrient timing. *Journal of the International Society of Sports Nutrition.* http://www.jissn.com/content/5/1/17

Kissane, J. 2011. Mastering the Marathon Qualifying Marks. *Running Times Online.* Available: http://m.runnersworld.com/masters-profiles/mastering-marathon-qualifying-marks?page=3.

Locke, E.A., and G.P. Latham. 2002. Building a practically useful theory of goal setting and task motivation: a 35-year odyssey. *American Psychologist.* 57, 705-717.

Locke, E. A., and G.P. Latham. 1990. *A Theory of Goal Setting and Task Performance.* Englewood Cliffs, NJ: Prentice Hall.

Marti B., and H. Howald. 1990. Long-term effects of physical training on aerobic capacity: controlled study of former elite athletes. *Journal of Applied Physiology,* 69 (4), 1451-1459.

McKean, K.A., N.A. Manson, and W.D. Stanish. 2006. Musculoskeletal injury in the masters runners. *Clinical Journal of Sports Medicine,* 16 (2), 149-154.

Moyer, C.S. 2012. Eating disorders an increasing problem in older women. *American Medical News.* July 9, 2012. Available: www.amednews.com/article/20120709/health/307099949/4/.

Pray, W.S., and J.J. Pray. 2004. Calcium supplements: benefits and risks. *Medscape.* Available: www.medscape.com/viewarticle/497826.

Robbins, L. 2010. Running for Charity Fuels a Boom in Marathoning. *The New York Times Online.* Available: http://marathon.blogs.nytimes.com/2010/10/21/running-for-charity-fuels-a-boom-in-marathoning/?_r=0

Rodgers, Bill, and Priscilla Welch. 1991. *Bill Rodgers and Priscilla Welch on Masters Running and Racing.* Emmaus, PA: Rodale Press Inc.

Rosenfeld, L.B., J.M. Richman, and C.J. Hardy. 1989. Examining social support networks among athletes: description and relationship to stress. *The Sport Psychologist,* 3, 23-33.

Running USA. 2013. *Running USA's Annual Half-Marathon Report.* Available: http://www.runningusa.org/index.cfm?fuseaction=news.details&ArticleId=333.

Running USA. 2013. *Statistics.* http://www.runningusa.org/statistics.

Schmid, S., M. Hallschmid, K. Jauch-Chara, J. Born, and B. Schultes. 2008. A single night of sleep deprivation increases ghrelin levels and feelings of hunger in normal-weight healthy men. *Journal of Sleep Research* 17 (3), 331-334.

Schulman, D. 2000. Fuel on Fat for the Long Run. Marathonguide.com. Available: http://www.marathonguide.com/training/articles/mandbfuelonfat.cfm.

Sheridan, M.K. 2012. Eating disorders in middle age bring unique challenges, treatments. *The Huffington Post.* March 2, 2012. Available: www.huffingtonpost.com/2012/03/02/eating-disorders-middle-age_n_1313791.html.

So, W-Y, and Choi, D.H. 2010. Differences in physical fitness and cardiovascular function depend on BMI. *Journal of Sports Science & Medicine,* (9) 239 – 244.

Trappe, S.W., D.L. Costill, M.D. Vukovich, J. Jones, and T. Melham. 1996. Aging among elite distance runners: a 22-yr longitudinal study. *Journal of Applied Physiology,* 80 (1), 285-290.

USA Triathlon. 2013. *2012 USA Triathlon Demographics Report.* Available: http://www.usatriathlon.org/about-multisport/demographics.aspx

Utzschneider, C. 2002. *Women Runners Who Became National Caliber After Age 40.* Ann Arbor, MI: Bell & Howell Information and Learning Company.

van Mechelen, W. 1992. Running injuries: a review of the epidemiological literature. *Sports Medicine,* 14 (5), 320-335.

Williams, G.N., M.J. Higgins, and M.D. Lewek. 2002. Aging skeletal muscle: physiologic changes and the effects of training. *Physical Therapy,* 82, 62-68.

Wilson, J.M., L.M. Hornbuckle, J.S Kim, C. Ugrinowitsch, S.R. Lee, M.C. Zourdos, B. Sommer, and L.B. Panton. 2010. Effects of static stretching on energy cost and running endurance performance. *Journal of Strength and Conditioning Research,* 24 (9), 2274-2279.

Wright, V.J., and B.C. Perricelli. 2008. Age-related rates of decline in performance among elite senior athletes. *The American Journal of Sports Medicine,* 36 (3), 443-450.

Young, A.J. 1991. Effects of aging on human cold tolerance. *Experimental Aging Research,* 17 (3), 205-213.

Young, A.J., and D. Lee. T. 1997. Aging and human cold tolerance. *Experimental Aging Research,* 23 (1), 45-67.

Young, W.B., and D.G. Behm. 2003. Effects of running, static stretching and practice jumps on explosive force production and jumping performance. *Journal of Sports Medicine and Physical Fitness,* 43, 21-27.

Index

Note: Page numbers followed by italicized *f* and *t* indicate information contained in figures and tables, respectively.

A

absolute times 6
Accelerade 190
Achilles tendinitis 17, 65-66
adaptation 105
adenosine triphosphate (ATP) 173
age grading 6-7, 101
age-grading calculators 91-92
age groupings 7
aging effects
      advantages to performance of 27-33, 100
      blood pressure and 13
      body temperature and 13
      bone and muscle loss and 15-16
      brain and 18-19
      cardiopulmonary function and 13-14
      effects of 12-21
      heart rate and 12
      metabolism and 17
      motivation and 21, 100
      performance decline 139-140
      recovery time and 17-21, 100
      respiration rate and 13
      stress on body 16-17
      $\dot{V}O_2$max and 14-15
      weather and environment and 21-22
      women and 22-26
alcohol 33, 175, 178
A march 51
anemia 24
ankle sprains 66
anorexia 24
aquarunning 58
Arbogast, Meghan 215-216
arm drive 43, 44*f*
A skip 51

B

Barbour, John 20
barefoot running 47-48
Barefoot Running (Douglas) 47
Barry, Kristin 131, 132
big-picture calendar 87, 89*f*
biomechanics. *See* form, biomechanics of
blisters 67
blood pressure, and aging 13
B march 52
BMI (body-mass index) 23, 39
body temperature, and aging 13
Bolder Boulder 161
bone loss, and aging 15-16
Borg, Gunnar 112
Born to Run (McDougall) 47
Boston Marathon 4, 5, 7, 173
bounding 54
Bowerman, Bill 4
brain, running and 18-19
breathing 45-46
B skip 52
Burfoot, Amby 9-10
butt kick 54

C

cadence 45
caffeine 33
calories, burned 17
carbohydrate 36-37, 173
cardiopulmonary function, and aging 13-14
carioca 53

Carlsbad 5000 7, 154
Cascadia Trail Series 214
Castille, Kevin 154
chafing 67
chiropractic 64-65
chocolate milk 190
clothing, temperature and 22
coaches, finding 97-99
Cohen, Susan Zwerling 4
Comrades Marathon 9
confidence 31
cool-downs 60-61
Cooper River Bridge Run 161
Cougar Mountain Trail Run Series 214
Crescent City Classic 7
cross country events 8
cross-training 58, 175, 177
cruise intervals 107, 108*t*

D

Daniels' $\dot{V}O_2$max and VDOT charts 108*t*, 113, 196, 219-223
dehydration 180
Derderian, Tom 4
De Reuck, Colleen 4, 171
discipline 98
Dominici, Francesca 98
Douglas, Scott 47-49
downhill form 134
duathlons 212-213
Dushay, Jody 210

E

eating disorders 22-24
Endless Summer Trail Run Series 214
Ericsson, K. Anders 31-32
Etzweiler, George 213
even-effort pacing 202
even pacing 199-202
events, masters running 7-9
expertise 31-33

F

fartlek runs
      about 108, 108*t*
      hill fartlek 135-136, 135*t*
fast feet 55
fat
      in diet 37, 173
      types in various oils and spreads 38*f*
female athlete triad 22-23
1500 meter race 149. *See also* mile race
5K race
      about 147
      periodization plan 106*f*
      training plan for 154-155, 154*t*-157*t*, 158
flats, racing 198
flexibility. *See also* stretching
      about 71-72
      yoga for 58-59, 73, 75
foam rollers 60, 175
foot strike 45
forefoot strike 45
form, biomechanics of
      about 41-42
      analyzing 64-65
      arm drive 43, 44*f*
      breathing 45-46
      drills 49-55
      foot strike 45

forward stride 43, 44f
    and injuries 63
    posture 42-43, 43f
    stride length and rate 46-49, 65
    tension 42-43
form drills
    A march 51
    A skip 51
    B march 52
    bounding 54
    B skip 52
    butt kick 54
    carioca 53
    fast feet 55
    heel walk 50
    high knee 53
    high skip with arm circles 50
    running backward 54
    shin grab 55
    side slide with arm swings 51
    toe walk 50
Freihofers 5K 154, 173
front running 202-203

G
gait. *See* form, biomechanics of
Galloway, Jeff 4
Georgia State Parks Trail Series 214
glycogen synthase 190
goals and goal setting
    about 85-86
    big-picture calendar 87, 89f
    flexibility in 87
    goal pyramids 87, 88f, 94f
    integrating running goals into life 87-90, 88f, 89f
    long-term goals 93
    postgoal analysis 94-96
    setting and writing down 86-87, 196
    setting outcome goals 92, 197
    setting performance goals 91-92, 196-197
    setting process goals 92-93, 197
    SMART criteria 86-87
    successive short-term goals 93
    support team for 97-102
    tracking goals 90
Gruca, Dorota 154

H
Haas, Kara 200-201
half marathon
    about 159-160
    hydration 35
    periodization plan 106f
    training plan for 164-165, 164t-167t
Harada, Mary 16, 27, 149-150
hard-easy rule 105
Hartshorne Memorial Masters Mile 150-151
healthy living habits
    about 33
    hydration 34-35
    nutrition and weight control 36-39, 38f, 40t
    recovery 34
    reframing 39
    sleep 33-34
heart rate, resting 12
heat, and aging 21
heel strike 45
heel walk 50
high knee 53
high skip with arm circles 50
hill running
    downhill form 134
    form 133-135
    hill fartlek 135-136, 135t
    hill repeats 108t, 109, 134, 135
    uphill form 133-134
Holmquist, Jan 70, 113, 161

Hussein, Mbarak 171
hydration
    about 34-35
    dehydration 180
    in marathon race 182-183
    in marathon training 175-180
    postrace 206-207
    in races 206
hyponatremia 179, 180
hypothermia 21-22

I
ice baths 62, 191
Iliotibial band syndrome (ITBS) 67
injuries
    Achilles tendinitis 65-66
    ankle sprains 66
    black toenails 66
    blisters 67
    causes and treatments of common 65-70
    chafing 67
    checklist for possible causes 63
    contrast baths 62
    ice baths 62, 191
    Iliotibial band syndrome (ITBS) 67
    massage 63-65
    muscle pulls or strains 67-68
    plantar fasciitis 68
    RICHE treatment 61-62
    runner's knee 68
    shin splints 69
    side stitch 69
    stress fractures 69-70
    whirlpool 62
injury prevention
    about 57
    chiropractic and 64-65
    cool-downs 60-61
    cross-training 58
    low-impact machines 59
    overtraining 61
    recovery 34
    running terrain 59-60
    track work 60
    training distances 59
    treadmills 60
    warm-ups 60
    yoga 58-59
interval training runs 108-109, 108t

J
James, Libby 110-111
joints, aging and 16
Joyner, Michael J. 141-143

K
Kelley, John J. 9, 10
Kerr, Matt 85-86

L
lactate threshold 104
Lamppa, Ryan 5
lemming effect (weight loss) 22-23
Lilac Bloomsday Run 7
Linov, Pam 112
long runs 107, 108t, 159-160, 172-174
Loomis, Amanda 4

M
Magill, Pete 28-30
marathon
    about 171
    checklist of items to pack 182
    day before activity 181-182
    delayed-onset muscle soreness (DOMS) 191
    hydration 35
    periodization plan 106f

marathon *(continued)*
 postrace refueling 190-191
 postrace running plan 191-192
 prerace dinner 182
 race day fueling and hydrating 182-183
 recovery 190-192
 stride rate *versus* length 46
Marathon des Sables 9
marathon training
 carbohydrate loading 180-181, 181t
 hydration habits 175-180
 injury prevention 174-175
 long and tempo runs 172-174
 long run fueling 180-181
 nutrition 180
 planning 172
 recovery and sleep 174-175
 training plans 183, 184t-189t
Martin, Kathy 168-170
massage 63-65
Masters Running and Racing (Rodgers and Welch) 6, 32
maximum heart rate (MHR) 12
metabolism, and aging 17
midfoot strike 45
mile race
 about 147
 periodization plan 106f
 training plan for 149-151, 150t-153t, 158
Miller, Joan 173
minimalist running 48-49, 65, 199
mitochondria 173
Monument Avenue 10K 161
motivation, and aging 21, 100
Mountain, Ultra and Trail Sport Council 213
mountain events 8, 213
Mount Washington Road Race 8, 16, 213
MOVE! How Women Can Achieve Athletic Goals (Utzschneider) 21, 87
muscle pulls or strains 67-68
muscles
 aging and 16-17
 delayed-onset muscle soreness (DOMS) 191
 foam rollers and sticks 60
 muscle loss and aging 15-16
 myofascial release (MFR) 60
 progressive muscle relaxation 204
myofascial release (MFR) 60

N
Navas, Joe 32, 147
negative splits 202
neurogenesis 19
New York City Marathon 5, 7
nutrition and weight control
 about 36-39
 fat types in various oils and spreads 38f
 long run fueling 180-181
 major nutrients 36-39
 marathon post-race refueling 190-191
 marathon race day fueling and hydrating 182-183
 postrace hydration and fueling 206-207
 racing hydration and fueling 206
 vitamins and minerals 39, 40t
 weight and running times 39
 weight control 37-39

O
overload 105
overtraining 61

P
pain, tracking 90
Parsi, Carrie 16, 213
patience 31
Peachtree Road Race 7, 161
perceived exertion 109, 112-114, 173-174
periodization
 about 86, 104-105
 aging and 20

 endurance phase 105-107, 106f
 sharpening phase 106f, 107
 strengthening phase 106f, 107
 tapering phase 106f, 107
periodization plans
 5K race 106f
 half marathon 106f
 marathon 106f
 mile race 106f
 10K race 106f
personal best times 6
Piers, Sheri 131-132, 171
Pilcher, Brian 148-149
plantar fasciitis 68
plus pace runs 107, 108t, 159
plyometric exercises, and stride rate 49
posture 42-43, 43f
The Power of Habit (Duhigg) 33
Pratt-Otto, Dru 109, 112
progress, measuring
 absolute times 6
 age-graded results 6-7
 age group placement 7
protein 37, 190

R
race time predictors 91-92
racing. *See also specific race distances*
 about 195-196
 day before plan 203-204
 hydration and fueling 206
 postrace goal analysis 207
 postrace hydration and fueling 206-207
 race day checklist 203
 race week 199-203
 recovery and rebuilding 207-208
 segmenting plan 199-203
 setting goals 196-197, 199
 shoes 197-199
 starting tips 205-206
Ratey, John 18-19
record keeping 90
recovery time
 and aging 17-21, 100
 guidelines for 34
 rest and recovery 105
relaxation exercises 33-34, 204
respiration rate, and aging 13
rest and recovery 105
resting heart rate (RHR) 12, 90
Riley, William 81-82
Ritchie, Tim 113
road events 7
Rodgers, Bill 4
roller sticks 60, 175
The Runner's Guide to the Meaning of Life (Burfoot) 9
runner's knee 68
Runner's World 9
Runner's World Complete Guide to Minimalism (Douglas) 47, 49
running backward 54
running clubs 102
running economy 104
runninginjuryoracle.com 61
running terrain, and injuries 59-60
Running USA 5

S
Samuelson, Joan Benoit 4, 140
segmenting plans for racing 199-203
self-knowledge 30
Shaheed, Nolan 151
Shapiro, Felicia 98
Sheehan, George 4
shin grab 55
shin splints 69
shoes
 barefoot running 47-48
 flats 198
 minimalist shoes 48-49, 199

orthotics 49
    racing 197-199
Shorter, Frank 4
side slide with arm swings 51
side stitch 69
sleep 33-34
Smith, Linda Somers 171, 176-179
Spartathlon 9
specificity 105
speed training
    about 107-109,112, 108*t*, 114
    Daniels' $\dot{V}O_2$max charts 108*t*, 113, 219-223
    determinants of speed 104
    perceived exertion 109, 112-114
    training intensities charts 221-223
spikes 198
sprints 108*t*
Steinbach, Coreen 151
Stewart, Barbara 98
strength exercises
    bench press 127
    bent-leg donkey kick 122
    bent over row 128
    chair dip 124
    front plank 129
    lunge 120
    one- or two-leg heel raise 126
    push up 123
    seated running arms 125
    side plank 130
    squat 119
    straight-leg donkey kick 121
    toe raise 126
strength training
    about 115-116
    body weight exercises 119-126
    45-minute program 117-130
    free weight exercises 127-128
    hill running 133-136
    indicators for 116
    isometric exercises 129-130
    machine *versus* functional 116
    scheduling 117
    for stride length 46-49
    10-minute circuit 133
stretching. *See also* form drills
    groin stretch 79
    hamstring and back stretch 81
    hamstring stretch 78
    heel dip 76
    hip and back stretch 79
    hip flexor stretch 80
    Iliotibial band stretch 76
    leg swings 73, 74
    piriformis stretch 80
    postrun static stretching 74-81
    prerun dynamic stretching 73
    quadriceps stretch 78
    shoulder stretch 77
    standing calf stretch 74
    sun salutes yoga sequence 73, 75
    upper-back stretch 77
stride length and rate 46-49, 65
strides 108, 108*t*, 109
surging 202
sweat rate 175-179

T
tempo workouts 107, 108*t*, 172-174
tendons, aging and 16-17
10K race
    about 159-160
    periodization plan 106*f*
    training plan for 160-161, 160*t*-163*t*
10-point running rating of perceived exertion 112
10,000 hours to excellence 31-33
threshold runs 107, 108*t*
toe walk 50
Torres, Dara 17-19

track events 8
track work 60
trail races 214-217
training
    attitude toward 140-143
    cutback weeks 89-90
    Daniels' $\dot{V}O_2$max charts 108*t*, 113, 219-220
    guidelines for masters 144
    increasing mileage 89-90
    mileage base 103-104
    perceived exertion 109, 112-114
    periodization 86, 104-107, 106*f*
    speed training 107-109, 108*t*
    strength training 115-116
    training intensities charts 221-223
training plans
    about 144-146
    5K 154-155, 154*t*-157*t*, 158
    half marathon 164-165, 164*t*-167*t*
    marathon 171-192
    mile 149-151, 150*t*-153*t*, 158,
        160-161, 160*t*-163*t*
Transitions: Making Sense of Life's Changes (Bridges) 209-210
treadmill pace conversions 224-225
treadmills 60
TREQ form 42
triathlons 210-212
Troncoso, Carmen 99-101
Twin Cities Marathon 7, 174
Type II (fast-twitch) muscles 15
Type I (slow-twitch) muscles 15

U
ultradistance events 8-9, 213-214
Ultra-Trail du Mont-Blanc 213
uphill form 133-134

V
vegetarian diet 37
Vibram Five Fingers 48
videos of running form 42
vitamins and minerals 39, 40*t*
$\dot{V}O_2$max
    and aging 14-15
    Daniels' $\dot{V}O_2$max charts 108*t*, 113, 219-223
    and speed 104
    $\dot{V}O_2$max predictor charts 91-92

W
weather and environment 21-22
weight control. *See* nutrition and weight control
weight training 46-49
Western States Endurance Run 9, 214
Whitlock, Ed 12
Winfrey, Oprah 5
wisdom 30
women
    age at start of running career 32*f*
    and aging 22-26
    diet and self-image 23-24
    endurance advantage of 26
    female athlete triad 22-23
    iron issues 24
    as masters runners 5
    menopause 25
    osteoporosis and osteopenia 24-35
    recovery time and 21
World Masters Athletics (WMA) championships 5
World Mountain Running Association 213

Y
yoga 58-59, 73, 75

About the Author

Masters runner and coach **Dr. Cathy Utzschneider** began running competitively at age 40. Between the ages of 40 and 50 she was ranked fifth in the world in her age group and won six USA Track and Field age-group titles and a silver medal at the Nike World Masters Games. She also placed third female overall and first in her age division in the 8K cross country race at the North, Central American, and Caribbean World Masters Athletics. For the past 20 years she has trained hundreds of runners ranging from beginners to Olympians and served as Boston Marathon coach to employees of John Hancock Insurance.

As head coach of the Liberty Athletic Club, the first and longest-operating all-women's running club in the country, Cathy has coached members to three world and six American age-group records, three world age-group gold medals, and 46 national masters age-group championships since accepting the position in 2006. She also served as president of the club for three years. In 2010, she and three other Liberty teammates set an American age-group record in the 4 × 1600-meter relay.

Cathy is certified as a level 1 USA Track and Field coach and in levels 1 to 3 in the Burdenko method of water and sports therapy. She is a national site coach for www.women-running-together.com, for which she has written training programs for the 5K through the marathon. In addition to coaching, Cathy writes a column for *National Masters News*, is a contributor to *Running Times Online* and *New England Runner*, and is a professor of competitive performance and goal setting at Boston College. Topics of study include exercise physiology, goal setting, theories of excellence, and human development. She also published *Move! How Women Can Achieve Athletic Goals at Any Age*.

Cathy lives in Chestnut Hill, Massachusetts.

John Keklak